"Don't Be So Sen

Surviving a Broken Boyhood in a Foolish Era

By Daniel Kupfermann

First paperback edition August 2023

ISBN 9798851409011 (paperback)

"Find the strength to be vulnerable. Embrace your scars."

Gordon Smart

"Having a Highly Sensitive Nervous System means that our nervous system responds longer and more deeply to external stimuli. When faced with excessive physical, sensory, or emotional stimuli, a Highly Sensitive Nervous System will go into over-drive and turn on the fight-flight response."

Alana Barlia

To sensitive boys and men everywhere.

I'd also like to thank Dr Elaine Aron and the late Dr Ted Zeff, psychologists and authors whose studies on highly sensitive people gave me the idea for this book. I never met you but your observations have enriched my life.

Contents

Introduction

Afterword

Introduction

"Life can only be understood backwards; but it must be lived forwards"

Soren Kierkegaard

This book was difficult to write. No account of alcoholism and neglect, especially one so convoluted, could ever be. When you write a memoir someone always comments that it must be "cathartic". Actually it's more like tearing the scabs off old wounds or, in certain cases, reconnecting to traumas buried in your subconscious.

A schoolteacher once commented that my home background was "a mangled maze". I'm trying to make sense of it by recalling key events as honestly as I can. There's no such thing as the absolute truth, however, only the truth through the memoirist's eyes, I admit. Both my parents were sensitive, kind people. But good people can do bad things and, if this account shows anything, it's that being "good" doesn't automatically translate into great works. Sometimes softness can be destructive.

I loved both my parents and part of my resentment came from not spending enough time with them when I was younger. Writing this has helped me to understand them. I hope I have approached them compassionately. Doubtless, my mother would have preferred me to write one of those lovely travel tomes on her bookshelves. But deeper psychological issues have always interested me more.

Forty-five years ago, issues like anxiety and depression, even alcoholism, in terms of its full repercussions on the sufferer and family members, weren't mentioned in depth. It was not only a foolish era but also one of concealment.

The purpose of a memoir is not to dish dirt or settle scores. After all, most of the people who figure in this story are now dead, or far gone. It's to clarify what happened and offer advice, to enable others to break a chain of destructive behaviour.

In some ways life has improved since the period detailed here. There's more discussion around mental health issues. But the old adage still applies; prevention is better than cure. If you create the conditions for stability in childhood, you're far likelier to produce stable adults.

Reading recent accounts of highly sensitive people (known as HSPs) opened so many doors.[1] Around 20 per cent of the population are believed to fall into this category. Even if it's just 10 to 15 percent that

---

[1] You can take the test yourself here. https://hsperson.com/test/highly-sensitive-test/

still constitutes a significant minority. Finding out about HSPs helped me to understand not only some of my behaviour but also that of my parents. It explained my inner landscape, both the good and the bad.

1. Three Wise Monkeys

"To leave is to die a little"

Gerard

I have this weird spasm before falling asleep. I'm about to drift off when I feel a jolt. Maybe it's the relic of my longstanding anxiety disorder. Or events from the distant past. Sometimes I reflect – how silly and immature to be haunted by what happened 45 years ago. Or is it? "God, you were sensitive," my half-brother said to me recently, recalling me as a child.

The "sensitive" label stuck. Then I thought it was a disadvantage but now I think, in some ways, "thank God!" My mother and I got on well towards the end of her life *but* we seldom talked of the past. When she'd had her bottle of wine she went to bed. Yet, if we locked eyes, I caught a flicker of pain and resignation.

***

Whenever I see Praia da Luz, especially the black rock marking the end of the beach and the triangulation station[2] (or trig point) atop the hill, the twin landmarks that scream "Luz", I feel a myriad of emotions. I see images first, like the most memorable scenes from a movie. My straw hat falling down the cascading limestone cliffs over Luz beach, my toy Tonka car rolling down the rock face, or wading out to sea on my gondola, the lone sailor battling the waves.

Praia da Luz (literally "the beach of light") in the Algarve region of Portugal is now sadly synonymous with the 2007 disappearance of Madeleine McCann. But back in 1977, when my story opens, Luz was a developing fishing village. Portugal was still only three years on from the revolution that had threatened our idyll in the sun and nine years away from joining the Common Market. You still saw donkeys with carts on the roads and women balancing laundry baskets on their heads. And the long winding road from Luz to Faro Airport was a 90-minute drive.

Our villa, which my mother had bought in 1969, had no phone. And the wait for one was eternal. One couple we knew in Luz (and, unlike us, permanent residents) requested a phone at their home in 1971 and only had it installed by Portugal Telecom in 1984! If you lived in the Algarve in those days you felt cut off from the rest of the world. If you wanted to catch the British news on the radio you had to

---

2 It's called Marco Geodésico da Atalaia, 109 metres high.

fine-tune carefully to hear the scratchy, scrambled BBC world service.

This seclusion carried dangers. Nowadays people are connected by technology but in those days, unless one had a job and a purpose, it was easy to see how the Algarve could render disconnected people even more detached. Yes, a perfect place for jumping into a pool or the sea … but also a bottle.

That summer of 1977 I'd taken so many photographs. The Algarve was famed for its luminosity and wall-to-wall sunshine and over-exposed tourist snaps. Gerard, my "stepfather", dubbed me "the Paki" because I was so brown. It was the end of August, that nervous time when (mostly British) villa owners looked north and fretted. Summer usually continues until the end of October in the Algarve. Then the rains come but there's no autumn in the British sense, no descent into dreariness and decay.

Many villa owners enjoyed longer holidays than the standard fortnight, enabling extended seclusion. But now they worried about what lay on the doormat and the prospect of returning to work. Had they overstretched themselves? My mother and Gerard, both London Blue Badge tour guides, had similar anxieties.

I also didn't want to go back to London but there were compensations for a 10-year-old boy: Arctic roll, Lyon's assorted cupcakes, Bird's Eye fish fingers, Penguin biscuits, those lovely Silver Jubilee buses, Liverpool football team, Mike Yarwood, Brian "bastard" Hayes on LBC's morning phone-in – the man who made skiving from school worthwhile.

Rich Man, Poor Man was the most famous imported series that summer on Portuguese TV. Otherwise, the country's reassuring Prime Minister Mario Soares,[3] known as "fat cheeks", was always on the evening news. The top drama series was *O Casarão*, a melodramatic Brazilian soap opera with close-ups of anguished-looking people, frequently alcoholics. Venture into the village and you'd see locals standing outside the homes of those with TVs so they could watch. But there wasn't much choice. We had a black-and-white television with two channels, fronted by sombre-looking presenters, probably clad in brown because this was the ubiquitous dress code in Portugal.

The last four weeks had been a giddy round of beach and pool, in and out of the Luz Bay Club, which was home from home for villa owners and tenants. The "Club", as we called it, had free access to an adult and children's pool, tennis, paddle tennis and mini-golf. I'd leave the villa, wander the 40 meters or so

---

[3] Mario Soares (1924-2017). Portuguese Prime Minister from 1976 to 1978 and President from 1986 to 1996.

into their grounds and my entertainment was provided for the day.

Other favourite venues in Luz included the Oxford pub in Rua da Praia, run by a friendly English couple. (Even they didn't have a phone and they had a business to run! They subsequently told me they'd use one of the (few) phones in the street belonging to a Portuguese neighbour.) I loved going to the Oxford, occasionally on my own, propping up the bar with my Sumol (orange), even ordering a Sagres or Super Bock lager on the sly, and always carrying a packet of Sugus sweets. Yep, Sumol, Sagres, Super Bock, Sugus, sun, sea, sand … and sometimes sangria with friends.

I'd spent most of my time swimming but I'd also befriended local stray dogs, despite public injunctions *not* to feed them. In the evening we went to restaurants on the beach. If you had dinner early you'd see Portuguese kids playing beach football, every strike punctuated by *"eh pá"* – an exclamation of surprise. Near Luz's main street you'd hear the constant roar of two-stroke engine motorbikes.

Then there was the occasional trip to Lagos, stopping off at Val Verde campsite en route to visit a Welsh friend, Mark, who lived there. I knew I was lucky when my friend's grandmother told me her favoured spot in their caravan was the toilet. "It's the only cool place," she would say. Another kid looked ill after being savaged by mosquitoes.

If I ever got bored there were other distractions: the lizard on the terrace that appeared nightly behind the lantern, and the omnipresent army of ants who encircled my bed as if planning a night-time raid.

My mother and Gerard both disliked the conventions of a summer holiday, shunning the pool and beach, because Gerard deemed sunbathing "crass" behaviour (one of his favourite words). They liked the water, but usually from a distance. So I was lonesome at times. I latched on to a family at the Luz Bay Club and they took me to nearby beaches famed for their high waves.

People behaved weirdly towards the end of August. I'd been thrown into the pool, even when fully dressed, a couple of times by "last dayers" as we called them. "Last dayers" were renowned for their practical jokes, undertaking midnight swims and stealing friends' clothes. "Last dayers" drank even more; I'm sure the Luz Bay Club testified to that.

Now it was *our* final day. From my bedroom downstairs I heard my mother going "clip clop" as she mounted the wooden floorboards on the spiral staircase, holding the handrail of white threaded rope. She took the early morning sun in her dressing gown on the terrace, sitting on the wrought iron white furniture above our tiled patio. I heard a "screech" as she dragged the chair to a favourite sunny spot, her back to the wall decorated with blue Azulejos (Portuguese ceramic tile work).

She would have had a fantastic view. Further on, below the hill and the trig point, you could see a parched football field. To the far right you could just make out the sea. On the other side of the villa was a field with a traditional Portuguese country house where cockerels would serenade us every morning. It was an idyllic setting, nestled on the corner of Luz. It felt like you were in the countryside – surrounded by orange groves – but still so near to the main Luz Bay Club and the sea.

I joined my mother on the terrace, passing through the lounge replete with books, the spines having paled under the force of the sun. That told the whole story of the impact of the Algarve's "blinding ball of fire", as Gerard called it. She said little. Something was gnawing at her. She looked up later when she heard our maid, Idilena, open the front door.

"*Bom Dia*," said Idilena in her sing-song voice.

"*Bom Dia*, Idilena," responded my mother from above.

Gerard too looked melancholy as he pottered around the kitchen. "I'm going to miss my babies," he said. He went downstairs after breakfast and opencd the French windows in the bedroom. I watched from the terrace as he inspected the flowers and potted plants in the patio below, occasionally stroking the petals.

"*Partir c'est mourir un peu*," ("to leave is to die a little") said Gerard, shaking his head. Speaking perfect French and Spanish came naturally to him because, although he was British, he was raised in the Basque country. He called my mother *"mon chou"* (my cabbage) or *"Chou"* for short.

The patio was ablaze with colour: hibiscus, bougainvillea, geraniums, begonia, blue morning glory, mimosa, eucalyptus and …

"What's this red flower called?" asked Gerard in Portuguese, calling up to Idilena who was sweeping the terrace.

My mother groaned. Our dear, faithful, illiterate maid whose total vocabulary extended to only a few hundred words, who wished us *"Boa Viagem"* (good journey) when we drove to Lagos seven kilometres away, was no horticultural expert. Even her ID card of the time was not signed but bore her fingerprint. So we knew what was coming.

"Não Sei, Senhor." ("I don't know", pronounced "Now Say".)

"Here we go again, the old one-two," muttered Gerard. He'd called *"Não Sei"* the "old one-two" so many times I wondered if he asked questions he knew she couldn't answer to poke fun.

Maybe Portuguese of a certain age said that because it was a cultural relic of fascism. Better to be on the safe side and claim to know "nothing", like Manuel, the hapless Spanish waiter in *Fawlty Towers*.

"It's poinsettia, bear," said my mother. "But do stop asking Idilena these questions. You're only embarrassing her."

"*Pois*," said Idilena in the background as she continued sweeping, oblivious to the exchanges. "*Pois*" means "yes", "ok", "of course", or "right". It was the most commonplace filler word used by "the peasants", as Gerard called Idilena and her ilk.

My mother appreciated Idilena's hard work and loyalty, occasionally treating her to gifts from the UK. A week earlier we'd dined at her blue-and-white cottage in Budens, a short distance from Luz. It was a simple meal of soup and bread with squadrons of flies competing for scraps. Nevertheless, my mother was effusive while Gerard kept looking at his watch and nudging her because he wanted to go home to watch *Rich Man, Poor Man*.

***

"Don't forget there's a letter from your son, bear," my mother reminded Gerard.

"I'll look at it later," said Gerard, still busy in the garden. He chucked a pebble at a stray cat scaling the patio wall. He patted his stomach and turned back to the bedroom. He looked like a bear from afar, hence my mother's nickname for him. He was five foot five, had no neck and a prominent drinker's distended belly.

"Who will look after the garden while we're gone?" I asked.

"I've enrolled the jungle bunnies in the Luz Bay Club to water the flowers," said Gerard. "Jungle bunnies" was his disparaging term for the gardeners who toiled for paltry wages in the Club. He came upstairs and put on a Dean Martin cassette; "Dino", as Gerard called him, was our staple summer soundtrack.

"*Arrivederci Roma, it's time to say goodbye ...*" Dino's seductive voice resonated around the lounge. The song was poignant now that it was our last day.

"Anyway, we'll be back in three months," said Gerard when he climbed back up to the lounge. This took us to the end of November, I calculated. He must have meant *four* months because we usually came out again just before Christmas.

Gerard took a few hundred escudos out of my mother's bag and counted some coins from his own wallet. He tossed them all over to me. "Now we've got the farewell party this afternoon," he reminded me. "Here's the shopping list. Off you go to the mini market and buy these drinks. You better be fast." He turned to my mother. "And, what do you say, *Chou*? Shall we have a snifter while we wait?" Gerard opened the cocktail cupboard and drained the last of the gin bottle into two glasses. "I don't mind if I do," he said as he added orange juice I'd squeezed the previous day. He always made the same little joke when he prepared spirits. It was now noon.

My mother, clicking her fingernails in the background, said nothing. On the coffee table, in a white folder marked Travel Club of Upminster, were three return tickets and black passports. I noticed something odd in my mother's personal details. Her passport, recently renewed, showed her birthdate as 1934 when we knew she was born in 1931. A few days earlier I'd seen Gerard amending it and I'd wondered what it was all about.

I returned from the minimarket and squeezed more oranges. The juice looked nutritious, although, gradually, I was realising it had unhealthy implications.

***

I always hate the last day of a holiday. When you know you must leave after a happy vacation, my inclination is to say – let's get on with it.

The guests arrived, Aubrey and Jennifer, who'd once been our neighbours in West London when my parents were married. Now my mother had enticed them into buying in the Algarve. They brought their son, Kevin, who was my age, along with three female cousins. I knew the boy's parents were heavy drinkers. I'd vaguely remembered my dad berating them across our little communal garden as they drank aperitifs opposite us in Porchester Terrace in Bayswater.

"Is that the only way you can stand each other? When you're drunk?"

I'd also witnessed some big afternoon drinking sessions with these friends in the Luz Bay Club. But nothing would prepare me for this. Aubrey had a foghorn voice, well-wetted with liquor. His face betrayed the signs too.

On top of the staircase was a small plot where Gerard could make the drinks. A round marble table had some canapés prepared by my mother in advance.

My friend and I and his three cousins were ushered out onto the terrace. Although the doors were open, the conversation was inevitably muffled. I glanced into the lounge and saw my mother playing with her glass, like a child with a toy, stirring the ice cubes. Gerard got up regularly to refill their glasses. It looked like everyone was drinking orange juice … but that was deceptive. When I went to the toilet he'd wink at me and point to my mother as if to say – "she's knocking it back this afternoon". But

Gerard was the barman and he could have stopped serving any time.

Something was up with Kevin and his three cousins. He was determined to humiliate one of them. "Fenella and Matilda I love, but Georgia I hate," he kept saying. Georgia took it well and tried to laugh it off but eventually she kept quiet. The baiting continued until Georgia, the offended cousin, left in tears.

Through the terrace window I could see my mother slumped in her armchair, looking misty-eyed. She'd lean over to slurp from the glass because Gerard had overfilled it. Then she'd wipe away a titbit of orange around her mouth. Her friends got into an angry, loud diatribe about the UK. I no longer had to strain to hear.

"Bastards in Britain – I don't see why we should go back there. With inflation the way it is, any savings will be worthless anyway." She nudged her husband. "We could sell the shop and the house and move out here permanently."

"Living on what?"

"Well, the proceeds from the capital. Come on, it's not so expensive here."

"That's a renter's mentality." But, even so, Aubrey looked to be mulling it over.

"I've got an empty glass," said my mother, banging it on the side of the chair. "Time for another refill," she demanded. "I wouldn't go back to England if I had a choice. In fact, I'm *not* going," she, said. "Who'd want to leave this lovely place?"

I was going to mention my school in London. But, looking at my mother, I could see conversation was pointless.

The guests ate a few crisps and Aubrey loosened his shirt, revealing a sweaty bellybutton. "We're all trapped there," he said. "Such a shame not to be able to use our villa more often."

"We've found a way around that," said Gerard. "So we can spend more time out there," he added.

"I don't want to go back to London at all. Ever!" said my mother, grimacing. She got up and fingered the Travel Club of Upminster folder. "I'm going to tear up the bloody air tickets and stay here," she shouted.

Gerard intervened and prized them off her. He turned to our guests, laughing, trying to make a joke out of it. "Come on, I'll fix us all another drink."

"I don't want to go back. It's one big financial burden," said my mother, referring to our house in Pimlico, South London.

"Look, *Chou*, we've discussed it so many times and we can find a way to get the best of both," said Gerard.

Our guests departed in late afternoon, the adults tottering down the stairs precariously. They had to start packing, and they'd become embarrassed by her meltdown.

"How's Daniel's father?" Jennifer asked my mother on the way out. My dad was then in London. "Still the same barrel of laughs, is he?"

My mother rolled her eyes.

Gerard headed downstairs and watered the garden for the last time. I went with him just to be able to breathe because the lounge reeked of gin and cigarettes. My mother had fallen asleep in her chair. Gerard watered every flower lovingly. I was wearing shorts and a T-shirt and flip-flops. He turned the hosepipe on me. We'd played that game many times before. On a hot August afternoon it was a welcome dousing but this time he drenched me. He looked genuinely resentful.

"You're omnipresent," said Gerard. "Useless baggage."

I ran back into the bedroom.

"Boarding," said Gerard. "There was none of this namby-pamby stuff when I was your age. I was already packed off."

I knew these terms Gerard used for boarding school. Depending on his mood, he'd describe being "sent away" or "despatched" or "kicked in the teeth". He was bitter about his own experience yet he never ceased wanting the same for me.

"But his father would never allow it," said my mother, appearing at the French windows, swaying slightly. "Maybe in a couple of years' time you could go to the International School here," she said to me. "We'd all be better off over here. Out of bloody London!" she shouted.

"His father would block that too," said Gerard.

My mother didn't answer. She went upstairs and poured herself another drink. It was unusual for her to shout. She rarely raised her voice and even when she did it had little effect. It was unbecoming in her case.

We went to the Club for our last meal. My mother was already drunk after downing gin throughout the afternoon. Gerard, also well oiled, appeared to be thinking deeply, which in his case meant contemplating how to improve his own circumstances. He saw life as a competition, an endless "struggle" in a worldview right out of Hitler's *Mein Kampf.* Any advancement for other people meant a retreat for him. Another man's happiness always seemed to be his misfortune. A zero sum game. After a good beginning we'd developed a mutual dislike. Something about his hard battlement forehead riled me, together with his constant callous comments. He'd spent the holiday belittling me and hissing whenever I was around.

Now the wine arrived, a bottle of Alentejo red, the *papo secos* (Portuguese rolls) and the main course. I can't remember what we ate and if we finished it. We were sitting there, surrounded by many "last dayers", the service exemplary as usual. But my mother couldn't shake her angry, depressed mood. I could see there was an obstacle to her and Gerard's dream of spending more time in the Algarve. My father. In London.

She reached for another drink and spilled it down her dress. Suddenly, without any precedence, she badmouthed my dad.

"I hope …"

"You shouldn't speak that way about daddy," I said. "How can you think such a thing, let alone say it?"

"You don't know the whole story."

"How dare you say that?" I got angrier by the second. "You … you … BITCH!" I screamed at her. Other diners banged their cutlery down.

Mum and Gerard got up from the table and left. I'd had tantrums before, which they ignored. And they were doing likewise this time. But a 10-year-old knows whether his anger is justified or not. And when you know it isn't, you calm down.

But this time I was convinced I was the wronged party. I watched as Mum and Gerard left the Club and turned right for the short stroll back to our villa. I shouted after them but they didn't answer. They were ignoring me, hoping I'd calm down. Not this time. They went inside and slammed the door. My mother was so drunk that – I subsequently learned – she went straight to the bedroom and crashed out.

It wasn't only her comments that upset me. I'd been working up to it the whole holiday. I felt I was becoming "a problem" to them, and my mother was now focusing exclusively on Gerard.

Now I was trapped outside our villa on a warm night. I was still fuming and looking to vent it. I picked up some pebbles and rang the doorbell. Gerard opened the door.

I threw them at him. "You cunts!" I shouted. I thought I'd got the right distance between me and Gerard to hit him. But I missed. So I went closer, a few metres from him, and threw them again. A few landed on his cheek and Gerard shielded his face. I moved closer. This was my big mistake. He was a nimble fellow and ran toward me, grabbed me and lifted me off the ground. He carried me through the door and into the bedroom. Now I was trapped. He struck me with the back of his hand and I fell onto the bed. Just as I'd recovered from the first strike, he thumped me again. And again, this time harder.

"Are you going to say that again? ARE YOU?" said Gerard.

I wouldn't cave in at first. I was so angry. But, gradually, as the blows rained down and the pain intensified, I knew I was truly beaten – in every sense.

"Please stop! Please!"

Eventually he did. He left me crying on the bed, nursing an aching back.

"You won't do that again in a hurry," he said.

Outside the window, through the mosquito netting, I'd hear the crickets. But, otherwise, the night was eerily quiet and I drifted off.

My mother slept through the whole ordeal. How typical of her to have dodged the unpleasantness she caused. The next morning I woke up early and I could hear my mother and Gerard talking in the lounge. I crept up the stairs. My back still hurt from the serial pummelling. Neither of them looked at me. My mother was ashen-faced and trembling, probably more from the hangover than anything else. I cravenly apologised to her and Gerard. Just because she indicated I should. Except I thought they should have apologised to *me* but that's more with hindsight.

No one ever mentioned the incident again. I doubt my mother could have recalled it anyway even though she had instigated it. If this drunken evening had had a happy postscript, she would have woken up the following morning, and been so horrified by her actions the previous night that she'd have phoned Alcoholic Anonymous, joined a support group and taken the pledge. But she wasn't in the UK, there was no phone and no support group – just Gerard standing there with a hair of the dog gin and orange cocktail. This was 1977. If you're old enough to remember Elton John before he had hair, you'll understand.

***

Children of divorced parents become the protector of the bad-mouthed parent. They grow up quickly. Should I tell? Thank God I didn't because it would have hastened my father's death. He died early enough as it was. When my mother criticised my dad I rarely repeated it to him. In any case, her words on this occasion were so vitriolic that I knew I was bound by a holy covenant. They could never be revealed. See no evil, hear no evil, speak no evil.

She believed my dad had serious emotional problems and he was, in words my father had allegedly used, "an endogenous depressive". That had more than enough credibility to it. My (Jewish) father was my mother's second husband and she came with "baggage", two sons from her first marriage, Michael and Colin. My dad didn't like them. And this was reciprocated.

At first they'd all tried to get on but it ended like two separate families living under one roof. Not that there was a formal demarcation but my half-brothers retreated to one part of the house and kept their distance. Of course, this must have been difficult for my mother. She told me he delivered an ultimatum. Michael and Colin should be placed in a children's home – specifically Dr Barnardo's – or the marriage was over. You can guess what happened.

My dad *was* wrong to suggest this, even in a moment of madness. But I also felt my mother was wrong to tell me because it cast my dad in such a bad light. Any more than her words about my dad that evening in the Club reflected her real feelings. Verbal *crime passionel* in both cases.

In truth, my dad divorced his *stepsons*. The two boys and my dad summarily loathed each other. (My dad later admitted there was a mutual dislike, although he didn't use those words, instead stressing "incompatibility".) He knew he'd defied his mother's wishes not to marry "out" of Judaism. I doubt he'd had much contact with "gentiles" except in the army. And these two English-looking boys reminded him of his "betrayal". But Michael and Colin weren't the easiest of teenagers anyway.

The marriage ended in 1971 when I was four. My half-brothers were then 15 and 17. Why did my mother tell me about the reasons for the divorce? The story, if true, acquitted her of any responsibility for the marriage's failure. But I wondered if my father ever guessed she was reporting these "details" to me. Probably not because he wasn't calculating and, crucially, he didn't realise how indiscreet she was in drink. (She hadn't drunk much during *their* marriage.) Naturally, I never cross-examined him. I never asked: "Daddy, did you ever insist on putting Michael and Colin in Dr Barnardo's?"

But such inhibited behaviour is not healthy. I had to conceal what I knew. The child of a hard-drinking parent learns to be the gatekeeper of his words. And drink was the key to all this. Yes, there were some happy times at the beginning involving my mother and Gerard, but gradually the mood shifted. It's difficult to pinpoint when playful banter became unpleasant. Mum had a strange habit of slapping Gerard on the stomach and saying "you've got a cheek, bear" – at first comically, then forcefully. Initially, it was horseplay but, gradually, it became more violent.

***

"Back to post and phone calls," said Gerard on the plane back to London the following morning.

"That's why I don't want a phone in Luz," said my mother. "It's our secluded bubble in southern Europe."

Yes, in Praia da Luz they were cocooned from news about sad old Blighty. Forget British Leyland, Blair Peach, Lib-Lab pacts, rampant inflation and the Yorkshire Ripper. The only crime recorded that summer in Luz was petrol being siphoned out of hired cars. Well, apart from beating the shit out of a child. But no one noticed.

Luz also provided many happy times. But I've never been able to say "Luz" without stammering. And for many years I always stammered over the word "mother". I buried the beating in my subconscious and certainly never told my father. It was as though it had happened to some other person. A protection mechanism. But from that moment on I always flinched when Gerard came near me. And many years later, long after we had sold the villa, I would return to have a look around. When the owners showed me my former bedroom, 45 years down the line, I reverted to that frightened little boy and started shaking.

2. The First Lotus Eaters

"Spain is different but Portugal is unique"

Gerard

Praia da Luz furnished so many drunken memories because we were all off-duty. Algarve-based photos of me from this period show me smiling happily. People comment on that when I say *most* of my childhood was painful. But photographs are never taken when people are miserable. If a couple has a drunken argument they don't stop right then to take a selfie to capture it for posterity, do they? "Let's take a snap of you slapping me in the face!" You're normally happy when a photo is taken, otherwise you wouldn't pose for it, would you? And photos, especially in a place like the Algarve, are taken during the day *before* major booze-ups.

Many years later I befriended an Australian prisoner in a Bulgarian jail, wrongly incarcerated on a murder charge. My friend, a real extrovert with a laugh like a machine gun, always beamed when we visited. His circumstances were grim and so people used to comment the same – it was strange he looked so cheerful. He'd say he was happy precisely because people were visiting him. And it's the same with photographs.

***

Luz had first become famous back in 1968 when Paul McCartney had spent time there, staying right by the beach in a house rented by his friend Hunter Davies.[4] A stream of famous visitors followed in the 1970s. We saw Pauline Collins[5] and John Alderton having dinner on the beach, and Bob Holness[6] by the Luz Bay Club pool. Comedian Dave Allen[7] arrived and asked the Luz Bay Club management for a secluded villa with an instruction to be left alone. Maybe he didn't realise residents had no access to British TV and so he was an unknown quantity!

But, outside the glitterati, buying a holiday home in the sun was still a precociously daring venture in 1969. My mother knew little of the Algarve when an advert was sent to her London home advertising a new development in Praia da Luz. I say "my mother" because it was her decision to buy an off-plan villa, I feel sure. My dad was not one to make a speculative

---

[4] British journalist and author Hunter Davies (b. 1936) who wrote the only authorised biography of the Beatles. He has also written extensively about his early days in the Algarve.

[5] Pauline Collins (b. 1940) and John Alderton (b. 1940), husband and wife acting couple most famous for *Upstairs Downstairs*.

[6] Bob Holness (1928-2012) was most famous as host of British quiz show *Blockbusters* but back when I met him (the summer of 1980) he was known as the co-host of a breakfast show on London's LBC radio called the *AM Programme*.

[7] Dave Allen (1936-2005) was a popular television comedian of his day.

purchase of any kind, let alone in Portugal. He only visited Luz two or three times.

In 1969, Faro Airport had only been open for four years. It looked more like a private airfield. But it soon became a familiar commute because, on average, I visited Praia da Luz three, even four times annually between 1970 and 1985. So 50-odd trips in total, spending about three months a year there.

Here I should pay tribute to her decision, or at least the *original* premise behind it. It led to inter-family schisms *but* also supplied me with great holidays. The communal nature of the Luz Bay Club, its accessibility only to villa owners, made it so easy to make "friends". I'd arrive after a gap of a few months, bump into other children I'd played with before, and re-connect as though there'd been no interruption. And it was easy to bond because of the guaranteed sunshine and the postcard-perfect pools and beach.

I loved Luz from the start. But even then there were inklings there could be trouble in paradise. My father, long after he'd stopped coming to Luz, once asked me about an American expat he'd met on the beach. My dad recalled this guy as "a keep-fit fanatic". That confounded me because, several years on, this expat was known to be a *chronic* alcoholic. And *so* many people I knew from there in the 1970s were drinking heavily. According to a bar owner, the town was "full of gin-soaked expats with nothing to do".

My dad was teetotal and so the gin and tonic brigade wouldn't have found him convivial. He didn't travel well. My mother told me he was "impossible" on holiday and I believe her. He hated air travel, long car journeys, changes and unfamiliarity. As a highly sensitive person (HSP), he also disliked surprises; creeping up on my dad unexpectedly was a no-no. He'd have reacted especially badly to any disruption to his routine. He also would have hated anywhere reeking of fascism and Portugal was, technically, still a fascist country.[8] So that "disqualified" him from enjoying it there on several counts.

If my dad wasn't happy, he tended to "grizzle": little complaints about the bathroom, the mosquitoes, the food, and the wind – whatever. My mother said he "grizzled" so much that she almost belted him. My mother, who had her faults, was undeniably easier to be with over an extended period, less nervous, more accommodating to change, unruffled by a break in habit and less "irritable", a favourite word my dad used to describe his own moods. He'd snap easily because, as she said, he couldn't help it. He was too exhausted by the day, from feeling everything over deeply.

---

[8] Portugal's longstanding dictator António de Oliveira Salazar had a stroke in 1968. He was replaced by Marcelo Caetano who ruled until the revolution of 1974.

Owning a house in London and a villa in the Algarve made my mother a catch after my parents' divorce. In 1973 we were in Luz when my late aunt's Jewish widower Adolf (yes, Jews were so named before the war!) called at our villa. I opened the door.

"I just happened to be passing and wondered if you were at home."

Even though I was only six years old I couldn't help laughing. No one "happened" to be passing by Praia da Luz back then. A trip took careful planning. We played mini golf together in the Luz Bay Club but evidently his courting didn't take off.

My mother preferred Portugal over Spain. Later, Gerard said he favoured Spain. This was a common division between the sexes. Portugal was less aggressive, less macho; maybe its brand of fascism had been marginally less brutal and its people gentler. Even the bull wasn't killed in a Portuguese bullfight, it was proclaimed. The centuries of seafaring had created the *Saudade* (loosely translated as a sadness or nostalgic yearning) for which the people are known. The Portuguese were quieter, without the famed "animation" of the Spanish.

In April 1974, however, our idyll looked close to being shattered. The Portuguese Revolution overthrew 40 years of dictatorship. We were walking in London one afternoon when an *Evening Standard* vendor   bellowed   "PORTUGAL   GONE COMMUNIST".

My mother burst into tears. She must have been distraught. For a while there was serious talk of properties being confiscated and foreigners – wealthy capitalists! – would have been first in line. Would we lose our villa? For a while the atmosphere was feverish and many overseas owners fled, taking their valuables. Motorists, usually assumed (correctly) to be foreigners because most Algarveans had a donkey or cart, found it difficult to buy petrol. There were inconveniences for sure but the communists, whose strongholds were in the Alentejo, gave up confiscating property down south.

"The Carnation Revolution", so-called because it was non-violent, fizzled out. A friend joked that the Portuguese deemed communism a great idea until they were told they'd have to share their pigs! Thankfully, the Luz Bay Club's British manager had managed to keep the Club running throughout because many locals relied on it for their jobs. So Portugal began clambering unsteadily toward social democracy. Foreign-owned properties were safe, after all.

My mother was agreeably surprised to find the villa untouched when we arrived later that year, 1974. Even our adopted cat, Bobby, knew we were coming, waiting for us on the doormat outside. The publicity in the UK had been so bad we'd half expected to find a Commie cat raising the red flag!

In the years between my parents' divorce and her meeting Gerard, I was happy. These were the halcyon days of my childhood. We visited Luz several times – sometimes only the two of us because my older half-brothers were working or studying – during this period. There's a picture of me as a seven-year-old reading a book while a fat Bobby lazes nearby, looking out over the sun-kissed terrace. I can date it to late 1974 because it's post-Revolution but pre-Gerard. Also, the furnishings were still makeshift, just before my mother lavished money on the place.

Our family doctor once dubbed me "a sensitive squaggy". There's no such word, of course, but it was oddly appropriate and onomatopoeic. Even my dad called me "squaggy". At this point I'd have been content to keep my mother to myself. Particularly for a *vulnerable* little fellow it's comforting not having to vie for your mother's attention. You look up and there she is. No competition, no rivalry, and no expectations … a "sensitive squaggy" nestling near his mummy in the Algarve, with reassuring smells emanating from the gas-fired stove and a friendly cat nearby. For me this was just p-u-r-r-f-e-c-t. (Yes, I know, I know!) When I look back at the time when I was happiest I don't hark back to big occasions but rather a mood of undisturbed innocence.

But this period wasn't so great for my mother. We struggled with the luggage on our return journey on the train from Gatwick to Victoria. She broke her fingernail, slamming it in the compartment door while trying to get through with heavy bags. Later she called an ambulance and had to spend a day in hospital. She was at a loss without a partner.

I never holidayed anywhere else abroad during the entire period in which my mother owned the villa in Luz. But I could see the advantages of having a home in the sun. You know where everything is; you kick off your shoes and the fun starts immediately. No recce is needed; restaurateurs recognise you as regulars and give you exemplary service because they like you and know you're likely to recommend them. And, in Portugal, sterling went a long way; in those days there were 50 escudos to the pound.

My mother was well-educated but Luz was not brimming with the intelligentsia. An exception was Alison Blair, whom we knew as Alison Hooper, who lived in a lovely rambling house in Boa Pesca, a quiet, elegant residential cul-de-sac. Alison, the Cambridge-educated co-founder of a popular magazine called Lilliput[9] in the Forties, was my

[9]Lilliput was a British magazine of humor, short stories, photographs and the arts. Alison died in 1995 in Praia da Luz and received an obituary in *The Independent*.
https://www.independent.co.uk/news/people/obituary-alison-blair-1621850.html

mother's closest friend in the town, sharing a love of art, travel and literature.

Luz housed more than its share of entertaining eccentrics. A retired army colonel, and his wife were Alison's neighbours in Boa Pesca. He and Gerard, who made his first trip to Luz at Christmas, 1975, would reminisce about the war. Gerard had been a bomber pilot in the RAF. Whenever I think of "the colonel" I can hear him saying "and then Monty said to me in the desert". We'd pass by his house and he'd be on the terrace, which Gerard christened "the bridge", giving a mock salute. *"Bow Tie,"* the Colonel would say, which was the best Portuguese he could muster, a pale imitation of *"Bom Dia"*.

"Permission to come aboard?" Gerard would ask and the Colonel would nod. Usually a long drinking session would ensue.

The Colonel and his wife lived the life of a stopped clock but maybe it was the life they wanted. One summer's day we had a picnic in their caravan in the countryside. The Colonel, who was a tightwad, noticed I was eating a lot. His wife kept offering me more but he stopped her.

"Come off it, you'll be offering him the Christmas pudding next."

Alison was amused by the eccentricity of her neighbours. One day we were at the Colonel's villa having drinks when through the wall we heard

Alison pounding on her typewriter. The Colonel's wife said: "I know that Alison is writing about us." Sure enough, as Alison later told us, she was!

Another semi-permanent (and educated) resident in Boa Pesca was a wealthy, softly spoken middle-aged American architect from Colorado named Jim Weaver. Variously known as "whispering Jim", "the quiet American' or "the weaver bird" to other expats – he'd speak slowly and only after consideration, propping his glasses back up the bridge of his nose. Gerard took him off to a tee behind his back but was (excessively) unctuous in his company. Gerard quickly realised where his bread was buttered – hence I inserted "wealthy" – because what was there not to like about regular buffets featuring spare ribs, English sausages and baked potatoes in a spacious villa overlooking the beautiful bay?

There's a photo of my mother and Jim Weaver chatting on the Luz sand of a winter's day, the water lapping gently at their feet. My mother, never one for lazing on the beach, has made a rare concession to her surroundings – by removing her sandals and treading barefoot! She has long cream-coloured trousers, rolled up at the ends, stockings underneath, a silk blouse and Hermes scarf, a cashmere cardigan, delicately rounded film star sunglasses and her obligatory gold brooch and bracelet. Weaver is wearing dark flared corduroys, a long-sleeved chequered shirt with gold cufflinks and a Lacoste Vneck sweater with a cravat. Nowadays, you don't see such folk walking around a public beach, at least not in the Algarve. But this was 45 years ago.

Luz, especially out of season, was not especially *exciting*. So you may well wonder what drew people like my mother and Jim Weaver to an uncharted, disconnected area of south-western Europe. The answer lay all around you, in nature, not in human company, and also in the allure of the seclusion itself. When the weather was clement, when the "toilet" (as Gerard christened the prolonged heavy rain) wasn't flushing, it was gorgeous. Most winter days saw mild and sunny weather with scattered clouds, the air suffused with delicate scents of jacaranda and oleander. In the summer, the weather was milder than in the Mediterranean with welcoming sea breezes and cool nights.

The Algarve had almost no rain at all between May and October, so when it did come it was welcome. The *"barragems"* (reservoirs) would be empty by summer's end. But for short winter stayers it was a nuisance. Sometimes the deluge would come without respite over a fortnight and if it coincided with your holiday, it was your bad luck. Damp was a major problem if you opened up an empty villa after prolonged downpours. But when would the rains come? *"Quem sabe?"* (Who knows)? Whenever it did, the locals would say *"bom para favas"* – "it's good for the beans (to grow)".

When I was a child I preferred the Algarve in summer, for obvious reasons. But, as I grew older, my favourite time was late winter when the almond blossom appeared, bathing the fields in pink. Sometimes the first blossom arrived as early as January, but peaked a month later. During cold, grey February days in London I'd close my eyes and visualise it. Later, I grew to love the flowers of the region. Many years later a week's holiday in Albufeira (by then my mother had relocated east, to a larger resort in the Algarve) saved me from total nervous exhaustion.

Even back in Luz days I realised that the longer the period spent in the Algarve's clement climate, the harder re-entry into the UK would be. It wasn't only the weather or the scenery, although the prospect of keeping winter at bay was enticing enough. It was also the relaxed pace of life and communion with nature. A riveting television drama series of the early 1970s called *The Lotus Eaters* related the exploits of British expats in Crete. The title comes from a saying to describe the lure of the Mediterranean. One of the characters says: "We've all eaten off the fruit of the lotus and lost the desire to return to our native lands." This could also have applied to Brits in the Algarve. *The Lotus Eaters*, filmed in 1972, was considered innovative for its escapist premise. But my parents predated it by three years. They *were* the first lotus eaters.

***

In the mid-1970s, when it became clear Portugal was *not* going to become another Cuba, the Algarve took off. My mother had helped to spread the word. Her erstwhile London neighbours had already bought a home in Luz – our "guests" in the previous chapter. One of her Dutch bosses in London visited us in Luz. He belted back a couple of Gerard's "vunderful" signature tumblers of gin and oranges, which Gerard prepared out of sight, and bought a place nearby the same day. I doubt it was the Vitamin C that loosened his grip on his wallet!

We had some "influential" guests. As far as the other villa owners were concerned, Luz was defiantly upper middle-class. Summer holidays saw us entertaining the Mountbatten prodigy for drinks at our villa, likewise Major General Lennox Napier – later chairman of the Central Rail Users' Consultative Committee – and his family.

One funny memory dates back to a hot afternoon at the Luz Bay Club. My mother and Gerard were having drinks when one bare-chested fellow drinker (but without the ubiquitous tattoos you see these days) leaned over toward us and without any preliminaries or provocation extolled his old public school. "You'll *never* meet a rotter who went to

Stowe," he barked a couple of times, jabbing his finger for emphasis.

My mother immediately responded – in her emphatic delivery which loses resonance on the page – "Oh, *I* have. A former boyfriend and he was a *total rotter* of the first order!" Our Old Stoic looked flummoxed and trundled off wordlessly. My mum had little sense of humour but she could also be *very* funny.

Out of season, actress and singer Pat Kirkwood,[10] a long-time Luz resident for part of the year, visited for a drink. I was chuffed because – although I'd never heard of her at the time – she was listed in one of my film reference books. She had lovely long fingernails and manicured hands to rival my mother's. I hope that Gerard, who was notoriously tactless, didn't ask her if it was true she'd had an affair with Prince Philip! Still, he was pleased to be entertaining a celebrity.

Gerard was less hospitable when another long-time resident, whom we shall call Mildred, dowdier and more anonymous than Pat, arrived one early afternoon, ostensibly for coffee. In Gerard's subsequent words, she "outstayed her welcome" which, in this case, was a euphemism for her not being sufficiently attractive, or wealthy, to engage his interest.

---

[10] Pat Kirkwood (1921-2007) was a British stage actress, singer and dancer. She was rumoured to have once had an affair with Prince Philip.

Mildred made her coffee last as long as possible, cradling it until the early evening cocktail hour which, in the winter, fell at around 5pm. She entertained us with local gossip. But it didn't win over Gerard who was reclining further back into his armchair, hands clasped on his stomach. Gradually, he fell asleep, even snoring lightly, only to stir when my mother told him to make a gin and tonic.

After the first round of drinks, Gerard rose to his feet and, with great ceremony, made an offer that Mildred could, it turned out, easily refuse.

"Well, it's nice to see you again, Mildred. You live near Baptista's supermarket, don't you? I have to go there to pick up some shopping and I'll HAPPILY run you back."

"No, I'm hunky dory," said Mildred, shaking the ice in her glass and draining her drink. "I'll have another gin, please."

Gerard rose to his feet, emitting a curdling hiss from the back of his throat. He poured a (deliberately) small gin and tonic and plumped the drink on a side table. He turned away from his guest, avoiding any eye contact, looking palpably bored. Another half hour passed. My mother had done all the talking, never once letting Mildred think she was in any way irritating.

Gerard tried again. This time he spoke with the enunciation of a stage actor who has broken character at curtain call to express his hope that the audience had enjoyed the performance. "Well, Mildred, it really WAS nice to see you," – the stress on the past tense too demanding of a reaction – "and it'll be my PLEASURE to run you back". He even thrust his hand into his pocket and took out the car keys.

Mildred was having none of it. "No, I'm A-Okay, thank you." She stayed where she was, extending her empty glass. My mother refreshed it and Gerard reluctantly fell back into his seat, his cheeks draining of colour.

Twenty minutes later, Gerard had a final shot at it – this time trying to make the occasion even more of a done deal. "It really HAS BEEN great. Now I'll get the car out and" – gesticulating to us – "let's escort Mildred downstairs." This time Mildred complied. Pat Kirkwood could have stayed all day and night if she'd wanted to!

***

Some members of Luz's small expat English community had fled from Rhodesia. According to Hunter Davies: "The more Right-wing members tried to treat the locals as they'd treated the Africans. One told me the only way to make a Portuguese maid understand things was to hit her on the head with a saucepan."

One couple from the colonies, Zé and Theo, who had a boutique on the beachfront, made no secret of their disdain for the locals. I doubt they'd have hit anyone with a saucepan but they'd sniff if any Portuguese tried to enter. But few did. They "knew their place", incredible since it *was*, after all, "their place", but that was how it was in those days.

Yes, aspects of life and behaviour, on all sides, were "antiquated" – turning on the water to find yellow sand, the electricity and water cuts, the lack of reliable public transport, and the air of poverty. The Portuguese, especially the older ones, initially found the tourist invasion unsettling and demonstrated it by rehearsing for what seemed to be a staring marathon. Brits, for example, will give passers-by no more than a momentary glance. We're taught that studying someone too intently is unacceptable because it's intimidating. But the dear old Ports felt no such compunction. They'd sit outside their homes and gaze at you unflinchingly as you walked by, disassembling you layer by layer until you felt like a pig on a platter being surveyed by starving diners.

Of course, it was partly because Brits would strip off to shorts, tank tops and flip-flops once the mercury nudged up to eighteen degrees. The pink skin and blond hair of the Dutch or Scandinavians would prolong the intensity of the scrutiny. You'd occasionally return their gaze, hoping to instil in them enough self-consciousness to make them stop but they just carried on regardless. Their eyes would follow you until you turned the corner and then – just as you left their surveillance – you'd quickly look back to find they were still staring.

But the backwardness of the place, and the lack of sophistication of the people, was also the key to its charm. Gerard and my mother would laugh about some quintessentially Portuguese artwork. A classic example was a statue in the centre of Lagos of Dom Sebastian, King of Portugal in the late 1600s. He looks like a figure from *Star Wars* even though it was erected long before the film!

One winter's day in 1978 the sophisticated veneer of the Luz Bay Club was stripped. A Jewish couple from London, holidaying down the coast, came for lunch. (Later, I gathered that Gerard disliked Jews but these were business associates, so he'd never let on.) My mother said they would complain about the hotel and they wouldn't drink much. They arrived and, sure enough, they compared their hotel unfavourably to one they had stayed in on Rhodes. He and his wife had a half glass of wine – tops. We went to the Club and ordered fish. A long wait ensued. Senhor Oliveira, the restaurant's manager, offered various excuses for the delay. Finally, he said the fish had only just been caught. After all, we had wanted it "fresh", right?

"So when might we expect it?" asked Gerard who was normally impatient, but strangely tolerant in the Club, maybe because he knew it was our local restaurant.

"It's coming soon," said Senhor Oliveira.

More waiting … and by now we'd been there well over an hour-and-a-half.

Senhor Oliveira came back to our table. "It's on its way now … from Lagos." (Seven kilometres down the coast.)

"From Lagos?"

"Yes, that's where they caught it." We must have waited at least three hours before it arrived.

In the 1970s there used to be an advertising campaign called "Spain is Different" and my mother and Gerard used to quip – "Yes, Spain is different but Portugal is unique."

All my family came to Luz, including Michael and Colin, neither of whom were great beachgoers, although Michael and I would collect shells. They'd usually arrive out of season, stressed out from London, sitting near the log fire while Gerard acted as barman. This type of visitor to the Algarve, first to Luz and, later, to her second home in Albufeira, became a longstanding joke. They'd either be suffering from burnout or recovering from a broken love affair. My mum used to say, stoically, that guests would arrive and she'd find herself cooking for them every night.

In later years, when she had grown disillusioned with the Algarve, she'd say some expats were there because they were running away from "something". And by "something" she didn't mean the standard grievances of bad weather and the extortionate cost of living but, more likely, debts and the law. And, yes, there were "shady" characters.

My friend Mark lived most of the time on the nearby campsite at Val Verde. He was a strapping Welsh lad, a daredevil with a broken nose. His dad ran a bar in Lagos for a while. Mark would oscillate between Lagos and Luz, often arriving unexpectedly at our villa whereupon my mother would treat him to a meal. We'd wander around the countryside, breaking into derelict houses and having impromptu games of football. One day he suggested walking from Luz to Lagos via what he called a shortcut. We climbed the hill opposite our villa, right up to the trig point, continuing east and skirting the cliff tops offering the most magnificent panoramic vista over the ocean. A beautiful day and one I'll never forget.

Being with Mark offered another reminder I felt "different" from other kids, in the sense of my reluctance to participate in their activities. One day we had a picnic at someone's country cottage. My friend and one or two other boys spotted chickens in the farmhouse. They grabbed some oranges and hurled them at the birds. They retreated, their wings fluttering frantically. An orange landed on the spindly neck of one of the hens, causing it to fall. I couldn't, or *wouldn't,* partake and the other boys sneered at me as if to say I'd failed an initiation test. This was another early sign I was a "highly sensitive person". It's not only a question of disliking seeing other creatures being hurt – although that plays a part – but rather the empath imagining transference, i.e. how would I like it to have to run for cover while creatures 20 times my size launch missiles at me?

Mark and I were once playing paddle tennis when a dishevelled-looking gypsy boy approached us to ask for money. I felt sorry for him but had no money to give. The gypsy assumed an aggressive posture. This didn't faze Mark who waved his fist at him, causing the boy to flee.

One winter I arrived in Luz to find Mark in a neck brace. He'd dived into the sea from a cliff somewhere near Lagos. The water turned out to be far shallower than he realised. He broke his neck and was lucky to have survived. Many years later an Old Alleynian (the name of former pupils of my old school, Dulwich College) had a similar accident nearby. But, in his case, he was paralysed from the neck down. He became a talented mouth artist.[11]

---

[11] Mouth artist Henry Fraser, educated at Dulwich College. He tells a similar story to my friend's here.
https://www.dailymail.co.uk/news/article-4870896/Story-school-rugby-star-left-paralysed-told-new-book.html

***

Naturally, there were funny times before everyone started over-drinking. Yes, a little wine might have added to the merriment. But I increasingly felt that Gerard had my number. He'd spotted my nervousness and enjoyed winding me up. One time we had lunch at the famous *Tasca* restaurant in Sagres, a favourite hangout for Portuguese fishermen. I played darts freakishly well, so much so that they all gathered around to watch. Gerard got jealous of all the attention. He put a five-pound note on the dartboard and said if I could hit it three times, it was mine. I could only ever land it twice. Gerard laughed in the background.

One day we found a heavily pregnant cat nestling in the flowerbeds in our garden. Unlike most cats who scarper when you approach them, this one snarled at us ferociously. Gerard – the bastard – wanted to chuck it over the wall. Fortunately, my mother stopped him. I can't recall if this was before or after the walloping he gave me but it only reinforced my dislike of him. No entertaining jokes, no fun times could ever compensate. I didn't feel comfortable with him. But in those early days I didn't dwell on him because I still loved going to the Algarve.

I had another reason for looking forward to my trips to Luz. Mum and Gerard had a couple of friends who ran a riding school outside Luz. They had a gorgeous daughter. She was 13 when I first met her – only a year older than me – but a 13-year-old girl looks *way* more mature than a boy of 12. She was tall and voluptuous with high cheekbones and sun-coloured silky hair. And she'd flick it back in such a sensual way, while pursing her nose and lips. She had the lightest freckles and a great figure, long legs, and buttocks like a ripe apple. I'd first laid eyes on her when she was coming out of the Luz Bay Club pool one glorious day. With her blond bob wet against the summer sun, her pink skin covered in droplets, she looked like a vision of loveliness unrivalled before or since.

One New Year's Eve we celebrated at the Fortaleza in Luz, an old seaside fortress converted into a restaurant. She was there with her parents and for a short while we danced together. I felt a frisson as, fleetingly, her breasts touched my chest. My cheeks were burning. Soon after we visited her parents on their farm. She'd made some mince pies, laden with sugar, and they were like an appetiser to tasting her. They were the most delectable melt-in-your-mouth, buttery, crumbly, pastry-perfect mince pies ever. She ate one in front of me, sitting on the carpet, her legs crossed. Her father, sitting on the sofa, hovered over her, stroking her shoulders. She licked a dried fruit and I … well, I must have looked a right sight, like any awkward and callow boy confronted with this exquisite creature.

Her parents suggested we go out riding, just the two of us. I was cantering behind her. Occasionally she'd turn her head right and left under her riding cap. She had the greatest profile I'd ever seen. We wandered alone among the fields, me still at the rear, watching her bottom bounce up and down.

One time we stopped to pick fruit. She placed a raspberry in her mouth. She looked at me with her ocean-blue eyes and twitched her nose and a bead of sweat fell over her lower lip. I was standing there, mesmerised. She half-smiled. Her tight T-shirt barely covered her midriff. Her bosoms looked like they were about to break out. I tried to speak.

"C-c-an I k..k…"

"Let's go back now."

I doubt she guessed what I was trying to say, probably never heard it, or spotted my infatuation. It's one of my signature memories. It was a huge chance for me and I'd blown it.

Another year passed and we were celebrating New Year's Eve in a club in Lagos when – oh my God! – she appeared again, this time in a party dress barely covering her breasts and long legs. With make-up on, and her beautiful blonde mane no longer tied in a bow but cascading down, she looked even more ravishingly beautiful than ever. Gerard kissed her. I could read his thoughts. My reaction was "oh yes, oh no, oh yes, oh no" not knowing which took precedence because … I desired her, I wanted to talk to her. But I also knew it was a big test for me.

There was only one other boy my age there that evening – Mark, my Welsh friend, a year or so before his near-fatal accident. She was sitting at the bar, her legs astride a stool, and a friendly barman was happy to keep her glass filled. Her parents were busy with other company. I so wanted to be her companion but as the booze flowed, and the noise increased, I couldn't find the opportunity I needed to talk to her. Or didn't know what to say. Noise always gave me a headache in any case.

At one point she was standing in the corner pressed up against the wall. She flicked her hair back. She moved back to the bar stool and Mark drew up alongside her. Neither budged for a couple of hours until the New Year arrived. After midnight a guy appropriately named Neville – because in my recollection everyone was posh – refilled our glasses. By 2am she and Mark were still locked in giggling conversation. I knew I'd failed.

I was only 13 and I'd had at least four or five glasses of champagne. But I'd been having a little wine with weekend meals and holidays regularly since I was 10. So, outrageous as it may be, this consumption wasn't enough to get me drunk. Nothing could tranquilise my sense of failure. We drove back to Luz. Gerard slammed the door on our return, and turned on me.

"I'm very disappointed in you."

I pretended not to understand. But, it was useless. He'd been eyeing me the whole time, essentially watching me watching her.

"You know full well what I'm talking about. I'm so disappointed," he repeated, shaking his head.

He was right. I'd always known.

"When I was your age I would have been all over that beautiful girl, suggesting we play at being sardines. Instead you allowed that fat boy to take over. Very, very disappointed indeed."

But not half as disappointed as I was in myself. Because that was the last time I saw her.

***

Gerard was extremely practical. Not only had he tiled the patio single-handedly but he was always busy with a saw, collecting firewood, doing jobs around the villa. You could look at his hands, those rough hands that had thumped me, and you knew he was used to manual work. Especially as I got older he obsessed over my lack of practicality. I was a clumsy "cack-handed" kid who must have broken a hundred cups and glasses. But I was outgrowing my strength and, in his words, a "beanpole" with "violin cases" for shoes who was always bumping into furniture. Gerard criticised me for "conducting an orchestra" while I was eating and also for my lack of interest if he was mixing cement or planting flowers. He'd made a similar complaint about his own son, so I wasn't the only one in his bad books.

I was never physically coordinated. People once said of former President Ford, that "he couldn't walk and chew gum at the same time". Snap! Gerard was outstandingly talented with his hands. I once saw him fashion a boomerang out of wood. We took it to the football field opposite our villa. Sure enough, he could launch it to a hundred metres away and it would come back. He never ceased trying to teach me practical chores but I was always failing. And in the Algarve he had the time to attend to them. Meanwhile, my poor dad toiled away as a solicitor in London in what was a mentally exhausting profession.

Gerard christened me "egghead" and used my gangly height and awkwardness against me. But, especially in my teenage years, I couldn't have done any better. Nevertheless the conviction that I can never bang a nail into a wall without chopping off a finger has stayed with me. It's funny how these admonishments stick. Gerard would give me a practical task to do and hover over me, increasingly impatient, shaking his head. Then if I continued to "muck it up" he'd lose his temper.

Given my increasing dislike of Gerard I enjoyed it when he got into trouble. My mother told me of a funny incident in a bar in Luz called Godots when the owner, tiring of Gerard's indiscreet comments, had ordered him out and called him a "shit stirrer". The owner in question was drunk, and so perhaps, for once, Gerard was wronged. Apparently he bumped into Gerard near the beach a week or so later and apologised.

"I've never liked you but I was on the wrong side of the bar to talk to you like that." This proprietor – I've since discovered – was not an especially popular figure himself but sometimes it takes one rogue to put another in his place!

A renowned larger-than-life character in Luz at the time was Bill Rees,[12] a former deep sea diver who had emigrated to Luz in 1970 and helped to promote the Algarve as a tourist destination. Bill was also a former Royal Marine commando who could, we were reliably informed, kill someone with one blow. Bill was around 50 when we knew him but he had an eye for the ladies and one time, so legend would have it, had a particular Portuguese girl in his sights.

---

[12] Bill Rees (1927-2011). He received an obituary in the *Henley Standard*, which was reproduced here on the site of his old school.
https://my.blundells.org/obclub/obclub/obituaries/bowen-rees_bill.htm

Perhaps she was earmarked for someone else because four young Portuguese guys decided to teach Bill a lesson outside a bar. Unfortunately for them, the encounter worked the other way. Bill's only complaint was that the fourth guy escaped because he couldn't run fast enough!

Bill was a Luz legend, his hairy, powerful chest and blue floppy hat adorning local postcards. He looked like Ernest Hemingway. When not taking tourists on fishing expeditions, he'd be giving swimming lessons at the Luz Bay Club. He was disciplined, even strict with tourists at work. But, off-duty, he was something of a reprobate, a womaniser and politically incorrect.

He and my mother got on well. His relationship with Gerard was tense because they both liked telling funny stories and disliked taking a back seat. Bill, a few years younger than Gerard, and too young for active service in the war, was determined not to be over-impressed by Gerard's endless RAF stories. And Gerard, for his part, didn't like to be upstaged by this manly Welsh guy who looked like he could break a door by running at it with his head.

Bill lived for 10 years in an old fisherman's hut. He'd be in and out all, often leaving the door open. No one worried about security. One day we were passing by (again, no phone) and Gerard called out for Bill. No answer came and so Gerard pushed open the door, which was ajar, and walked in. Bill appeared from the rear, carrying a full gas bottle, looking like an angry bull.

"Don't you ever knock on someone's door before entering, you rude little man?"

Gerard, rarely lost for words, was taken aback. "Oh sorry, Bill, I saw the door was open and decided ..."

"That's not the point. Do me the courtesy of knocking. Who do you think you are?"

Gerard also had "wandering hand trouble" when it came to women. Nowadays, in the age of political correctness, his behaviour would be deemed scandalous. If my mother had a half-way attractive female friend, he'd be pressing her about whether she'd "had her bottom pinched" – a curious line of questioning. One time, Zé, the snobbish proprietor of the beachside boutique, arrived for a drink at our place. As he was saying goodbye, Gerard kissed her and with his right hand gave her a soft but tangible slap on her bottom.

She recoiled and in a voice worthy of Lady Bracknell, said: "Gerard, don't be so familiar!"

I now had three people in Luz whose hands I wanted to shake: drunken bar owner, Bill and Zé.

Sadly, so many characters in the Algarve proved transitory. Bill was top of the list. He met a Welsh lady and in 1980, after a rumbustious decade in Luz, he and his new fiancé returned to the UK. On his last day I helped him load everything into his van: sofas, fishing tackle, nautical and diving and landing equipment, mattresses, tables, ropes and inflatable dinghies. I've *never* worked as hard as I did that day. I'd never have toiled like that for Gerard. But I was glad to do it for a guy who had Gerard's number. Bill got into his Blue Volkswagen and drove off. He'd kissed goodbye to a decade of his life. But he never even glanced over his shoulder. Bill died in 2011, aged 84. Now the little road where he lived in the town is named after him.

My mother was a strange choice for the Algarve. I've already noted she never swam. But she never even *accompanied* me to the pool; she'd just tell me to "go and enjoy it". When it was the two of us, pre-Gerard, I'd enter the sea and she'd look at me from the Concha, a restaurant on the beachfront.

But unlike other expats, notable the "bow tie Colonel", she was determined to go native. She learned Portuguese and was able not only to guide in it in the UK but also converse with everyone without misunderstandings. She attended an evening class in London with an elderly Portuguese teacher and he was always delighted to see his star pupil. The other "students", admittedly 20 years older than my mother, sounded stilted by comparison.

My mum later claimed to have bought the villa for me but, ironically, as we shall see, she spent more time there *without* me than with me. My "stepfather" Gerard also loved Luz and the villa when he saw it for the first time in 1975. He quickly took up the garden lawn and made it into a Spanish-style patio. It hadn't occurred to him a child would be happier in a conventional garden, kicking a ball about, not a patio brimming with overgrown plants. Or maybe it *had* occurred to him and he realised the conversion would get me out of the house. He also hated cats but Bobby had disappeared by then. Gerard had probably scared him off.

Up to 1977 my mother and stepfather used to travel with me out at Christmas time and other times of the year. But times were changing. Gradually the villa was no longer a traditional holiday home but a lavishly maintained second residence. The tiled floor in the lounge was carpeted, a third bedroom was added to replace the porch facing the farmland at the back, and hundreds of quality hardbacks were shipped from London along with some paintings. We had an elegant marble coffee table that doubled as a chessboard, and a beautiful pine desk. Our original chairs were replaced by a cream-coloured sofa and the white shutters were repainted yellow. The incremental improvements to the villa were in tandem with my mother's growing disillusionment with London life.

Michael and Colin normally visited over Christmas, both drinking heavily. Michael once arrived, moping around, and getting sozzled over a girlfriend in the

UK before promptly running off with a Brazilian lady two doors down. Both Michael and Colin had been abandoned by their father, my mother's first husband. Michael even changed his name to my maternal grandmother's maiden name. It was a spur-of-the-moment decision to spite his father and I never gave it much thought until one day I realised my two half-brothers and myself now had *three* different surnames *and* my mother also changed her name *three* times.

Holidays in Portugal were better when Gerard wasn't there. August from 1980 onwards was a fun time because he stopped going out for the summer, pleading excessive heat. Our last Christmas in Luz, the last family holiday there I can recall, was at the end of 1984. Gerard had (technically) broken up with my mother by this stage. It was another booze-filled yuletide. Only this time I was the main offender and ended up vomiting over the carpet. But the example had been set by the older adults. None of us drew a sober breath. Just after Christmas I bought *The Daily Telegraph* which reported the deaths of two hard-drinking British actors, Peter Lawford and Ian Hendry. "The vodka bottle cost Lawford his life at 61" proclaimed an inside spread.

"I'll drink to that," said Michael, raising his vodka and tonic.

"Let this be a lesson. Drink in moderation," chimed in my mother.

Yes, indeed, always drink In Moderation. I bet they had a bottle of that in their cocktail cabinet. Even then, by the age of 17, I was already hooked. I had my first drink when I was 10. "You should get used to drinking early," my mother told me, "so when you go to university you'll know how to handle it". (Ironic, given what happened when I went to university.) I first got drunk when I was 12, again in Luz over Christmas, drinking most of a bottle of white wine, and Gerard, uncharitably but typically, laughed uproariously.

That first drunken session was strange. I can't say I enjoyed the taste *per se* but I liked how it loosened my tongue. I giggled insanely and Michael was laughing at me laughing. I became quite the entertainer, pulling funny faces and even telling a couple of stories which I didn't usually do. I drank at every subsequent opportunity.

My mother and Gerard imbibed every day, lunchtime and evening, if they weren't working. Gerard was always encouraging me to drink, saying it would "put hairs on my chest". I don't know about that. But I *do* know it was to eventually cause liver cirrhosis in one half-brother, trigger a massive stroke in another and, in my case, render my twenties a lost decade. But Gerard had a good head for drink and so each session saw him emerging the following morning unscathed while we nursed our heads.

Sometimes in the villa I'd go to their bedroom when Mum and Gerard weren't there. You had to pass through it to reach the garden. My dad had once occupied the same room but, sadly, I could never remember him in the Algarve. He'd been "replaced" by Gerard, a little man whom my mother would later concede, wasn't "a patch on your dad's character". So what accounted for her vile drunken outburst against my dad that night in the Club? My mother and Gerard wanted to run away to the Algarve. But, in her mind, my dad stood in their way.

But who was Gerard to usurp my father?

3. Hysterectomy

"I don't think I'd be very good with someone who's ill."

Gerard

One day in the autumn of 1978 I was crouching at the top of the stairs in our London house when I overheard my mother telling Gerard something important.

"I have some bad news, bear," she said, matter-of-factly. "I need an operation for cancer of the uterus and it has to be done quickly. At the Royal Marsden Hospital."

As I peered through the banisters I could see Gerard sitting in his normal place at the far end of the sofa nearest the TV, clasping his stomach. *The Evening Standard* was on the table and he'd circled the evening's entertainment according to the order of play. Early autumn had been a difficult period in British politics, with worse still to come. Recently, he'd been fulminating against the Callaghan-led Labour government, regretting no election had been called.

He lit a cigarette and, as usual, when someone else was talking, his eyes rolled around in their sockets.

He didn't say anything, just drew deep on his cigarette and stroked his chin.

"Did you hear me, bear?"

"Er…yes, *Chou*, but I don't think I'll be very good with someone who's ill." He said this with no malice in his voice, like a throwaway comment.

My mother laughed and that was rare for her. But it was a strange laugh. And when she told her friends they also laughed the same way.

She had her operation in November 1978 and we visited her in the Royal Marsden in the communal lounge. A TV was on in the background. Gerard was pleased because he had a keen eye for the schedules and one of his favourite programmes, *Return of the Saint*, was on later. He wanted to return in time and so he was rushing the conversation, doing small talk while glancing furtively at his watch.

My dad was alarmed when he heard the news of my mother's impending operation. It was time for a rare call to Gerard.

"It's nothing to worry about. Everything will be fine. It's a minor procedure," Gerard told him.

Later, when I was 15, I had a retrospective conversation with Gerard regarding that minor "procedure".

"It's good they caught the cancer early. Because, if they hadn't, Mum might even have died," I said.

"Oh I don't know. It's easy to exaggerate these things and get them out of proportion."

My mother soon came home. (She lived another 42 years, so the "procedure" must have been a total success!) The NHS operation meant she had been unable to work as normal in her capacity as a London guide. And when you're a freelancer if you don't work you don't earn money. It was now late autumn.

Gerard told me they might have to stay in the UK for the winter, after all, and cancel their planned trip to Portugal. That would be "a disaster", he told me. Everything hinged on the result of a post-operative scan.

One day, in the earliest days of her convalescence, I found Gerard had circled some items in the *Evening Standard* and, for once, to my surprise, they weren't on the television page.

"I'm looking for suitable jobs to tide us over if we have to stay here," he told me. "It's important to keep the cash flow rolling over."

My opinion of Gerard went up a notch. He was obviously more big-hearted and considerate than I'd allowed, putting on a brave front while my mother was ill. Tough but tender. Maybe his dismissive stance on hearing the news was an aberration.

"What jobs are they?"

"There's a traffic warden … oh God I've always hated them, bloody bluebottles …but it's a possibility… wait a second, this could be interesting too" … He read out the exact wording. 'Evening housekeeper required for an elderly man – to cook, clean and attend to all domestic duties'."

I couldn't see Gerard doing that. When he was alone in the house the Chivers marmalade, margarine and dirty plates remained on the table until lunchtime.

"And there's a waitress job that doesn't pay too badly."

Finally, I saw we had our wires crossed. No sooner had my mother signed her discharge papers from hospital than Gerard was ready to send her out to work.

***

My mother later told me they'd met in 1974 while both were on London guiding jobs. Gerard had asked her out for a drink. His opening gambit was to ask her what she thought her greatest "assets" were.

Her reply, which she later confided to me, made it clear that she had taken "assets" to mean "qualities". "I'm a people person. I get on well with everyone and I'm popular. People like me. And that's my number one asset," she said.

Later, I wondered if she'd misconstrued what Gerard meant by "assets". I'm sure it didn't take long for her to reveal her principal real estate "assets": a mortgage-free house in Pimlico *and* a villa in the Algarve, the latter still exotic in that era. They'd been in a pub, after all, and I knew how loose-tongued she could be after a couple of drinks.

Or had Gerard meant physical "assets"? Maybe his eyes were fixed on her chest the whole time. I say this because Gerard never tired of mentioning how well-endowed my mother was, regaling friends and even strangers with the same joke. "If she had to play golf, she wouldn't be able to see the ball!" How everyone laughed at this (slightly risqué) humour. It must have been vaguely amusing the first time. But when I heard it 100 times, it started to pall.

Our great friend, actor Carlos Douglas,[13] also a qualified London tour guide, later told me that, when my mother had met Gerard, he and some fellow guides who knew them both, had puzzled over the relationship. "That just can't be right," they'd said.

My mother couldn't see anything much wrong with anyone, even though I suspect she knew from the outset that Gerard wasn't exactly the world's most upstanding citizen. She had little cynicism herself

---

[13] Carlos Douglas (1935-2004) was primarily a supporting actor, best known as the waiter in the television series *Duty Free*. He won a scholarship to RADA. One of our closest family friends. He supplemented his income from acting by working as a London Blue Badge tour guide.

and so had a problem spotting avarice. She was manipulative but also malleable. She loathed arguments. She once told me she could never do jury service because she couldn't convict anyone. I didn't dwell on this revelation at the time. But now I see it as pivotal to her whole life. She could *always* see the other person's point of view. I later saw it as a destructive softness because if you can't look evil in the eye and call it out, you can do damage. I always thought if my mother – who wasn't Jewish but who married a Jewish man (my father) – had met Hitler, she'd have tried to "understand".

"Tell me, Herr Hitler, why do you dislike Jewish people? I have met some lovely Jewish people."

She wasn't aggressive or confrontational. Even when she was angry her manner and voice were so soft that few guessed how she felt. She needed booze to make it seem real; then there was a huge mood swing and her anger was frequently misplaced and irrational.

Sometimes, when I got older, her softness only riled me. If I went on a political demonstration and I told her of the strength of feeling that day she'd smile and say: "Yes and what a great day for a walk around London. I passed by St James's Park today and the flowers looked wonderful."

She had a strange lack of *conventional* humour. Brits of a certain age may remember *The Two Ronnies'* classic Four Candles sketch when it first aired in 1976. My mother and Gerard were sitting on the sofa with their gin and orange, me with my coke, passing around the nuts. Gerard and I were falling off the sofa as Ronnie Barker made all his (misunderstood) requests. She paled because she couldn't understand why all the *double entendres* were so funny. Eventually she trundled off sheepishly.

It wasn't only the famous Four Candles sketch that passed her by. Others gems of 1970s British comedy – Jimmy revealing his cache of arms and threatening a counter-revolution in *The Fall and Rise of Reginald Perrin* didn't tickle her. Neither did Basil Fawlty berating an elderly guest who complained about the partial sea view from her hotel bedroom: "What do you expect to see from a Torquay hotel window – Sydney Opera House perhaps …?" Not a chuckle from my mother. Yet these were iconic laugh-out-loud moments for most families, the apogee of the British sitcom during a profoundly grey decade.

Humourless people can be dangerous because they can't see the ridiculousness of their own actions. She could tell a funny story, and she was a gifted mimic, so people mistook this for humour. But it wasn't. She knew how to make others laugh and repeated the same stories by rote. But if she was in a group of people and someone made a funny remark, and the others also didn't "get it", then she was silent. If the others laughed, my mother would get her "cue" and say "that was very funny". [14]

But she had buckets of charm. My God, did she have charm! The dazzling smile and glowing eyes when she met a friend, her soothing hand placed on someone's shoulder if they had a troubling story to relate, the generosity she bestowed on others, and her quality of radiating goodness. "Charming" was also my mother's favourite word for people she liked. She would say that (so-and-so) was "absolutely c-h-a-r-m-i-n-g", with an elongated emphasis.

When the breakaway Social Democratic Party (SDP) was formed in the UK in 1981 my mother supported its four founding members. She wasn't a political animal at all and I doubt she knew much of their platform. But she had always liked Shirley Williams,[15] Roy Jenkins and David Owen, all of whom she found to be "c-h-a-r-m-i-n-g". She never mentioned Bill Rodgers at all, presumably because he lacked this quality. We attended the launch and, I have to

---

[14] I'm reminded of a great quote from the late Martin Amis. "A sense of humor is a serious business; and it isn't funny, not having one. Watch the humorless closely: the cocked and furtive way they monitor all conversation, their flashes of panic as irony or exaggeration eludes them, the relief with which they submit to the meaningless babble of unanimous laughter."

[15] Shirley Williams (1930-2021), Roy Jenkins (1920-2003), David Owen (b.1938) and Bill Rodgers (b.1928).

say, the so-called Gang of Three – sorry Four – were indeed "c-h-a-r-m-i-n-g" company!

If this makes her sound superficial, this wasn't so. Charm is an endearing quality but she could never have forged lasting friendships without genuine commitment, interest and hard work. She was endlessly patient and solicitous with friends. After her retirement, and after her job had morphed from being a tour guide to being a tour director, a close friend and work colleague phoned. She'd been offered a tour to Ireland. She wanted to accept it but the stipulation was it had to be someone who had been before which she hadn't. So she had to con her way in.

My mother was in Portugal when the call came through from London. She spent the afternoon detailing Dublin's hidden treasures, telling her what to say in the Waterford glass crystal factory, offering insider tips about the best shops and the most picturesque routes around Bantry Bay. She even coached her on answers to likely questions. The conversation lasted over *three* hours.

She also looked out for others proactively. When another friend, a gentle middle-aged Scottish widower, confided his loneliness to her, my mother thought of a Scottish lady who could be a compatible partner. They've now been married 10 years. How many people these days bother to act as matchmakers?

***

Gerard moved into our three-storey house in Pimlico, in 1975. You could see the Houses of Parliament and the spires of Westminster Abbey if you climbed the ladder on our roof terrace. In contrast to his slavish devotion to our patio in Luz, Gerard lavished scant attention on our roof terrace. This was an early sign of his intentions.

At the beginning he tried to ingratiate himself. He appeared at the 1975 sports day of Connaught House School,[16] my first main school in London. My mother and Gerard were standing at one end of the venue in Hyde Park and my dad at the other. When I'd finished participating in a race or event, I was unsure which way to turn. Most children would have dashed to whichever parent they wanted to but I remained in limbo, my head bobbing both ways, straining my neck like a spectator in side-line seats at a tennis match, waving to both ends.

Part of me was too eager to please. I was already a nervous little boy, ostensibly reeling from my parents' divorce. I felt more vulnerable to external stimuli than other children. Towards the end of my time at Connaught House I'd feel apprehensive as

[16] Connaught House, independent school for boys and girls, still at 47 Connaught Square, London, W2.

my mother drove me from Pimlico and around Hyde Park Corner on the way to the school. As we passed by the Odeon Marble Arch I could feel my heart racing, my "sensitive" nervous system reacting to the imminence of the school day and all the sounds and noises about to come my way. It was the pre-multiplex era and Oscar-winning movie *One Flew Over the Cuckoo's Nest* was enjoying an unusually long run. A huge colour poster featured a scarlet-faced Jack Nicholson, gritting his teeth and sweating. When I saw the film a few years later I realised it was McMurphy – the character in the film – trying in vain to lift a water fountain. The image disturbed me and got me even more tentative. But it didn't take much to unnerve me. The opening credits of a TV show called *Survivors* were enough to make me feel uneasy for the rest of the evening.

I was still at Connaught House when Britain baked in the great heat wave of the summer of 1976. We'd troop off to nearby Hyde Park, wearing T-shirts and shorts, holding clammy hands in pairs. Often, my "partner" would be SF Said,[17] who would join me at my next school, Sussex House. (He later became a successful writer of children's fiction.) Trouble is, no one thought about water for us in the park with the mercury topping 30 Celsius. We'd return to school with a raging thirst, jostling to reach the kitchen. No sooner had one boy raised a beaker of

---

[17] SF Said, successful children's writer (b.1967).

water to his mouth than those behind him would be prodding and jabbing him to get out of the way. I too felt like doing the same but when I watched the boy in front drinking quickly, desperate to quench his thirst, I waited patiently.

During school holidays I'd accompany my mother on tours. I could see first-hand her winning ways, answering tourists' daft and repetitive questions with infinite patience. She disarmed difficult clients with her charm and warmth, quietly defusing any potential altercations. But grievances were rare because people liked her and her reports (post-tour evaluations filled in by the tourists themselves) were invariably glowing.

One time, after a long full-day's sightseeing, my mother was tipped to such an extent that there was an "embarrassment of riches". She had trouble finding somewhere to put the coins, pound notes and dollar bills. "Does anyone have a doggie bag?" The only problems I can ever recall involved Irish-Americans, one of whom once unleashed such an anti-English diatribe that she (politely in her soft voice) asked him why he had decided to visit London in the first place.

Gerard was different. Sure, he was amusing with his ever-expanding "joke book" of ridiculous questions asked by dim-witted foreign tourists – usually Americans if only because they were the majority visitors. "Why did they build Windsor Castle so close to the airport?" was a perennial favourite. A sign on the London underground instructing that "dogs must be carried on the escalators" perturbed another American tourist who said he didn't have a dog and therefore couldn't travel. Then there was the American who had "corrected" him for mentioning something about "World War One". "You must mean World War Two. There was no World War One." My mother's favourite story (and here we note the old adage about the UK and the US being divided by a common language) was that of a male American tourist who asked her, while they were staying in a hotel on an extended tour of the UK: "Can I knock you up during the night if need calls?"

"No, sir, you certainly *cannot!*"

Yes, plenty of material for funny stories. But, as I accompanied Gerard on *his* tours, I noticed his strange ways. One time, returning from Stonehenge, which was a full-day's sightseeing, he snored loudly on the front seat. I suspect he'd been drinking wine at lunchtime. During Silver Jubilee year he sold commemorative coins at heavily marked-up prices. Likewise, if tourists didn't want tickets to visit the Tower of London he'd re-sell them, again at inflated prices. He made too many stops at souvenir shops where it was clear he was on commission. At the end of every tour, as the coach wended its way back to the hotel, he'd say: "If you'd like to extend a token of your appreciation to me and the driver, this would be gratefully received." Of course, he was never tipped as generously as my mother!

Gerard's "difficult" character was containable when he had Americans. But he also did tours in Spanish. One time, in charge of a group of elderly Spanish tourists, he steered a sickly-looking lady of ample proportions down the steps of the coach. "Come on – you fat old cow!" he said under his breath as he took her arm, smiling broadly. Gerard, always something of a gambler, bet on the elderly passengers not understanding English.

One time we came home and the phone rang. It was the head of Spanish Speaking Services. It might have been a follow-up to the same incident, but I can't recall. I answered. He asked for Gerard and then all I could hear was SCREAMING. And screaming in Spanish sounded especially frightening. It was no surprise Gerard wasn't requested for tours subsequently. He spent most of his time in his top floor "office" (in reality, a third bedroom and this was a luxury to use it as an office) perusing photographs.

Back in the days before digital photography, Gerard's first port of call on return from Luz was to run to the chemist to have his many reels of film processed. He'd pick them up a couple of days later and go through them with the salesperson. "The colours of the mimosa look over-exposed. It's the incredible luminosity, you see." The assistant would twiddle her thumbs and look the other way, interrupting him to serve other customers, but Gerard wouldn't budge. No one could deny he was a talented photographer but this was no reason to force sales staff in Pimlico to witness a private exhibition!

At home, Gerard could be amusing, finding laughs in everyday situations, but usually at someone else's expense. For months on end we would visit the same wine shop in Lupus Street to buy a red wine called *Prince Noir* (Black Prince in French). The lady there didn't speak French and pronounced it Prince Noy, deeming it a proper name. We used to play a game. How many times could we coax her to say "Prince Noy"?

He was also oddly fickle with his loyalty. A great Italian delicatessen was round the corner in Sussex Street, selling the best salami. A Sicilian guy named Salvatore ran it with his sidekick, wearing white overalls. Gerard would go there to buy a few items and be gone an hour because "great" discussions would ensue, often about football. Gerard, who liked to back the victor, was a Nottingham Forest fan in the era when, under Brian Clough, they were winning international competitions. Gerard would bait Salvatore about the outcome of a match until our Italian friend lost patience and demanded a more formal bet.

"Putta da money on da table …"

Gerard resisted. He'd grimace if you asked him for 10 pence and take out 20 half-penny coins he'd put in a jar. So he declined.

"Putta da money on da table!" Salvatore would repeat, banging the counter.

The Italians proved great friends, helping us out with an ice box and legs of lamb when we went to Portugal, even bringing bulky orders to our door. Gerard would send him a postcard of some attractive nubile lady from Luz. Salvatore would become all coy on Gerard's return, complaining his wife hadn't approved. It all seemed like good-natured boyish banter between friends. And for years Gerard and my mother were daily customers.

One day, a new delicatessen opened nearer our home. Gerard stopped going to the Italians. Just like that, as Tommy Cooper would have said! After six years of regular visits. There was no falling out. It was just more convenient for Gerard to go a shorter distance. So he transferred allegiance on the spot. My mother chastised him, reminding him of everything the Italians had done for us. But she was so embarrassed by Gerard's rejection of "the Italians" that she too stopped going because she didn't know how to explain his absence.

A few months later we happened to be passing by the Italians as a family and Gerard breezed past wordlessly. From inside the shop I could see

Salvatore and his partner raising their palms and looking at each other in bemusement. I couldn't hear what they were saying but it was obvious – "Did we do something wrong?"

Another time a boy kicked a ball into the inaccessible deep basement of our large house and rang our doorbell. Gerard, who was having an afternoon siesta, opened the window and told him to get lost. Later, the doorbell went again and it was the boy's mother. Get lost again! Strangely enough, it remains one of my iconic memories.

Gerard's gruffness was exacerbated by drink. If he had a morning sightseeing tour of London, and I was on school holidays, there was an unspoken assumption that I would have squeezed a few oranges in time for his return at lunchtime. If I had "neglected" my duties he'd start shouting. The liquor must have occasionally taken its toll because there was the odd day when he would abstain. A popular fad of that era was the Beverley Hills diet and he would sit there eating grapefruit, strictly without alcohol.

Deep down, he was bitter about his childhood. His father had died when he was nine and he'd been dispatched to boarding schools. Ironically, although he'd been through a tough time at boarding school, he was eager to inflict the same experience on me. He wanted me out of the way, especially as I neared 13. My mother once said a strange thing, referring to

Gerard's own lonely childhood. He'd had, she thought, "an emotional hysterectomy".

The more I saw of Gerard, the more suspicious I became. He decreased with knowing. He was only interested in beautiful women, wealthy people, people who could help him in his job, and in having a good time in the Algarve. He did offer to do some repairs in my dad's flat. But there was always the sense that he was trying to curry favour with people for his own ends.

We played darts, scrabble and even, in Portugal, paddle tennis. He had to win every time. If he didn't, he'd insist on playing on until he *had* won, punching the air repeatedly while baiting me about my loss. He might have loved his "babies" in the garden in Luz. His real babies he treated with disdain. He'd write to his son with an electronic typewriter from his "office" to tell him he'd never wanted children. My mother intercepted the letters and made him erase the hurtful content.

Those who knew Gerard only vaguely would have said he was very funny. Yes, he could make people laugh. He was also a talented mimic. One day he overheard me practising my French 'O' level oral. I'd once told him I'd been called "a wanker" by some kids on the way through Brixton one day when there was a train strike and I had to return by bus. Big mistake. Every such revelation would furnish Gerard, the great raconteur, with a story at my expense. To a roomful of friends Gerard once imitated my English accent and my stammer: *"Je veux devenir avocat ou j.journaliste. Je prend le train a l'école et on m'appelle w...w...w...wer...wer...wanker."* ("I want to become a lawyer or a journalist. I take the train to school and they call me 'wanker'.") Gerard could use humour effectively – in a way winning them over by making them laugh.

He was rather like Jean-Marie Le Pen: the forceful stare, the cynical shrug of the shoulders, the disparaging hand gestures to dismiss someone he disliked. When he shouted it would have reached the Churchill Garden Estate across the road. His personality was so powerful that when he told a funny story you couldn't help but be carried along to the raucous finale.

I hated Gerard's ability to make people laugh because I'd grown tired of him and his relentless abuse. He had sociopathic tendencies. By this I don't mean he was preparing to shoot people in Pimlico but that he did what he wanted. By 1980 his work had dried up. He spoke perfect French but when the phone rang for a guiding job in French it was invariably for my mother whose French was excellent but not at native speaker level, like Gerard's. At first he resented it but then his natural aversion to work kicked in. He'd spend the day in his "office" where his "above average" wartime

RAF certificate took centre stage, alongside photo montages of the Praia da Luz skyline and ex-girlfriends. "That was Angie back in 1960. She had lovely legs, didn't she?" he'd say to me. A picture of my mother when they first met was also on the wall. "She looked better back then," Gerard once commented to me five years or so later. "So did you, pal!" I thought, looking at his fat belly. I suppose a cheekier stepson would have said it.

He disliked black people. Even at Connaught House he was banging on about "Mbutus", as he called them; later, his language became far more obscene. His favourite tourists were white South Africans. One day he returned from a tour in fine fettle, cackling to himself and repeating a line he'd heard. "You can take the black out of the jungle but you can't take the jungle out of the black."

His racism wasn't confined to black people. He called me "Yitzhak" or "Yacob" to emphasise my half-Jewish ancestry. One time I questioned the price of an item and he replied this was "a Jewish question". He told me I'd end up fighting for Israel. If he saw a Jewish name when the credits rolled on a film or TV programme he'd say "he/she is one of yours". He also mentioned my "ski-sloped nose" and said he was sick of hearing about the Holocaust. Also on Gerard's hate list were trade unions whom he assailed for their "crass bloody-mindedness". His views were extremely reactionary although he never voted.

Life in the UK in the late 1970s could be depressing. Not so much knife crime but strikes, unrest, and constant talk of industrial decline. (Some might say the UK in 2023 isn't any better but that's another story!) Whatever view you took of the cause, Britain was lost.

One day I came back and murmured something about how nice it was to be "home". Gerard shook his head and said he viewed our house in Pimlico as "*a base*". This resonated with me. I knew it carried implications, like someone in the military describing temporary accommodation. My mother, in the background, did not demur. A big change was looming.

4. Abdication

"… it's always November and it's raining and it's three o'clock in the morning…"

Richard Burton reflecting on bad times on the Dick Cavett show in 1980

I got summoned to a meeting in the lounge in Pimlico in October 1977. This was shortly after the punishment beating in Luz. My mother and Gerard were sitting side by side on the sofa. She told me to pull up a chair, so I was now opposite them.

Gerard spoke first. My mother was looking down at the coffee table and out of the window. Anywhere, but at me. "We're going to be leaving for most of the winter." (It turned out to be the whole winter and more besides.) "We're be spending it at *the villa*. Michael will look after you in the run-up to Christmas. He'll move in here. And you'll be flying out to see us over the holidays. You'll be king of the castle. It'll be good for you; you'll be able to forge your independence and it will be" … I knew what was coming because he'd said these words before when announcing some form of punishment … "character-building".

My mother took over: "I'm sure we can stretch out your stay to four weeks over Christmas. Then, when you come back in January, we have an absolutely wonderful, c-h-a-r-m-i-n-g lady who will move in and look after you. You'll like her. Her name is Jill. She'll be your housekeeper."

I just sat there.

"And we can get you out again for half-term week in February," added my mother, sensing she wasn't winning me over.

I still couldn't say anything. Didn't know what to say. Neither had mentioned the words "Portugal" or "abroad", simply "the villa". It was as if they were relocating to a country cottage. But this was right at the tip of southern Europe. 1500 miles away.

"Ideally, we would have waited until before Christmas and we'd all go *together*. But the snow would make the journey difficult. So we'll be leaving in November," she added.

"I'm sure you're mature enough to understand all this," added Gerard. "Mature enough" meant understanding the need for separation from one's mother. It was his pre-emptive strike so that if I whined I'd be classed as "a cry-baby".

They waited for my reaction. I laughed and tried to make a joke out of it. "That's a long holiday." I looked at my mother intently, sitting there with her usual manicured fingernails and gold-leaf broach pinned to her chest. She averted her gaze. She had the word "GUILTY" etched all over her face in blazing capital letters, illuminated with neon lights.

Even Gerard looked nervous, the *only* time I can ever recall him like that. He was glaring at me, waiting for me to respond. This must have been his idea, I knew that. And the whole plan was precarious. Maybe if I'd kicked up a stink that would have been the end of it. But in those days children accepted things. Now I wish I'd thrown the coffee table at them. For everything, I realised later, hinged on collective compliance. All parties had to be signed up. If my father had protested vigorously my mother would have abandoned the idea. Or Michael, fickle-natured as he was, might have balked at the prospect of having to move in and cook for me. Or Jill, this "c-h-a-r-m-i-n-g" lady whom I wouldn't meet until January, might have had to change her plans. Then their dream of spending the four coldest months in the Algarve would have been kyboshed. This was never going to be a consultation. They were never going to ask: "Would you be ok if we left for the entire winter?" This was a *fait accompli* – or at least they hoped so.

My mother continued, offering further rambling explanations. There was nothing much, she claimed, in the way of work between November and March (true, there was less work but it wasn't non-existent). I was now old enough to let myself in from school (true), and fix myself some tea (true). My separation from her would be less time on an annual basis than endured by boys at boarding school (true). I'd be able to speak to my dad on the phone every evening (true), I'd have free run of the house (in a way, yes), I could watch all my favourite programmes (most of the time), I could invite friends back whenever I liked (I hardly ever did), and the time would pass by quickly. (It didn't). It could even be, and here she paused, "fun". (It wasn't). She had a knack of deftly defining this and other (abysmal) scenarios so they seemed unthreatening. And also telling you how you should feel.

I didn't buy any of it. I only saw loneliness ahead. But, in a strange way, I could see from their point of view it *was* a comprehensible choice. Yet I still have trouble accepting how my mother's conscience didn't stop her. I can *understand* it but can't *excuse* it. Also, a deeper reason, but one I didn't grasp at the time was that this was a great way for them to drink themselves senseless. Without a phone, they'd have few responsibilities. The only contact was through the phone and telex at the Luz Bay Club next door.

I rang my father later and told him the news. Typically, my mother was probably hoping I'd do so first. He responded as he always did when he disliked something, with his trademark 10-second pause and a heavy sigh. "Come again," he said. I'm sure he'd heard what I'd said but he couldn't take it in.

I'd expected him to explode. But he was wrong-footed. He was a solicitor, not a barrister, and not quick verbally, *and* he had little communication with my mother. I was the go-between. Maybe he also thought there was little he could do to stop them. In a follow-up conversation he said he regretted I couldn't stay with him. But he lived in a cramped one-bedroom flat. I had to agree. And he couldn't move into our house because it wasn't his to move into. Agreed again. It was a Catch-22.

My mother and I seldom broached these events later in life. But, when we did, her explanation only made me laugh. "Gerard was entitled to spend some time alone with me. After all, he'd taken on you three boys." How typical of her to explain her actions by saying she had made a sacrifice for someone else. In any case Gerard hadn't "taken on" Michael or Colin. They had largely fled the nest by the time he arrived. She would never have said, "I need to have a good time and I hate London in winter" which would have been nearer the truth.

Later, I pondered other potential motives for them to spend four months away. Was it an elaborate tax dodge? No, 120 days away wouldn't have made a difference for tax purposes. As I grew older, I even wondered: Was something going on during those winters I was unaware of? Algarve-based orgies? It crossed my mind. Yet my conclusion, 46 years down the line, was they wanted to escape and, as for the phone, I suspect they weren't unduly bothered by its absence, even welcomed it.

The lack of a phone was always perturbing for me. I'd never get used to not being able to chat to my mother. It's impossible now to contemplate life without it, especially in the smartphone era, when one touch connects you. Back then, in Luz, if she and Gerard wanted to meet friends or book a table in a restaurant, they'd have to see the people beforehand and arrange it in person. But that was not the key point – from my point of view. What if there was an emergency, such as a sudden illness or an attempted break-in? Or what if something went drastically wrong with me *in London* and *I* needed her? But what could go wrong? Well, quite a lot actually. I was in the slippery hands of my alcoholic half-brother.

***

My mother always had escapist tendencies. She couldn't face unpleasantness. She hated woolly jumpers, icy winds, coughs and colds and dark, dismal days. She loathed domesticity. So this would be her getaway. This four-month sojourn was no one-off. It was repeated for the next five years. A double whammy enabled it: both her and Gerard having a seasonal, summer-intensive job, and, above all, the availability of *that* villa in the sun.

Also, she lacked wise counsel. Her parents were both dead. Her mother had died when she 10, coincidentally the same age as I was when she chose to leave me. But was this a "coincidence"? Sadly, I'm not so sure. She'd had no mother to guide her through her second decade. Now, ironically, she was inflicting some of that on me. No family member was there to say her behaviour was unacceptable. (Both sets of my grandparents had died before I was born.)

Would I have been tempted to do the same if I'd been in her shoes? It's easy to say "no". I believe the answer *is* "no". But I can't be sure. One time I was looking at a documentary about Hitler's Germany. A Jewish guy appeared, a German Jew, and he asked a novel, rhetorical question: "When I looked at all these handsome young German soldiers, fighting fit, marching proudly for their *Fuhrer*, I've often thought, if I'd been one of them, would I have done the same? Fortunately, that didn't happen."

I'm not drawing a direct parallel between the two situations. Just that, in my mother's case, temptation and the desire for an easier life had gotten the better of her. Whenever kids at boarding school ask their parents later in life why they were dispatched to these cruel institutions, someone says "it was in your best interests". She could never say this. So instead she made out it was necessary to keep Gerard happy.

The way I saw it – although admittedly more with hindsight – was I'd already been separated from my dad and now I was separated from my mum *and* during the winter, which is a tough time for kids. Colin and Michael never complained about this period. But they were not in their formative years, being 21 and 23 respectively, whereas I was only 10.

These winters apart ran counter to every value my mother preached before or since, namely the importance of family togetherness. For her this period doubtless passed by quickly and without incident. (Well, if you secluded yourself in a place like Praia da Luz in wintertime back in 1977 there wouldn't have been many incidents!)

My half-brothers would say these events only accounted for a few weeks and so what's the big deal? And so, dear reader, as you are invariably addressed when the ball lands in your court, you must decide whether this was over-reaction, or something different.

I saw it as an early example of gas lighting. It was ingrained in me how to respond. I wasn't allowed to have a voice or an opinion. I was told how I *should* view the situation. "You'll find the time will pass by quickly. Don't be so sensitive about it all ..."

Her decision also marked the culmination of her submission to Gerard. Her soul had been captured. My mother had already changed her surname to his in the summer of 1976. (Gee, that hot summer in London must have made people mad!) – And she was now his. Her maiden name was left behind when she took the names of her first and second husbands. And now she had taken Gerard's name.

I'd assumed they were married but this was naïve of me. After all, Gerard loved photos and any wedding pictures would have surely featured prominently on the mantelpiece. She told me she'd changed her name to protect me at school. But a boozy household holds no secrets. The real reason, she later confided to me after a bottle of wine, was she disliked Kupfermann as a surname. "It was making my life harder in the business because people assumed I was Jewish. And I'm not. I had Jewish tourists approaching and talking to me about Judaism, asking me about synagogues in London. It was a complication I didn't need."

I felt this was insulting to my heritage.

Did Gerard destroy her? This is no throwaway question. People *can* be destroyed by other people, sometimes literally. Women can be strangled by abusive partners. Gerard didn't do that. But he did strangle her moral compass. My mother once told me she'd never been a big drinker until she met Gerard. "I knew little about alcohol." This soon changed. If she returned after a morning's sightseeing then the lunchtime aperitif ushered in generous helpings of wine, an afternoon siesta, and more booze in the evening. She once said that drink served to conveniently "delineate" the day from the evening. Trouble is, the "delineation" gradually became between the morning and any time from noon onwards!

My mother's escape plan also suited my half-brother Michael who disliked me but could live rent-free for a couple of months. Michael had been renting a flat in Stockwell but his chronic drunkenness had riled the landlords. Moving into our home in Pimlico, while he looked for somewhere permanent, suited him. Colin, then at Oxford Polytechnic, could also stay there when he was on breaks. There were three bedrooms, after all. And although Gerard had converted the top bedroom adjoining mine into an office, anyone could put a sleeping bag there. So all the dominoes fell into line.

These winters in the sun became the norm. It wasn't just the absences I loathed. She and Gerard *lived* for these four months away. We rarely ate out in London between March and November. Gerard would have said: "What's the point?" We seldom went *anywhere*. In the summer she was always working, apart from in August when we went away on holiday. They were saving up for their "sabbatical" in Luz.

I dreaded the prospect of her leaving. That first winter I even resorted to hiding her keys and handbag. At heart I was a mummy's boy and loathed the long separation.

***

It was an early morning in mid-November. My bedside radio alarm clock said 5.21. My room at the top of the house was decorated with orange flowery flock wallpaper, the carpet stained with ink from a fountain pen. The cupboard was full of dirty clothes even *before* her departure.

I had woken with a start. Was it the door banging? More likely a telepathic link. I went to the condensation-filled window overlooking Lupus Street. It was still dark, blustery, and some paper bags were flying around. An autumn shower was yellow-filtered, visible only through the street lamps. I heard movement downstairs. Sure enough, there was Gerard in his zipped-up golf jacket, coughing serially in his trademark foghorn way, like three punctuation marks. He popped a Fisherman's Friend lozenge in his mouth and loaded the boot. My mother followed, her high heels clicking the pavement, holding a headscarf against the wind.

"Keys?" asked Gerard.

I was minded to open the window and shout downstairs. I don't know what I was going to say …

but as it turned out they were too quick and they never looked up. If I'd turned on the light they might have done. But I didn't. She and Gerard got into their silly silver Simca and slivered away. I stared down at the street for a long time.

Michael was, I knew, sleeping in the next room. But this was no consolation. There's nothing lonelier than a London street at 5am in November. *Nothing.* At least in December Christmas lights abound and the holiday season beckons. And in January, dull month that it is, you can convince yourself spring is within reach. No wonder when I look back on my time in London it was always a dark, squally autumn day as I kick my way through fallen leaves.

I imagined them driving over Chelsea Bridge toward Southampton to board their ferry to St Malo. Did my mother have last-minute guilt pangs? What would they have discussed? Perhaps Gerard would have said – as they drove south through the morning fog – "We'll be away from all this in a few days."

The scene will stay with me forever. Total abandonment. With hindsight, their choice of vehicle to cross the Pyrenees and take the long trek down to Portugal was as ill-judged as their decision to leave in the first place. But this was the age of foolishness. Nothing made sense.

I went back to sleep. I woke up a couple of hours later to the familiar cheery voices of Bob Holness and Douglas Cameron on LBC's morning show, the sing-along adverts, "the Houndsditch warehouse … with five floors of bargains all waiting for you at our stores". I washed and ate some *Ready Brek*. Michael staggered into the kitchen, made me a marmite sandwich for my packed lunch (it took him under a minute), cigarette dangling from his mouth, and stuffed the bread inside an orange Hovis wrapper. I looked at it and dreaded eating it in front of my classmates. In my first year at Sussex House they'd abolished cooked lunches, a fait accompli I hadn't mulled over at the time but which now hit me hard. My neglect would now be visible to everyone.

I wasn't keen on inviting friends back. There would be no tree in the run-up to Christmas. What would be the point? Even Michael was planning to fly out to Portugal over Christmas – but after me. So the house would be empty. Besides, Michael never cleaned properly and the place was a mess.

Both Michael and Colin had gone to boarding school, likewise my mother and Gerard. So this was my version of boarding school, as she would have it. But at least at boarding school you knew someone was in attendance. What would happen if I was ill? Who would look after me? But London, although dark and drab in winter, has a merciful climate and I was seldom sick. Once, that first winter in the run-up to Christmas, I feigned a high temperature because I was being bullied at school. Michael called my dad who came to see me from his law firm in the West End. He stayed into the evening and Michael wasn't sure if this was right. It wasn't his house, after all. I do feel bad about my "performance" now.

My dad had to compensate for my mum's absence in other ways too. He'd attend weekday school coffee mornings to discuss topics related to Sussex House, the posh private preparatory school I attended in Cadogan Square. At times he was the only man there. I'm surprised he wasn't picked up. How I wish he had been!

One Sunday evening, again wet, dark, and cold, my father drove me back home after our usual afternoon outing. Michael wasn't there and maybe I'd forgotten my key, I can't recall. Dad was fuming. We stayed in the car as the rain lashed down, waiting for Michael to return. It was a long wait. My dad got out of the car and told me to stay inside. I was sitting in the back seat. I could see him stamping his feet. He walked a few steps away toward Lupus Street, turning round to see if I was still watching him. I ducked in the car seat but kept my eyes glued on him. When he thought he was out of earshot he again stamped his foot angrily and shouted "Bitch! Bitch!" several times at the top of his voice. He assumed I hadn't heard. I dutifully played innocent.

He got back in the car, still enraged, and then Michael arrived, collar up, head down, scurrying through the squall, carrying his signature "dinner", a four-pack of Special Brews and some cheese. My dad ushered me in while shouting at Michael: "This is a total abdication of responsibility for her child!" I knew the meaning of the word "abdication". My father was a gent; he probably didn't realise I knew what he was talking about. Michael cowered in the background. Eventually he murmured: "You're quite right!" My mother had achieved something incredible, uniting my dad and Michael, who loathed each other, in agreement!

I was used to my mother defining my father's behaviour. Now my father was defining hers. I did convey to her what he had said but not the "bitch" part. She shrugged it off.

The weeks up to Christmas dragged by. I never liked Pimlico, particularly Lupus Street, and the adjacent streets which were like one giant concrete maze. It was a sorry cousin to Chelsea, so grey by comparison to those lovely red-bricked buildings, and less exciting than Victoria which at least carried the promise of travel and hustle and bustle. And Pimlico in November was drabber than normal. Lack of trees and green spaces meant playing football in the street. But even that was a no-no because the clocks had just gone back.

One afternoon, walking back from school in my tweed jacket and mulberry tie, I was attacked by a group of local hooligans. All I heard was "toffee nose" and the next thing I was kicked to the ground and my school satchel fell open, exercise books scattering around the pavement. I had my fair share of that, kids from the Churchill Garden Estate asking me "Do you wanna figh' abou' it, mate?" I could never work out what "it" was.

Pimlico's most famous resident, as far as I knew, round the corner from us in Denbigh Street, was actor Wilfred Brambell[18] from *Steptoe and Son*. Occasionally we'd see him in the Sussex Restaurant in Sussex Street for Sunday lunch. He dressed dandily off-screen with a carnation in his lapel. Kids used to ring his doorbell and run away and he'd open the window and shout – in a much posher voice than his screen character – "piss orf"!

An Italian friend lived near Westminster Cathedral in a modern block. His father worked for Esso and his mother was a warm Italian lady with a lovely undulating voice. Their flat was cosy and she made great homemade pizza. I began spending more and more time there, not wanting to go home. I'd get on the tube at Sloane Square and go to Victoria or even journey round the Circle Line on my own, for the adventure. The days went by slowly …

But that first separation from my mother eventually passed and I was reunited with her and Gerard for a month-long Christmas holiday. I flew to Faro on a TAP (Air Portugal) scheduled flight as an

[18] Wilfred Brambell (1912-1985).

unaccompanied minor. My special status meant a helpful stewardess escorted me throughout after I'd said goodbye to my dad. He looked sad to see me go. I had a nice little "necklace" with a badge.

I relished the singularity of it all but there's something undeniably odd about being an unaccompanied minor. You're cargo being despatched through the skies, a solitary little human being tossed around. It crystallizes your situation. Back to the Connaught House sports day again where I got ambivalent about my allegiance. I felt sorry about leaving my dad but I so looked forward to seeing my mum.

A family friend from Luz was sitting a couple of rows down from me on the flight and even though I was only 11 there was a surge of maturity in me and I wondered if I should approach her. I didn't because I was captivated by a majestic sunset as we descended over the marshlands surrounding Faro airport.

The in-flight lunch included a miniature bottle of Alentejo red wine. The crew probably assumed I'd leave it. But I drank it and arrived distinctly tiddly. Mum and Gerard didn't notice and asked me about the post. The holiday went well and, to be honest, my overwhelming emotion was happiness at seeing my mother again.

Gerard behaved better towards me after not seeing me for a while. Maybe he'd got what he wanted, time alone with my mother, and he'd accepted he'd have to be accommodating. Or my mum, mindful of the separation, had laid down the law and reminded him I was entitled to a warm welcome.

A few days into the holiday, however, I was in the garden trying to help out with a couple of chores. I was being my normal cack-handed self and Gerard lost his temper. My mother leaned over the terrace balcony and told him in no uncertain terms to "leave the boy alone". Her intervention surprised me because she wasn't usually so assertive or confrontational when sober. Although heavy drinking can make people angrier (if they are feeling angry to begin with) it also has a soporific effect. Yes, she and Gerard would have drunken quarrels but they were forgotten the next day. Booze made her drowsy, apathetic, compliant and non-confrontational, except at the peak of drunkenness when the dam burst.

Much attention is devoted to abusive behaviour resulting from alcoholism – and for sure this has a devastating effect as I have already recounted. But booze is also a huge "influencer" in the way it softens people up, making them more likely to agree to terrible decisions they'd never have taken when sober.

All behaviour is affected and undermined by chronic heavy drinking. It's well known that after a few drinks your driving is impaired. Yet you convince yourself you're manoeuvring more confidently. The same applies to everything else. When you're drinking – or you've got one eye on a pre-lunchtime cocktail – you don't clean as meticulously. Your brain is rewired to scan ahead for the next "injection", so routine domestic chores are put on the backburner.

In drink, you may fantasise about your great deeds to come but they never materialise, just like the pledge (if it's made at all) that starting from tomorrow it's all going to be different. Promises, duties and dreams are unfulfilled as you recreate that anaesthetic day after day, that endless party zone in your head. Social life dwindles as teetotallers and moderate drinkers feel uncomfortable around you. You betray a hurried self-consciousness as you ferry out the empty bottles. Above all, in my mother's case at least, she became more amenable to suggestion, especially the tantalising prospect of escaping from responsibility. Yes, alcohol changes people …

It suited Gerard to mould her into this unassertive person. Hence his solution to every event – victory, defeat, rain or shine – was to uncork a bottle. He had her wrapped around his little finger or, more accurately, the prick had her wrapped around his little dick.

***

This four-week separation over Christmas must have further depressed my dad. Yes, divorce is commonplace but it was compounded by my long absence and the lack of a phone. There'd been a communication breakdown over the holiday. I'd gone to the Luz Bay Club at the pre-appointed hour on a Sunday to speak to him but … no call came. If you phoned from the UK, you'd sometimes hear a well-spoken female announcer telling you "all lines to the continent are engaged – please try again later". But this could last all day. Perhaps I'd also tried to call him back and been unable to get through.

One day, after he hadn't heard from me for a while, he sent a telex to the Luz Bay Club saying "silence is not helping". I sympathised with him. His Christmas must have been lonely; he took himself off to a health farm and I hoped he might meet someone, but no such luck.

I flew back from Faro in the second week of January in 1978, again as an unaccompanied minor. This time I sat next to another British unaccompanied minor, who was a year older than me, on his way back to boarding school in the UK. He'd developed the first pangs of love for a Portuguese girl. So he was doubly distraught at having to leave the

Algarve. Every few minutes he'd put his head in his hands and say "I will miss Alexandra…I will miss Alexandra…" We consoled each other.

My return heralded a confluence of opposite feelings because I *so dreaded* returning to the grey, motherless English winter. But there, at Heathrow, was my father looking *so pleased* to see me. He was crying with joy, whereas I was crying at the thought of that lonely house in Pimlico. My dad must have detected my downcast mood because I could sense he was hurt. And I felt disappointed in myself for disappointing *him*. So many times in my life were like this – I'd catch myself feeling a certain way and think, "perhaps I shouldn't be feeling this way".

My extended time away in Portugal riled the school because I didn't return for the start of term. My mother had been determined to "maximise" my holiday. The lack of out-of-season flights meant you had to come back on a certain day of the week, so giving me a choice of three or four weeks away. Unsurprisingly, we chose four. The first morning back at school I was chatting to another boy in the assembly room about my new pocket calculator or digital watch or whatever – then considered innovative technologies. The headmaster shouted at me to go to his study. Ostensibly it was for talking out of place but I felt I was really being punished for my delayed return. Everything, I realised, had a price tag.

But my circumstances in wintry London DID improve, at least compared to the period before Christmas. (Mind you, that wasn't difficult because I'd been entrusted to Michael!) Jill, my new "c-h-a-r-m-i-n-g" housekeeper, was already ensconced. On the first evening back I'd had dinner with my dad, came home late and had only had time for introductions. But when I came downstairs the following morning she was kneeling on the carpet, in a pink dressing gown, in front of the blow heater fire in what was to become her trademark position, smoking a nourishing fag and smiling broadly. She'd already prepared me a decent packed lunch, so we got off to a great start.

Jill was the granddaughter of a Conservative MP and daughter of a famous tennis player.[19] She'd fallen on lean times after her ex-husband had been declared bankrupt. At this stage she was temporarily homeless. Like my mother and Gerard, she was working as a London tour guide, but in Italian. In those days, Italy was her dreamland to judge from her favourite food and wines. Many years later she wrote a book about her lone travels in India where she met, and subsequently married, an Indian taxi driver.[20] Her trip to India was a courageous move.

[19] Jill Lowe (1937-2004). Her father was tennis player Arthur Lowe (1886-1958) who played with his brother Gordon in the Wimbledon doubles' final. Jill's grandfather Sir Francis William Lowe was Conservative MP for Edgbaston between 1898 and 1929. Jill received an obituary in The Daily Telegraph when she died.
https://www.telegraph.co.uk/news/obituaries/1471285/Jill-Lowe.html

She relished challenges and was able to bounce back from misfortune.

Back in 1978 she must have been down but she never allowed it to show. Over the next few weeks the house grew busier as her (five) children breezed in and out. I instantly liked her because we were able to chat in a way I couldn't with Michael. She had an attractive way of laughing shyly when she heard something funny, and vaguely snorting with amusement. She was interested in what I had to say. She would cock her head, lean forward and say "oh, really"? She treated me as an equal.

Jill had the air of an aristocratic lady but she was able to talk to anyone. She was also a chain smoker and one time I was so tired of the fog that I hid her cigarettes. It was the only time she lost patience with me. She often seemed bemused but maybe this was an act to conceal her embarrassment at her reduced circumstances, a feigned shyness so people would help her.

I soon realised I could depend on her. When I forgot to take my gym kit to Sussex House one morning, and sneaked out to call her from a payphone, she was at the school door within half an hour. I repaid her by calling the fire brigade when she accidentally

---

[20]*Yadav: A Roadside Love Story* was published in 2003 by Penguin Books India.

locked herself in the bathroom. It was one of those narrow bolts that could tear the skin off your forefinger and it wouldn't budge. She panicked. I dialled 999 – they thought it was a woman calling because my voice hadn't yet broken. Jill was so effusive in thanking me after they broke the door down. "Thank God you were still here, oh thank you, otherwise I'd have been locked in the whole day," she said, clapping her hands repeatedly. That's when we bonded. I was pleased to bask in the applause as her "rescuer".

I was becoming precociously political, although my interest really lay with the personalities involved. My devotion to current affairs and politics was sublimation, a way of forgetting my loneliness. For me, aged 11, politics was about individuals seeking preferment. Heath or Wilson? Come on – it's clear! (My mother must have been similar because back in February 1974 I recall her announcing Labour's narrow victory by saying "Harold is back in.") Callaghan or Thatcher? Again, no contest. On one side there was this avuncular figure, tried and tested, and, on the other, a housewife (yes, the prejudice against a female politician was widespread) with a precious manner and accent who had won the Conservative leadership by default.

Even Jill, a Tory to the core despite her straitened circumstances, agreed Thatcher didn't stand a chance and she'd be trounced by Callaghan. She liked former Home Secretary Reginald Maudling,[21] another figure forever trapped in the 1970s, who had fallen from grace after a scandal earlier in the decade. Jill was convinced the Tories would come to their senses and dump cheeky upstart Thatcher and replace her with dear old Reggie.

This, like most of our forecasts and conclusions in the 1970s, was wrong. Maudling had a great future – behind him. Within a year Maudling had drunk himself into the grave and, soon after, Thatcher was Prime Minister. Another hard-drinking Reggie, namely Bosanquet,[22] was staple viewing on *News at Ten*. Jill had no qualms about allowing me to stay up to watch. I had a TV in my room but I enjoyed seeing her reactions. "He's such a great character, isn't he?" Jill would say. "I'm sure he'll be on our screens forever." Wrong again! Within a couple of years, Bosanquet was off the TV and also died young.

For some reason *all* our mainstream perceptions in this decade *were* wrong. As a kid I loved Gary Glitter,[23] jumping up and down to *I'm the Leader of the Gang* on *Top of the Pops*. And Jimmy Savile[24]

[21] Reginald Maudling (1917-1979). Conservative MP, Chancellor from 1962 to 1964 and Home Secretary from 1970 to 1972.
[22] Reginald Bosanquet (1932-1984). ITN newscaster.
[23] Gary Glitter (b. 1944) British glam rock star, frequently on *Top of the Pops* in the 1970s, later imprisoned for downloading child pornography and child sexual abuse.
[24] Jimmy Savile (1926-2011) British DJ, television and radio personality, later revealed to have been a prolific sex offender.

seemed a "cool" television personality to me. I liked Savile's Clunk Click advice on TV adverts (to fasten your seat belt) more than his signature programme. I was impressed he cared so much to warn about road safety and I was always imitating his funny yodel. Did we take everyone at face value? When Hughie Green[25] on *Opportunity Knocks* said "I mean this most sincerely, folks," it was difficult to see what is so clear now – he couldn't have looked more insincere if he'd tried. Why was everything the reverse of what we thought?

I also don't remember a single reference to diet, i.e. what was good for you, to the importance of fresh fruit or vegetables. My mother's only edict about food was to ban butter –"it's no good for your heart, bear" she'd say to Gerard through the haze of smoke, surrounded by empty gin and wine bottles. That turned out wrong too.

***

After a full day's sightseeing Jill would do a wonderful Italian meal complete with Chianti or Valpolicella red wine. The booze flowed freely with Jill as well but I don't recall her ever drinking spirits, the lethal knockout blows that had rendered my

---

[25] Hughie Green (1920-1997) British television personality and game show host.

mother senseless. But those times were strange. At one of her parties Jill sympathised with a 14-year-old boy whose parents wouldn't allow him to go to the pub.

She was indeed a "c-h-a-r-m-i-n-g" lady (after all, my mother had befriended her) and even my 11-year-old self could see Jill was special. A vague plan crossed my mind. My dad was a lonely soul and too introverted. His home needed a woman; everything was so dark, the chair propped up with telephone directories. He told me he had the same dinner every night, cold chicken and coleslaw from a delicatessen in Bayswater and, he'd say to me, "sometimes I treat myself to Ribena" which sounded even more pitiable.

One day, after one of our Sunday afternoon outings, my dad drove me back to Pimlico. This time, unlike the infamous occasion with Michael, Jill was at home. It was already dark. He asked me to stay in the car. From the back seat I saw my dad and Jill in extended conversation on the doorstep. It was still difficult to see what was going on but he appeared to be asking her something and she kept declining. It was like an elaborate mime because I couldn't hear anything. But my dad kept pressing her and Jill, in her shy manner, would flutter her eyelashes, recoil, and wave her hand dismissively. I wondered if my dad was asking her out. Or was he asking himself in? To have coffee? God, this was exciting! Come on, daddy, get in there! Into the lounge, I should stress, not her knickers, necessarily, because what I had in mind was *companionship*. Dad was 18 years older than Jill, but so what? Gerard was at least a decade older than my mother. No one noticed the age difference with an older man anyway.

As I peered more closely, I saw my father had his wallet out. Jill drew back again. But then, surreptitiously, he gave her some banknotes and, reluctantly, after the fourth refusal, Jill accepted them. He'd almost had to thrust them in her hand. My dad opened the car door and I went inside the house and he left. So that was what it was all about! Just money! I was *so* disappointed.

Michael was supposedly staying somewhere else by now. But he kept turning up on the pretext of collecting clothes. I thought nothing of it because he'd been staying there for six weeks. One morning I came down early on the landing and the bedroom door flung open. I saw a belly button and a draft of air hit me as Jill quickly wrapped a dressing gown around herself. And, fleetingly, I saw Michael's acned back. He was lying prostrate on the bed. Jill shut the door.

I was surprised. But kids wonder how something will affect them. And, in this case, I concluded it wouldn't. I was looking forward to watching *Star Wars* that weekend. I was more shocked by the suffocating stench of cigarettes and the musty smell in their sealed bedroom after a night of drinking.

I was still standing in the corridor when a few seconds later Jill opened the door. They must have had a quick whispered exchange and decided concealing it all was pointless. Jill looked at me benignly with a shy half-smile – a bit like Purdey at the beginning of *The New Avengers*. She bore a strange expression, as if to say (but she didn't) "let's not make a fuss over a little display of affection". She never openly referred to it again. Michael grunted "mornin'" in the background.

They'd spent the night in the marital bed, the one normally occupied by my mother and Gerard. Jill was 17 years older than Michael. And, even today, that's odder than a man being 17 years older. So still the double standard. Back in 1976 a controversial TV series called *Bouquet of Barbed Wire* (whose theme tune instantly evokes the 1970s to me) was all the rage. I'd watched it alone in my bedroom when it first aired, with the light off and the sound down, because my mother and Gerard's bedroom, was directly below. This was getting kinky, like Cathy Manson's affair with her son-in-law in the follow-up series *Another Bouquet*. Jill even looked like actress Sheila Allen; she had the same English rose look.

Naturally, I didn't tell my parents. In any case my Sunday phone calls to Mum at the Luz Bay Club were within earshot of Michael who was also waiting to speak, so this wouldn't have been feasible. I'm sure the news leaked out but it was the following winter before it became family knowledge.

For the next couple of winters, Jill would be a mainstay. It was funny because, at first, Michael was there. Then he was supposed to have moved out but he lingered on – for obvious reasons. The following two winters it was the other way around. Michael was in and Jill was supposed to have moved out. But it turned out they were together in reality. She'd bought a place around the corner but Michael would ring her and she would capitulate and visit. One evening Michael couldn't persuade her to come over. He looked so miserable and tried to cuddle *me*. I rang Jill. "Please come over," I pleaded. She did.

Perhaps she didn't want me to see them canoodling on the sofa. But I soon got over that. I still liked Jill, despite my reservations about her taste in men. She and I made a wonderful trip to Dorset in 1980 to see her daughter at her convent boarding school. That first winter we'd watched Alan Bates in the television serialisation of the *Mayor of Casterbridge* and now I was visiting all the locations depicted in Hardy country. I treasure memories of our time together and was devastated when she died, aged 67, in 2004. But at least she did manage to see a copy of her book about India in print before her death.

For all Jill's great qualities I still missed my mother dreadfully. But it was increasingly tinged with anger. In January 1978 I had a letter from her saying how much she had missed *me* on the day I'd left for London after the Christmas break. "Gerard and I walked up Meia Praia" (a long beach in Lagos, east of Luz) "and he comforted me while I cried." This was my first "sod you" moment. My reaction, voiced inwardly, was simple. Why did you go away for the whole winter in the first place, if you "missed" me so much?

In February I received a densely written letter: "Rip-roaringly warm, cloudless skies, almond trees blossoming." My second "sod you" moment. I saw it as grossly insensitive and my father agreed. She was loading on the colours too lavishly, rather like Gauguin accused Van Gogh of doing.

I re-read that letter many times. I made the mistake of taking it with me to Sussex House and looking at it again in the locker room. Someone snatched it from me, and scanned it. It was then thrown around and I was left pathetically trying to retrieve something that angered me anyway. Soon everyone was laughing and my secret, confided only to a couple of friends, was out. I'd been abandoned.

Around this time, 1978, a photographer came to the school's gymnasium annexe and snapped our class, both us as a group and individuals. In my close-up I'm caught standing near the ropes, looking mournful. It wasn't just the ropes, which I could never climb. Nor was it the horrendous horse over which we had to jump, an iconic image of 1970s schooldays. (That wretched horse became an object of fear because I developed a hyper-vigilance about hurting my delicate parts!) I have a lonely air; it might even have been taken during one of my mother's lengthy absences. I look weary from having to fend off endless preconceptions. The reality of my life was different from how it was framed by others. The gym master was another of his era who assumed all boys at the prep school were privileged and "mollycoddled". So he gave us a hard time. But he knew nothing of my home circumstances.

But, yes, it's true I looked "sensitive". In the group photo – like my dad whenever he stood with other people – I seem to be standing apart from the others. My mop of unruly hair and dark, hooded eyes set me apart from my (mostly) blue-eyed classmates. And although I'm the tallest boy in the class I look the most vulnerable.

***

Winter eventually turned to spring. And around the third week of March I spent the afternoon of their announced return gazing expectantly out of the window, waiting for the little Simca to re-enter our street. I was so overjoyed to see my mother that all anger quickly dissipated. It was over.

Yet this winter away was recurring – an annual four-month exodus. Was the anticipation worse than the separation itself? The following year (1978) I lived in dread of their departure from September onwards. By now I had mixed feelings about Gerard but I hated seeing my mother go. I loathed the build-up. This began in October when she and Gerard dropped me off at Sussex House. "You're arriving on a real autumn day," she said on one occasion, pointing to the fallen leaves. Gerard slapped the steering wheel, with relish, and piped in – "Yes, and we'll be off soon." The countdown had begun. I came to hate Guy Fawkes Day because I knew "D-Day" was near. As we walked to the off-licence, sparklers all around us, Gerard said how much he was looking forward to the trip, even playfully impersonating the sound of the ferry's horn by blowing through his fist. He sure was a jovial character when he wanted to be! A part of me wished he'd been knocked down by a firework. But there was a spanner in the works…

That year, as it turned out, I did accompany them down to the Algarve in December in the Simca because that was the autumn of my mother's cancer diagnosis which I have already described. I now saw how a few weeks' delay *did* make a difference. And I also realised a friend of hers was right when I overheard him citing the folly of doing the journey in such a vehicle.

Our trip began well enough. We boarded the overnight ferry. I loved our dramatic early morning entrance to the rocky harbour of St Malo. We drove through Brittany, stopping at Barbezieux, to the north of Bordeaux. The next day we continued on to Biarritz and St Jean de Luz, arriving there at lunchtime. Gerard kept disappearing to have a few drinks with friends. Or we'd be driving along in town when Gerard would recognise someone, stop the car, and tell my mother he'd be back soon. It was usually more like an hour, or even longer.

On the morning we were due to cross the Pyrenees he met a friend for what later transpired was an early liquid lunch, several glasses of wine on an empty stomach. Nevertheless we began our ascent around lunchtime. Gerard would painstakingly overtake some heavy trucks only for me to ask to relieve myself at the side of the road. The trucks would overtake us again and Gerard would seethe in Spanish at the wheel (he always swore in Spanish) as once more we were stuck behind these slow-moving monsters. This was an ongoing problem because my bladder had no powers of retention at all.

We climbed the Pyrenees, a perilous journey along twisting, spiralling mountain roads. I gave up looking out of the window because it made me dizzy. It was already icy but the snow got thicker and the blizzard more intense. Higher still, the rear windscreen blew out; it now had stress cracks all across it. I made another toilet stop and as I was getting back in the car, Gerard warned me not to bang the door. It was too late. This time the window shattered more profoundly, so it looked like a mosaic of fragile glass. Cue more Spanish expletives from Gerard. If my knees accidentally brushed his driver's seat he'd start shouting.

We climbed farther, the narrow roads grew icier and more precarious and, suddenly, we were mired in the snow with a huge drop at our side. We all sat there, motionless for a while. Gerard was banging the steering wheel with his fist. He tried again to start the car. Nothing. We were stuck.

"Get out and push!" Gerard said to me. "And I'll stay here and try to start her up."

I got out. It was freezing and there was the ridiculous spectacle of an 11-year-old boy trying to push a car out of deep snow. I couldn't. Gerard started the engine again but the Simca wouldn't move. At one point I saw Gerard's reflection in the car mirror and I caught a look on his face, not exactly of murderous intent, more one of wilful abandon. It was as though I was extraneous, superfluous, two's a company, and three's a crowd, something like that. If I'd stumbled badly and fallen over the cliff (which was not inconceivable) I felt he'd have written it off as bad luck.

As it turned out, we were all in danger. A truck hurtled down in the opposite direction toward us on what was already a narrow road. Incredibly, it was gaining speed as it approached us. The driver had lost control. He managed to brake only a few metres away from us. If he'd hit us, our little Simca would have been sent flying over the mountain. And you wouldn't be reading this!

Eventually some emergency crews arrived and several guys with spades dug us out. I was shocked and remember little of what ensued except we drove down through "sunny Spain", staying overnight at Talavera de la Raina, outside Madrid, still in freezing conditions. The next day we continued south until, around Badajoz, the snow melted and the sun came out. We crossed the border and made the long trek down to the Algarve via winding roads, arriving in Luz late into the night. The signs everywhere at the Luz Bay Club read "*Feliz Natal*" – "Happy Christmas".

When I look back at the incident – and I know "with hindsight" is a phrase one inevitably over-eggs in a memoir – I realise the whole trip was foolhardy. You needed a sturdier vehicle with winter tyres. It would have been better to have got the ferry to Bilbao or Santander. We'd only gone to France to satisfy Gerard's whims. He'd sacrificed our safety to have a good time in St Jean de Luz. Also, Gerard had been drinking beforehand, not drunk as such, because I have to say I *never* saw Gerard fall down drunk. But, yes, enough to miscalculate a few manoeuvres.

My poor dad must have had grave misgivings about the whole trip. Scaling the Pyrenees in the winter was, after all, no mean feat. Doubtless too, his reservations would have been pooh-poohed by my mother who would have said "you know what he's like; anxiety is his middle name and he likes to keep you in a bubble".

I never told my dad much, except to say we'd had a few "problems" owing to severe weather. It was all ironic. I've already written how the previous winter they made this trip on their own. I'd always wanted to accompany them. But that was in November. They'd been right that a month made all the difference. This only made the question more pertinent. Why did they do it? It must have been at Gerard's behest. Everything was.

5. A Mangled Maze

"...he has allowed himself to drift ..."

My school report – circa 1978

Our escapade on the Pyrenees was soon forgotten. Well, not by me actually. To this day I don't like heights. But my mother never mentioned it again. Early 1979 saw the usual routine. Her post-operative scans gave her good news, so she and Gerard spent January and February in the Algarve, returning at the end of March. I flew back to London in January 1979 as an unaccompanied minor once again.

Britain's infamous "winter of discontent" passed them by. And, in the best tradition of unpleasantness-avoidance, my mum never alluded to it either at the time or since. I mean, *never*. But Britain had been in a bad way with disruption to London transport as well, starting in late January, amid freezing temperatures and snowfall. So sometimes my father had driven me to school, crisscrossing the capital to get to Pimlico from Bayswater and on to Cadogan Square and back to his office in Great Marlborough Street.

I was declining sharply at Sussex House after a good start. I was not exactly popular with the senior staff. During the May 1979 election, I openly supported the Labour Party. I knew little of substance, only the personalities involved. Most importantly, I relished annoying the two "upper-class Tory" headmasters. When, a few days before the election, a rogue poll showed Labour had nearly caught up with the Tories, one of the headmasters came to me and said "your lot are almost level pegging now". I loved his reference to "your lot". I felt like a rebel. On the day of the Conservative landslide victory, any boys interested were invited up to their private flat to watch Thatcher walking up Downing Street, with both headmasters cheering her on in the background.

By the end of 1979 even entering Dulwich College (the independent school I eventually attended) was a long shot. For the third winter in a row, my mother and Gerard left, as usual in November. My behaviour at school was poor and I found inventive ways to rile the teachers. One was by writing deliberately illiterate letters in collusion with a friend to two football weekly magazines of the day – *Match Weekly* and *Shoot* – using the addresses of headmasters and teachers. We found their contacts from the telephone directory; it wasn't difficult to locate teachers' whereabouts. They usually lived in the SW3 catchment area. Also, the more unusual their name, the easier it was to trace them. The staff member would receive a reply from the magazine editor thanking them for their contribution but saying that, sadly, it couldn't be included on this occasion. The implication was their contribution was not up to the required standard. I'd forget the letters once I'd sent them. The editor of *Match Weekly* was named Melvyn Bagnall and one of my favourite "victims" was my English teacher.

One morning I was busy boring a hole in the classroom wall with my compass (as you do) when the English teacher burst in, shouting: "Any friend here of Melvyn Bagnall is no friend of mine!" The others, naturally, didn't get the reference at all and continued with their business. But I did and laughed loudly. So it couldn't have been hard for the English master to identify the culprit. And he'd probably guessed, hence he had charged into *my* class. Meanwhile, in other hanky-panky, a friend would come over to Pimlico and we'd ring up teachers, ask for them by their first name if their wives picked up (nearly all our staff were men) and hang up when they answered.

You may conclude these juvenile, even cowardly pranks, didn't amount to much. You'd be right. *But* I wasn't a rebellious kid naturally. I wasn't a risk taker at all and now I see I was demanding more attention because I felt neglected. So I can trace this period as the beginning of my downfall. I'm not even sure the school realised I wasn't living full-time with a parent. We never made a formal declaration to the headmasters. But my dirty little secret came out when I had my Michael-made sandwich. We'd have our lunch in the classroom with the teacher and I'd hide my inedible stale bread behind my desk lid. God, desk lids were wonderful!

But I concede that rebellion in a posh school in Cadogan Square was not exactly Mutiny on the Bounty. I indulged in *safe* rebellion. Hardly anyone was ever expelled. There was only one case of expulsion during my time as far as I know. He was a friend of mine. His parents summarily dispatched him to Orley Farm, a boarding prep school. But he was uncontrollable, a tearaway.

I never took part in the usual haranguing or bullying of teachers perceived as "soft". I never liked the thought of a vulnerable person being hounded. My "misbehaviour" stemmed from a strange susceptibility to eccentricity. I lacked self-possession. I couldn't control myself in the presence of certain teachers who had funny mannerisms. Strangely enough, to make my ordeal worse, they were the senior staff, in this instance one of the headmasters.

I was only beaten once at Sussex House. I'd thrown some clay at other boys during one of our art classes. I was thumped with a gym shoe by one of the headmasters who told us to expect "a short, sharp shock". It certainly was; I clambered up the back stairs, my bottom stinging so badly I couldn't walk. My expelled friend fared worse. "In my time at Orley Farm I was beaten bare bottom with a gym shoe and run up, six strokes, once a week like clockwork," he told me.

Bring back the 1970s? The mind plays tricks on you. People sometimes say a good flogging "didn't do me any harm". But maybe we should turn this round. The real question is – "did it do any good?" The answer is, unequivocally, "no". Beating a kid into submission doesn't solve any problem. But it may serve to satisfy the latent bloodlust of a teacher, turned self-appointed judge and punisher. Corporal punishment was later abolished in Britain for good. Do I resent being beaten by Gerard and my old headmaster? You bet I do!

Don't forget that parents *paid* for the likes of the regime inflicted on my friend at Orley Farm. Back then a hilarious advert for instant mashed potatoes showed aliens laughing at primitive earthlings peeling potatoes. If aliens *were* laughing at us, it's over parents paying for their children to be beaten black and blue at supposedly prestigious segregated boarding schools. (I don't include Sussex House in the list of offending institutions, by the way, because corporal punishment was administered rarely.)

Other aspects of my wellbeing went by the wayside. My diet was inadequate. The food wasn't great anyway but I was eating especially poorly. I suffered badly from constipation. A doctor made a home visit and told me to lie on the couch prostrate and take my trousers and underpants down. He took out a couple of metal utensils, longer and weightier than your traditional knife and fork, and I felt him prodding me deep in my anus until I defecated. I made the mistake of telling my mother and Gerard. He always referred to it as "a spoon and fork job" and regaled everyone with this hilarious story. Oh boy, that guy sure had a great sense of humour!

Michael's behaviour when drunk was wearisomely predictable. When he was sober he said nothing or sniffed sullenly. Every evening, if Jill didn't come over, he'd consume a four-pack of Special Brews. After one can he was able to progress beyond monosyllabic utterances. But he still made little sense. After two cans, he "knew", or thought he did, the answers to all the major political conundrums of the day. After three, everyone was "useless" apart from him, and "bloody commies" (his favourite bugbears at the time). After four cans he'd shout that Menachem Begin[26] was a "terrorist" and I should join him in Israel – because of my Jewish origins. He'd also start badmouthing my father to me. If he moved on to wine with his dinner he'd be paralytic.

Although Gerard had stopped frequenting our Italian friends in the delicatessen, I still ventured there occasionally with Michael. One day I noticed Salvatore had pinned Michael's bounced cheques on the wall. That was the end of a beautiful friendship.

---

[26] Menachem Begin (1913-1992) was Prime Minister of Israel between 1977 and 1983.

Sometimes Michael varied the routine by cooking dinner early and heading out to the pub. This was my preference by far. At least it spared me his drunken rants. And he could never help me with any of my maths homework. One night, lonely and in mourning, he said: "There's an equation in life – man and woman equals happiness". For Michael this was a real profundity. It was the only equation he'd ever mastered because even basic arithmetic was beyond him.

One evening we ran out of money. My mother must have given him an allowance but, presumably, he'd spent it on drink. Instead of phoning my dad, I emptied my piggy bank of coins and we managed to buy a couple of portions of chips.

Michael's drunkenness was also getting me into trouble at school. Not only was he *not* making me a proper packed lunch (a sore point) but he'd started writing comments in my homework books. One time I wrote a political essay and handed it in. The English teacher returned it with meticulous corrections and notes. Again, I forgot about it. A few weeks after the "Bagnall" incident, and after we'd handed in another essay, the same English teacher charged in and threw my exercise book on my desk.

"What on earth is this? WHO wrote this?"

I looked at the book. Beneath my essay, and the teacher's comments, someone had written "you comunist! (sic)". I knew immediately who that someone was. I recognised the scraggly handwriting and, in addition, "communist" was misspelt. No need for Hercule Poirot. I'm sure if I'd smelt the paper up close it would have reeked of Special Brew too. I feigned ignorance. I could only say, truthfully, I hadn't written it.

After dinner and a phone call with my dad, when Michael was out at the pub or at Jill's, I'd wander around the block. A favourite late evening destination was Dolphin Square. I swam there on weekends with my dad but he never knew of my late evening visits during the week. I liked it because it was so orderly and pristine, in contrast to my life. I spent so long at Dolphin Square between 1975 and 1983 that I recognised residents, staff, regular swimmers, squash players, bar hoppers and even a few famous politicians. But I never saw paedophiles, at least as far as I know. I'd go swimming on my own and, yes, encountered one or two weird characters there, but nobody that perverted. Hence I doubted allegations by alleged abuse victim "Nick" that a high profile VIP paedophile ring was abusing children there. Coincidentally, the years in which he claimed these horrific events occurred were exactly the ones in which I was a thrice weekly visitor.

Perhaps I was lucky, because I spent so much time on my own, *not* to have run into worse trouble. Otherwise, this memoir might have been called

Pimlico Paedos. One time I was up at the squash courts in Dolphin Square when I bumped into my French teacher from Sussex House.[27] He took me aside and wondered what I was doing out alone at night. I lied and said I'd been swimming with my dad and he was having a drink with a friend.

A pressing problem during these winters was that every evening a parent had to sign off our homework. When I saw my dad on weekends he'd sign my "prep" (as we called it), using the name "Kupfermann". When my mother was there she'd sign it using Gerard's surname. Some of my classmates soon figured out there had been a divorce in my family. But that was no big deal. But when Michael and Colin were there, they signed it using two different names because Michael had changed his name. This took further explaining to perplexed teachers.

The first winter with Jill took this to new levels. She signed her name as "Gibbons", after her divorced husband. So there were five surnames in total, making my home circumstances look extremely convoluted. One day a teacher took me through the long list of various surnames and looked at me strangely. "Your household seems like a rather mangled maze." That it was. If there was no one to sign my homework I forged my mother's signature – and became quite good at it!

---

[27] A superb French teacher named Hugh Duvivier.

The same teacher also noticed my school uniform was dirty and quizzed me about my diet.

"Are you eating fruit?"

I looked at him blankly.

"Oranges?"

I could only think of gin when he asked me this. I didn't know what to say.

I was spending too much time alone during those winters. Coming home to an empty house, getting my own tea while watching *Grange Hill* wasn't so bad. But you know something is odd when this stretches to the early evening news, *Nationwide* and *Superstars*, and you still haven't spoken to anyone. My first conversation would be with my dad when he'd phone in the evening.

Being alone was even the subject of an essay I wrote at Sussex House. When I compared notes with other boys I deduced that, for them, being alone was an anomaly whereas for me it was becoming normal. My solitary confinement made me feel none of my feelings could ever be validated. If I felt angry, hungry, or scared, there was no one to confide in. Was I still there? Am I? I soon started talking to the TV to relieve the boredom, even reliving the conversations I'd had at school during the preceding day, imitating the accents to amuse myself.

What got me, and continues to bug me, is people saying "you come from a good background" when they didn't know me. Yes, I'm grateful for a good education (academically) but much in my background was not enviable. Michael wasn't equipped to look after me. I know also that to contextualise this, living in a large house in Pimlico, attending a top-notch private preparatory school in Chelsea, and travelling to a holiday home in the Algarve, would have seemed an enviable upper-middle-class existence. And compared to the material deprivation experienced by many people worldwide, even in England, it *was* privileged. But your childhood is *yours*. You don't have anything to compare it to.

As Sean Connery once said, everything becomes apparent with hindsight. In his case, he meant he didn't realise how poor he was until he looked back. I don't know what it's like to be a refugee from Somalia. All I can do is supply pass notes about my experience. In the UK, if you don't have a regional accent, or a cockney accent, you must come from "a good background". But it ain't necessarily so!

It was also a difficult period for my father. Only a few years earlier he'd been married but by this stage I was returning to a large house without a parent. And he was going back to an empty flat. It must have reinforced his own sense of failure about the divorce.

Meanwhile, my school reports tracked my decline. "Socially, he has allowed himself to drift," was an early summation. Music classes were my cue to muck around. "A feeble effort in so far as one can be discerned at all," wrote the music teacher. I deliberated over the meaning of "one" for some time before I got it. In 1979, we put on a musical production of *Noye's Fludde* with all the pupils dressed in animal costumes. "Perhaps, after the Fludde, the word co-operation will take on a more positive meaning?" the same teacher wrote. By 1980 my science teacher had given up on me. "Another remarkably indifferent term's work," he wrote. My form master also wrote "he is remarkably uninvolved in school life". But what *was* this school life – I still don't get it, stamp club?

In many ways I was mature for my age. One day the headmaster told us tragic news. The father of one of the boys in our class had been killed the previous night in a car crash. We should be mindful of this when he returned and act accordingly. Even in the intensely cold atmosphere of the times, there was still, to my surprise, room for thoughtfulness for a bereaved pupil. The boy was absent for a few days and another teacher informally told some of us that he'd be irreversibly changed. But, when he did return, he was still the same jovial kid we'd known.

One afternoon, returning from school, a friend and I chatted about the unfortunate boy and I'd said he was putting on a brave front and cracking jokes was his way of coping with grief. Another parent heard me talking like this and, when my mother once met me at the school gate, conveyed to her what she'd overheard. She noted my "exceptional sensitivity". It had *never* occurred to me that my "sensitivity" was praiseworthy. It was the first time it was cited as an asset. I'd always been damned for it – and told to "toughen up".

My vulnerability to others' eccentricities – my excessive sensibility to something or someone I deemed funny, was also part of my "sensitivity" and not praiseworthy – at least in the eyes of one of the two headmasters. The other headmaster had billed him as "a six-foot-four rugger player" (but, as it turned out, cricket was his favourite sport). He had brylcreemed hair, a severe parting, pinstriped suits, and a strangely over-emphatic delivery, spitting words out in assembly as he peered at us over his spectacles.

And here I admit to a susceptibility to "eccentric" characters. I used to have to run the gauntlet of greeting him every morning at the school entrance where he waited for us to arrive. Another boy found him equally funny and if we locked eyes when this headmaster was present we couldn't breathe. It was beyond laughter. He quickly realised he was the butt of our jokes. He was looking for excuses to punish me. I even wondered if his eccentricity was staged on purpose. He'd swing an imaginary cricket bat as he was striding along the hallway, or on the station platform at Sloane Square. When we had our carol service in a nearby church on Friday mornings, he'd stand behind me, bellowing hymns in a croaky, guttural voice. He sounded like a laryngitis-stricken toad. One boy standing by him fainted during one of these renditions. Supposedly, he had an asthmatic attack but I wonder if it wasn't more like shock. How did the others keep a straight face? This problem afflicted me throughout my life.

This headmaster's vocabulary also set him apart. Once we were making a din in the cloakroom. "What's all this malarkey?" he said. He also reprimanded us for "loutish" behaviour and "tomfoolery", and in my case, my "slovenly" appearance. My vocabulary was broad for a 12-year-old but his chastisements had me regularly consulting a dictionary.

He lived in a flat at the top of Sussex House, "institutionalised" within the establishment itself. Did he, I wondered, exist outside the school walls? He must have done because one day a friend told me he and his mother had bumped into him near Harrods. Ok, I conceded that one. But then, I wondered, did he exist outside Chelsea/Knightsbridge?

Not only did I dread our daily morning greetings, but if he came into our classroom I spent most of my time hiding behind my desk lid. Again, thanks be to God for desk lids! But in his eyes, I was a troublemaker and so, especially on school outings, he made sure to keep me near to monitor me.

In spring 1979 this headmaster took us to Eastbourne for a day trip, armed with ordnance survey maps. He called it "Exercise Mayday", a typically pompous way to describe what should have been a fun day. We stood on a windswept hillside while he addressed us through a microphone. "You are here to work, not to play, this is Exercise Mayday." I survived, just, even though he insisted on sitting near me on the train from Victoria to Eastbourne and back again.

His face also cracked me up, so the mere sight of him was dangerous. When he spoke, and especially when he spotted a miscreant boy, his mouth would curl up, and his eyes would narrow. He looked like a bespectacled British bulldog that had smelt something untoward and was homing in on his prey.

George Orwell[28] once wrote a memorable essay about his schooldays. He noted that "an adult who does not seem dangerous nearly always seems ridiculous" (so true) and also explained why this was so from a young child's perspective. "People are too ready to forget the child's physical shrinking from the adult. The enormous size of grown-ups, their

---

[28] The essay by George Orwell (1903-1950), *Those Were the Days*, was an autobiographical account of his schooldays, written in 1939.

ungainly, rigid bodies, their coarse, wrinkled skins, their great relaxed eyelids, their yellow teeth, and the whiffs of musty clothes and beer and sweat and tobacco that disengage from them at every movement! Part of the reason for the ugliness of adults, in a child's eyes, is that the child is usually looking upwards, and few faces are at their best when seen from below."

This headmaster wasn't ugly. Neither did he reek of tobacco or beer but he was undeniably eccentric. I had a *terror* of laughing in his presence. I note this because I've always been susceptible to laughing at inappropriate moments. But the real reason I dreaded giggling uncontrollably was that I lived with the possibility my dad would be summoned. I didn't want to embarrass him, especially during these winters when my mother was away, because he had enough to handle as it was. I learned to master techniques to control myself: avoiding eye contact with my friend, biting my tongue if he passed us in the corridor, and thinking about something entirely different.

One day my world collapsed. All my self-induced psychological ploys came to naught. In my last year at Sussex House we did frequent mock exams, including what they called a Common Entrance French dictation. Our normal French teacher was absent. But we were told we had a stand-in. Another staff member spoke excellent French. This particular headmaster. Yes, *him*! Total terror gripped me instantly. I felt like Winston Smith in Room 101 when confronted by rats. Oh no, P-E-R-L-E-A-S-E! If I'd known beforehand I'd have skived because this would be unendurable.

So far I had survived because he didn't *teach* us. He only addressed us in assembly where we (among the other 120 boys in the school) could hide more easily, curling up in a ball. He arrived and started the dictation. He began: *"Quand je fais un long voyage à bicyclette."* ("When I make a long cycling trip.") The first time I managed to hold myself together. But, in dictations, every phrase had to be repeated to ensure understanding. This time he enunciated *"BICYCLETTE"* with gusto, as if he were trying to spit towards the back of the classroom. I collapsed laughing. He told me to leave the room. After he'd finished the dictation he beckoned me to the study. He berated me standing up, still furious.

"If there's something funny about me, I'd love to know what it is. I haven't had a good laugh in ages," he said while twirling his glasses. I suppose the truthful answer would have been "how long have you got"? But that would have merited instant expulsion.

To be honest, I was crying while laughing. I knew it was a serious situation for me. Small wonder that his parting shot to me on my departure in 1980 when the leavers had a summer party and we presented all the teachers, including him, with a bottle of claret, was "*goodbye* and thank you for the wine". I can't do justice on paper to the way he said it. But his intonation made his feelings clear.

My last day at Sussex House was strange. I'd gotten used to this little closeted universe and was saying goodbye to a close school friend. I figured I was now unlikely to see him often – a correct assumption because my friend was going to boarding school. I became tearful. But perhaps bristling at the headmaster's dismissal of us, my mother told me "this isn't the place for that kind of emotion".

I should add that Sussex House had some excellent teachers thanks to whom I made precocious strides, especially in English and French. It's true – you never forget a great teacher.

***

In early 1980 I was fascinated by a documentary series about the independent boarding school Radley College, erroneously called *Public School* (just to confuse foreigners because it's *anything but public*) with Jill and Michael who were by now into the third year of their relationship. Michael kept drunkenly shouting "bastard" at the screen when he saw a master he didn't like. I was interested because I knew I was going to a fee-paying "public" school that, I assumed, would resemble Radley. For those out of the loop, private preparatory schools like Sussex House "feed" public schools – like Radley, St Paul's, Harrow and Eton. This is the strange word they used in their promotional materials. You're on a trajectory to these elite establishments which derive their sustenance from the equally elite private prep schools. There was little to no chance, of course, that a bog-standard state school could "feed" Radley.

It was one of the most revealing programmes I'd ever seen. It was the first inkling that these enforced separations punctuating the lives of my mother, Gerard, Michael, Colin, and, in a different way, myself, were unnatural.

The first episode showed a mother delivering her offspring to Radley and departing rapidly. It all looked so perfunctory and cold. Radley's headmaster, Dennis Silk,[29] taught them the importance of clean fingernails. One moment Silk was talking about extending courtesies to each other. Next, one of the teachers, David Goldsmith, was calling a new pupil "a vile boy". Some of the parents reminded me of something one of the characters said in the movie *The Wild Geese*. "If his back was any straighter, his spine would snap."

---

[29] Dennis Silk, (1931-2019), warden of Radley.

Incredibly, interest in Radley soared after this programme aired. Many viewers had missed the point. To me, Radley was nothing more than a "luxurious lock-up" (although some might even question that, depending on its provision of creature comforts) for parents who wanted their children out of the way.

Now I recognise a pattern. My mother too had gone to boarding school and been bullied at the beginning. My half-brother, Michael, had boarded between the ages of 8 and 13. Then he'd gone on to a co-ed grammar school, but the years of boarding had left their mark. My other half-brother Colin, who had boarded at the age of 8, continued with the same regime at a public school where he was picked on badly at the beginning. So he was a boarder for 10 years in total. This was while he was living with my father who didn't get on with Michael and Colin. But he'd been supportive of Colin when he was being bullied.

Gerard had been sent to a preparatory boarding school, aged 8, at around the time of his father's death, and went on to Eton where, as a diminutive foreign-looking boy, he was fair game from the outset. "I was bullied out of my mind," he once told my mother. Gerard told me he'd learned attack was the best form of defence. He took to hitting them for no reason. "That's for doing nothing – now try something," he had apparently told them.

Unfortunately, he continued this pre-emptive strike on me, grabbing me in an arm lock or digging his fingernails into me. He'd say "pain was all in the mind". I'm dubious.

The more I saw of Gerard, the more I concluded he was still a little boy at heart. He once said to me. "You never tell me your secrets, why should I tell you mine?" Another gem: "I never had a happy childhood, so why should you?" Even as a kid, such words had me concerned for his mental state.

Boarding school was the norm for the affluent set. Few questioned it. Yet this insanity helped to destroy so many in our family. Ironically, Gerard always wanted me to attend boarding school despite his own misery. Is this how the abused can become abusers?

The boarding school experience, shared by all family members, excluding my dad, also shaped their wider attitudes. Significantly, the only person who spoke out against these long winter separations was my dad. The others either initiated it or tacitly supported it. Colin once told me that his experience of boarding school had "toughened him up" which could be a euphemism for "taught me to conceal my true feelings". He once ridiculed therapy as for "wimps" only. Looking back was, according to this theory, a waste of time. Therapy might remind you of bad experiences but you should be "man enough" to override them.

Those who attended boarding schools choose not to analyse situations or feelings precisely because the whole experience teaches them *not* to. You're supposed to grin and bear it, to battle through loneliness, homesickness and bullying. Certain family members put the drawbridge up when it came to analysing their reactions or even understanding depression. The denial of feelings, or an unwillingness to admit their experiences had triggered depression, meant bottling up resentments. They needed a catalyst, usually drink, to release them. Equally, I'm sure that the heads of these institutions felt likewise – that releasing feelings was unmanly and the road to self-destruction.

Many who boarded will have learned to conceal emotions. But even more insidiously, and implicit in their "training", was refusing to discuss them. And they couldn't deal with their own children's problems, in turn, because they were ill-equipped to do so. Some who undergo this experience claim it did them little harm. Well, that's as far as *they* know – because self-designation is unreliable. It may be better to ask others how they perceive you.

I was glad not to be separated by boarding school but I already was separated for at least a quarter of the year. And my mother once said to me I should treat these winters as others would view boarding school. Although I attended Dulwich College as a day boy I felt like a boarder because I went home to a house without parents. This is where the ambivalence sets in. Yes, there were good times in Luz, but they enabled my mum to "abdicate". I never saw her much even when she was in London. In the summer she was usually working and our conversations were interrupted by phone calls.

In November 1979, when my mother and Gerard went off to Luz again, my dad said it was a strange decision bearing in mind my likely entrance exam into Dulwich the following February. He said she should be in London to help me prepare. A fastidiously detailed letter he dictated to his secretary on office notepaper before I went to Portugal for Christmas couldn't hide the friction in the run-up to the exam. "I would be grateful if you would send me a telex if possible on Monday after Daniel's arrival (in Luz) giving me a telephone number where I can speak to him, say at noon, on the Sundays that he is away. As you know, I have had enormous problems in the past in getting through to the right number and it may well be that certain offices in the Club are closed on Sundays."

Later, he wrote in his own hand: "He affects (he may feel it) a self-assurance and an independence which is a constant source of pleasure but, of course, he misses you and his nightly talks with me when he gets back from school is the best substitute I can offer."

... "affects" was the right word.

In the letter, shortly before I was due to turn 13, my father also rued his "remissness" in being unable to get me to a bar mitzvah, the ritual marking a Jewish boy's initiation into manhood.

And yet when I read those words I'm also puzzled because the only Jewish people I had met were my dad and my aunt, the latter only for tea a couple of times a year, and also a couple of Jewish kids at Sussex House. My parents had divorced when I was five, my mother had not officially converted to Judaism and I was raised in a gentile household with Gerard and my two half-brothers. In addition, as one of my half-brothers told me, technically I'm not Jewish because under the rules of Judaism, it descends down the matrilineal line. Others pointed out my lack of religious affiliation, i.e. active worship in a synagogue.

Yet my half-brother and other helpful advisers were mistaken and missed the point. I may be only half-Jewish but to the outside world I *am* Jewish. I've lost count of the number of conversations with strangers, or first meetings with people who later turned out to be friends, who have interrogated me, not necessarily with hostility I should stress, about being Jewish. My name is a giveaway.

To the outside world, I'm to all ostensive purposes a Jew. Also, Jews are a *race* with discernible characteristics. Although some Jews may be at pains to deny such a thing exists, I *do* look Jewish. So, irrespective of religion, Jewish people remain Jewish to observers. They may be atheists but they are still perceived as Jewish and vulnerable to anti-Semitism. And anti-Semitism, wearisome and perversely durable phenomenon that it is, tends to make the Jew feel Jewish.

Because Jewish lineage is supposed to descend down the matrilineal line you could have the surname Smith if your father wasn't Jewish and had married someone called Goldberg. But you're less likely to experience anti-Semitism in the outside world if you have a gentile name. For example, Stephen Fry is not perceived as Jewish, even though he *is* half-Jewish (on his mother's side) because he has a British-sounding name. But some would say Fry is more Jewish than me because his ancestry came from his mother's line. So Jews like me who are half-Jews (but on their father's side) have the worst of it. Also, if they are not part of a religious community, and isolated from other Jews (as in my case), this could reinforce a sense of alienation.

Gerard had enjoyed teasing me that one day I'd be in a tank, fighting for "my country" – as he put it – Israel. But, as I got used to the idea of attending Dulwich College I was unprepared for the anti-Semitism about to come my way.

Dad took me to Dulwich to do the exam in February 1980. I did pass – and so I *should* have done – but I should have done better, and domestic instability didn't help. I'd already failed the exam for the City of London School which would have been a better environment for me. In subtle incremental stages, I'd lost confidence even in my academic potential. So I was a Jewish guy heading to a south London school. Michael told me I'd have my teeth knocked out playing rugby. This didn't bother me unduly. But I was glad that Saturday morning school at Dulwich was abolished in 1980, just before I started, because waking up early six days a week would have been too much.

I'd already "learned" to quash feelings of loneliness and neglect. I wasn't supposed to express feelings. I'd already had that installed in me through my time alone those winters. One time I sprained my hand so badly I couldn't write. My half-brothers reacted with scorn. "Ah, diddums. Don't be so sensitive!" Ah yes, every time you feel crushed and try to articulate it, you're "diddums". Feelings were girly things.

6. God's Gift?

"I once heard him address the assembled school on the equal dangers of masturbation and borrowing other boys' bicycles without permission."

Playwright David Hare on David Emms at Cranleigh. From his book *The Blue Touch Paper: A Memoir*

"Some people say men are much more themselves when educated without girls. That is what I'm terrified of. I think we've had more than enough of men being themselves and knowing they are right."

Film critic and Old Alleynian David Thompson

"Dulwich was remarkably uncaring - sink or swim"

Former Dulwich College teacher of that era

Dennis Silk, headmaster of Radley College, was known as "the warden". Captain Mainwaring's main antagonist in *Dad's Army* was also a warden. But that had a custodial, proprietor-like ring to it. David Emms, headmaster of Dulwich College, was known as "the master" This sounded to me like something out of *Dr Who*. Yet, so it transpired, the Doctor's arch nemesis was far more earthbound and grounded in reality than our headmaster. Dulwich had a broader social mix than Radley, yet Emms acted as though it were an old-fashioned public school of the same ilk.

I'd "met" Emms twice already, at Sussex House prize giving in 1977 and, subsequently at my interview at the end of 1979. He reminded me of Silk in certain ways, even looking and sounding similar. He had a bald domed head, little round spectacles and broad shoulders, and wore a black gown. His voice was metallic and booming (although we usually heard him behind a microphone) enunciating every word with punctilious precision. He would sit up on the dais in the Great Hall, emitting a faint smile and a radiant confidence that was hard to prick. He was forever trying to knock some enthusiasm into his pupils. But it never worked. He affected intimacy with us by making a point of eye contact with every boy he passed and saying "hello" (which, in his case, sounded more like "heller").

Nothing he said resonated with us, or had any relevance to my life then or since. Broadly, Dulwich was composed of two groups, the old-fashioned public school-type kids who'd pretend to listen attentively (but I suspect even they *didn't*) and the "sarf" London set who thought Emms was risible. A former teacher told me that "he (Emms) didn't understand South London and the racial and social mix".

Even the school's main literary hero, after whom the library was named, meant little to us. Were London kids interested in the adventure of Jeeves and Wooster? They'd relate more to the characters in *Only Fools and Horses*, not to PG Wodehouse's period novels. A quick review of fathers' professions in our 'O' level year revealed a broad cross-section. They were a policeman, a fire-fighter, a bookie, a wine merchant, and an anarchist intellectual writer. Emms probably thought our dads were all country squires.

Emms' most salient rejoinders were on political issues. He'd bang on about the danger posed by Labour and Michael Foot in the run-up to the 1983 election. "I can only reiterate that the Labour Party is committed to the abolition of private education." He never mentioned why Labour would be a danger in the broader context, in the "outside world". If he'd expanded on why Labour was dangerous for the UK, maybe we would have listened. But nothing. It was always about *us*, protecting our exclusivity. The only supposed words of wisdom he imparted were about the importance of getting "the magical three A's" which were prerequisites for entrance into Oxford or Cambridge. This was abbreviated to "Oxbridge" in our terminology.

Emms made a habit of repeating several jokes during my five years there. One was he was determined that *capital* punishment should be brought back to the school. He'd wait for the reaction and then mutter over his glasses, "you didn't get it". The other, if it can be considered a joke, was that "tomorrow is the first day of the rest of your life". He said this several times, each time anticipating an ovation.

Nothing Emms ever said hit "home" when he addressed us in the Great Hall. Or hit Planet Earth. One day, the head of a big British banking group was a guest speaker. He held us spellbound (at least in comparison to Emms) as he offered practical, sensible advice on how to approach interviews and challenges in the workplace. After the speech, Emms wondered about that. "I could tell you were really listening," he said. Yes, perhaps because he spoke with an accent most of the kids could relate to. And also because, unlike Emms, he gave the impression he existed *outside* the school. Private school headmasters were cosseted in ivory towers, living as they did on the grounds. You could never imagine Emms in a supermarket or post office or on a charter flight or queuing up at a petrol station. Nothing "normal" at all. Even his choice of hobby – "radical gardening" as listed in *Who's Who* – sounded odd. What did it mean?

Back in 1980 the roughly 100-strong staff contingent at Dulwich College was all white and (nearly) all male. "The master" and the deputy masters (by which I mean the most senior staff after Emms) had "luncheon" on a raised dais in the dining hall. Ordinary teachers, on the other hand, dined with the pupils and were sometimes belittled by their seniors. The pecking order was strictly observed. One time the Deputy Master (Terry Walsh[30]) berated an "ordinary" teacher, who was sitting alongside the pupils at our long tables, for wearing a raincoat. "You shouldn't be wearing that in here." Walsh also regaled us in assembly with some illuminating advice: "You get out of an establishment what you put into it!" I bet you know what I think of that!

One day someone daubed graffiti in large capital letters on walls on the periphery of the school grounds. "Emms sucks cocks. Walsh is fat," some disgruntled, ex-pupil (or present one!) had written. For some reason Emms and Walsh made a point of inspecting the graffiti. I looked out of a top-floor window to see great commotion downstairs as the two walked off to see this "outrage". Walsh was cracking a joke and Emms was at his side, looking down, affecting a shy giggle over his Himmler glasses. Perhaps it was an attempt to show they could "take it" and had a sense of humour. Whatever the reason, their little walkabout did no good at all and even publicised the words in question. Everyone

---

[30] Terry Walsh (1929-2019) was Deputy Master at Dulwich College, i.e. the deputy headmaster.

flocked to see it before its hasty removal; it was like a billboard for a coming attraction.

And what was the great attraction? Shortly afterward, in early 1985, Emms gave himself the starring role in a tribute in the Great Hall to the late Lord Wolfenden, chairman of Dulwich College governors.[31] Emms praised him for his stand on homosexuality, rightly so, but in this environment, few would have dared to agree. Maybe, they thought, Emms really *did* suck cocks. Emms continued. "He was someone without any pomposity at all." That brought the south London set laughing because in the words of a former classmate, reflecting 40 years down the line, Emms had a reputation for being "a pompous old fool".

The Times's obituary in 2015 noted that Emms "filled a room with his presence"[32]. Perhaps, but to no discernible effect, I'd say. The same obituary added he acted as the informal school counsellor before such was appointed formally. I'd need hard evidence in a court of law for that. It was also noted that he had "educated" Nigel Farage.[33] That's a

---

[31] Lord Wolfenden (1906-1985) was a British headmaster. He was most famous for chairing the Wolfenden Committee whose report, recommending the decriminalisation of homosexuality, was published in 1957.

[32] *The Times'* obituary of David Emms can be read here in its entirety. https://www.thetimes.co.uk/article/david-emms-xdxrnhvckdb

[33] Nigel Farage (b.1964), former leader of the UK Independence Party. More than any other individual, he was the driving force behind Britain leaving the European Union.

strange description because it implies Emms *taught* at Dulwich which he never did. But, yes, he "educated" him in the wider sense of the word. He *was* responsible for making Farage a prefect, for better or worse. I won't attempt to link Farage's supposed far-right sympathies with his later advocacy of Brexit because these are different issues. But I note in the correspondence that some teachers wanted to expel Farage because of his cheekiness and supposed fascist sympathies. Emms claimed he saw his "potential" and made him a prefect. Another teacher had supposedly piped up in Farage's defence when someone claimed he was a fascist, saying this was no reason why Farage wouldn't make a good prefect!

One of Emms' parting salvos was his bid for more actively attended reunions. His idea was to stage reunions not of the whole school but of, say, "the class of 1985". In such a way it would be a meeting point for people who already knew each other. This was an extension of his belief that Dulwich should be run as a "family" with the close involvement of parents and staff.

***

School reunions are awful. In the case of Dulwich there was little feeling of any "union" to begin with.

Perhaps the disparate social backgrounds of the pupils went against it. But there was no sense of solidarity, merely an acknowledgement we were there because our parents could afford it. Certainly, many pupils were *not* there on account of their academic brilliance because the standard was not particularly high. I'd bet few Old Alleynians have returned for any "reunion". After all, if you made friends at school, you'd see them regularly, outside reunions. So what's the point? No matter what your status at the school, reunions spell disaster. And the longer the distance between your time at the school and the reunion, the more ludicrous these get-togethers appear.

If the school's "great sportsman" returns 30 years later it's likely he'd be running to fat, with a drinker's red nose after too many post-rugby drinking sessions. If you were a school bully, and a surprising number of supposedly "nice" adults have bullied someone, you've long since found out that not many people *liked* you. If people hung around you it was only because, especially in a boys' school, the hard man or the loudmouth offers some protection. Bullies disappear in any case.

If, on the other hand, you were bullied yourself, you'd arrive with a chip on your shoulder determined to prove you've survived the experience and prospered. But your chance of running into your oppressor is negligible. And even if you did attend a reunion with the idea of flaunting your success (if you've attained it) it would be pitiable, as if you have an inferiority complex. Or maybe you want to re-live that scuffle you had in the locker room back in 1983? "Now, try that again! I've developed quite a punch in the past 40 years!"

If you've done well, you don't want to come across as bumptious and self-satisfied. If your life has gone south ever since, you're likely to come away feeling bitter once you discover those you deemed to be less capable than you are now on six-figure salaries.

Comparison ultimately does no good and, yet, beyond the supposed joyful camaraderie of these junkets, this is what reunions foster. It's a loser all-round. If you were charismatic at school, a golden boy of a kind, chances are the rest of your life has been an anti-climax. If the teacher perceived as soft, the one who couldn't control the class, is attending a reunion he may expect to meet kids who've seen the folly of their ways, and may apologise. No chance. If you were a senior staff member, one whose every command was obeyed, by the time you waddle back into school as an aging relic, you'll look pathetic. The only case left for attending a reunion is to "network" but, let's be honest, if you're reduced to relying on the old school tie and connections for advancement then this is pitiable too.

I never went to a Dulwich reunion but did try one at Sussex House. I arrived nine years after my departure and met one of my old headmasters, *not* the one who made me laugh, by the way.[34] He asked me how I was but he clearly didn't remember me. Stupidly, I told him I'd been through a rough time since leaving the school.

"Oh right," he said. He hadn't heard what I'd said or didn't know how to respond.

***

Independent schools were supposed to be for the privileged. But, in reality, sending a half-Jewish boy to a south London school was madness. Added sneakily to the bill for my first term at Dulwich was a history of the school called *God's Gift* by Sheila Hodges. The book contained a ludicrous claim, supposedly expressed by some pupils, that "there's no bullying here". This was nonsense. The train back from West Dulwich to London was like letting Combat 18 supporters into an Auschwitz memorial service. One boy broke the wall of a train compartment with a hockey stick. I especially came to dread the first day back at school. The kids looked more threatening when their hair was cut short, usually in anticipation of the new term. I hated the cacophony of noise, the outpouring of boisterousness

---

[34] And not the current headmaster of Sussex House, as of 2023, Nicholas Kaye, whose memory is excellent.

– suppressed during the holidays but now unleashed in its full fury as the pack reunited – the pushing and shoving, the chair pulled out from under you, the derision of disability, the farting in your face.

Wait a minute, I hear you saying, this was "posh" Dulwich College. Well, yes, the school *looked* great and the sports facilities *were* fantastic for sure.[35] *But* I didn't go to school to admire buildings and I was not a talented sportsman. I was a nervous Jewish kid with a bad stammer and starting to feel different from my peers. It wasn't only my reluctance to get into brawls but that prolonged exposure to noise and too many speaking occasions tired me. One time, a decade on from leaving, I met an old Alleynian, who predated my time by 15 years. He told me he hated his schooldays because he had "a sense of dignity". I'll second that!

The most striking aspect of Dulwich College – as far as I was concerned – was its anti-Semitism. One day Emms told us a Jewish kid had been thrown out of a window. To be fair, he did look shocked when he revealed this in assembly. But there was little reaction. Hatred of Jews was widespread and again I protected my dad who sometimes wanted to visit or even meet my "friends" (the term loosely applied)

---

[35] Good sportsmen might have had a better time at the College. Among the staff at Dulwich in this era were Paul Ackford (b.1958), later England rugby union international, who taught me English in my first year. Also Roger Knight (b.1946) who taught me French in my first year. At that time he was also captain of Surrey County Cricket Club.

because even he, someone vigilant about anti-Semitism, would have been surprised at its prevalence. Anyone walking around the college at that time would have heard the word "yid" everywhere as a routine term of abuse alongside "spastic", "square", "wanker" and other pejorative terms. There weren't many Jewish kids at the school. Even staff members were not immune from the racist virus. A mother of a Dulwich boy, whom I encountered many years after leaving the college, told me she'd overheard a senior master saying, regarding that year's intake, "we have a wog, a coon, and a yid". One day, another boy at Dulwich told me I wouldn't last five minutes at your average comprehensive. But, in retrospect, I'd have been happier at a state school in North London where at least there were some Jewish kids.

My first class at Dulwich College was with the school's veteran, tyrannical physics master who screamed at us for being late. (It was a vast school and negotiating one's way through the science block, which was a newly built annexe, was not easy.) I was useless at physics and this teacher, who kept reminding us he was nearing retirement, delighted in belittling us. His diatribes went down in school folklore. "Stick to Latin, stick to play away drama, become a civil servant, work at British Leyland but don't waste my time." This was funny because I was good at Latin, later dabbled in drama (in the same way the cripple hovers near the athletics track because I had a bad stammer) and I did work for a while as a civil servant. All three were the lowest of the low for our physics teacher. As an opening introduction to Dulwich College, it was hardly auspicious. The same teacher was lauded as "inspirational" in his obituary. And, given his political views, I suspect he was the one who piped up to say – regarding Farage – that being a fascist was no bar to being a prefect!

The senior masters seemed stuck in procedures. Our Latin master, generous of girth, reminded me of an overweight walrus. He'd stand there, both hands on his braces like Rumpole of the Bailey addressing the court. He'd walk up and down the classroom aisles, kicking any extraneous satchels out of the way. Every lesson would start the same way. A pupil had been assigned to tell him about homework set for that day.

"Any prep for today, Hendy"?

"Yes, sir, *Civis Romanus*, page 52. "

Of course, he knew full well what the prep was. He'd been operating the same procedure for 320 years for fuck sake.

***

Around the age of 15, my stammer grew markedly worse. I'd always had a problem speaking but teenage self-consciousness exacerbated it. Ironically, but inevitably, the more aware I became of my stammer and the more I tried to force fluent speech, the more it deteriorated. Stammering is what you're doing trying *not* to stammer, so this was an inevitable corollary of my obsession with dysfluency. In my 'O' level year the problem peaked because I did so many subjects involving reading aloud – English, French, Spanish, and German. These were my best subjects but a stammerer couldn't have made life harder for himself if he'd tried.

Every time, in one of those classes, we took turns to read, I would be scanning ahead and wondering how long my blocks would last. If we did a paragraph each it was easy to anticipate my section. By the time it was my turn, I'd be shaking and gasping. Speaking became an emotional experience, not an automatic one. The prelude to my reading was a long, silent, strangulated block. Like 15 seconds – which is a long time for the rest of the class who wouldn't have given a second thought to stammering. Any oral exam, in French, German and Spanish, was something to be dreaded but, particularly, my 'O' level English talk when I had to give a presentation to the class.

I should have asked to be excused from reading or sought some dispensation when I had an oral exam. But, especially during classes when I had to read aloud and each boy did his stint in turn, it would have looked strange if I'd opted out. And, naturally, given the sadism of teenage boys, others pounced on my misery. Nevertheless, my father did visit the school to see if something could be done to help me. He got short shrift from Emms' other deputy, Ray Payne. Basically, what do you expect us to do about it? "Don't be so sensitive about it all."

Dulwich had failed someone who would now be categorised as a special needs pupil. I should have been granted the option of skipping reading aloud. But, in the words of one teacher whose career at Dulwich spanned 25 years, the school was "remarkably uncaring, sink or swim".

This "uncaring" nature was especially found in the senior staff, the ones who were called upon to add a postscript to your end-of-term school report – inanely, because they never knew you. One such nugget came from the head of the Middle School. My results in the arts subjects were good, but dismal in maths and physics. Granted, a certain lack of application on my part might have been to blame but also the putdowns of the aforementioned physics master hadn't helped. The head of the Middle School felt obliged to offer his opinion in my report. "I find it difficult to understand the dichotomy displayed by someone of his obvious potential and ability. Has he no sense of pride?" The last remark, I felt, was gratuitous and *insensitive* but typical for the senior staff who felt at liberty to rush to judgement without knowing you.

Possessing sensitivity does have its advantages, for sure, but there would be little point in denying that it's a disadvantage at an all-boys' school, or, for example, in an extreme situation such as war. I never went to boarding school, a fact always commented on by my half-brothers and stepfather – this, in spite of being separated from my mother for three months a year. But I'll freely admit that, given my sensitive disposition, and the separations I had already endured as a result of my parents' divorce and these solitary winters, going to boarding school would have compounded it.

I'd strongly advise against sending sensitive children to such institutions. I once read an insightful quote from Dr Sagar Mundada, an Indian psychiatrist. "In a sensitive, isolated, emotionally scarred child, the chances of developing childhood depression, anxiety disorders, and social phobias are very high," said the doctor, adding that the child could also subsequently develop problems with substance abuse.

Every time I visit a school I think of the law of natural selection. We fill our world with mitigations, unlike in the jungle, but ultimately, life roots out those incapable of making the grade. The vulnerable, the nervous, the disabled, the ugly – are not discriminated against officially but they get spurned quickly. School is, in essence, where the laws of natural selection hit. Schools should at least try to mitigate a disability. But Dulwich did nothing.

Gerard, too, had always ridiculed my stammer. "Spit it out!" he'd say. Or "we don't have all day". Or "start again". I especially resented his imitating my stammer in front of others and his constant insinuations that my stammer rendered me inadequate. I'm sure my stammer was exacerbated by Gerard and his belief, constantly repeated, that my disability implied some deep-seated inadequacy. Perhaps I felt there was something deeply unacceptable about myself and this came out in my speech, which, after all, is our foremost form of self-expression as humans. Also the expression "struck dumb" is oddly apt here. This is often said when someone, especially in their formative years, has been traumatised.

Not all the staff at Dulwich were unsympathetic to my speech problem. One of my favourite teachers was for Spanish. I was doing Spanish on my own because I had transferred classes at Dulwich midstream while having bi-weekly consultations with my teacher to monitor my progress. All went well until my oral exam. It was me and my Spanish teacher in a room and he explained he'd have to record my examination to send it to the governing body. He'd start the tape and the only sound emanating from me would be a strangulated spasm.

My benevolent teacher merely smiled and began again and we must have done that 10 times.

This teacher also gave one of the few standout sermons in assembly. He recounted how he'd witnessed bullying at his own school but had never done anything about it and how, in later life, he'd regretted it. This was the type of human interest story, with a salutary lesson, that was missing from the top Dulwich brass. This same teacher, who lived during the week on the school grounds, grew increasingly disillusioned and took to drink. In the words of another staff member, "he just lived for his house in Suffolk" to which he would go at weekends to be near his mother. He retired early and died at 65. I'm guessing he was also a highly sensitive person.[36]

Another teacher, tender-hearted and intellectually brilliant, had trouble controlling the English class during our 'O' level year. Gradually, the disorder and chaos must have filtered its way to the other staff. First, our form master reproached us for our behaviour, followed by the head of English. Later, the head of the Middle School, whose office was just above us, took to lurking in the corridor outside our class. One day he came in screaming, "This is Dulwich College, not a ragamuffin comprehensive", a funny phrase that stuck in my mind because I

---

[36] Alistair Slabczynski (1949-2014). An inspirational teacher of Spanish.

sometimes wondered if I hadn't accidentally drifted into Kingsdale, the local state school.

None of these interventions helped and our teacher struggled to maintain order. Eventually, and predictably, as the chain of command works, David Emms himself walked in during one of our classes, his black gown swishing like the caped crusader. This time, unlike on his daily rounds of the school, he made no contact at all but went around examining our work. "Have you got a notebook?" The word "notebook" betrayed his detachment because they were called "exercise books". None of these interventions, carefully staged so that all the upper echelons of the school were involved, paid off. And our English teacher was replaced by two others who managed to restore discipline. This dear English teacher, by the way, praised me in a school report as producing "mature and sensitive" essays throughout this period. It was only the second time the word "sensitive" had been used to describe me in a complimentary way. For once it implied something praiseworthy about my nature. But, overall, I still interpreted the word as unflattering.

A couple of months after out dearly departed English teacher had been humiliatingly ousted, one of his replacement teachers failed to show. We waited and no one arrived. Then, from the window of our classroom, I saw our old teacher walking tentatively toward our block. I don't know whose sadistic idea it was to make him stand in again for one more class. As soon as he walked in the old chaos erupted once more and one of the worst offenders – the muscle man of the form – did a happy jig when he saw he could torment his former teacher once again. It was not the first time I'd fantasised about shooting people. The final scene of the film *If* sees pupils on rooftops opening fire at senior staff on Founder's Day. I'd have started with some of the pupils.

So, for all these reasons, I'm suspicious of those who say they *enjoyed* their schooldays. Schools, especially all-male ones, are fascist institutions in that a leader emerges by dint of physical strength or his ability to impose his will. Rugby, for example, which was compulsory from the age of 13 until 16 when I was there, was a ritual weekly humiliation of the weak. We had one boy, pencil-slim, who looked like a concentration camp survivor and was ill-equipped to run with the ball, let alone tackle others or battle his way through the scrum. I'll never forget him cowering on the sidelines.

Single-sex schools also (self-evidently) do not stand you in good stead later on when you encounter the opposite sex. If you spend the rest of your life with women, it seems stupid to be segregated from them at school. One of our most charismatic teachers at Dulwich, Dr Ian Walker,[37] later headmaster of Rochester at the tender age of 35, subsequently

---

[37] Dr Ian Walker (b.1951)

noted that boys behave more "oafishly" at single-sex schools. So he decided to introduce girls into the school.

Even at Sussex House, an attractive female art teacher caused a commotion among us 13-year-olds. It would have been better if we'd developed early adolescent crushes on other girls in our class.

Apart from single-sex schooling, something was profoundly wrong with the Dulwich education of that era. Yes, some of the teachers, especially the younger ones, were knowledgeable and efficient at giving us the rudimentary knowledge to pass exams. Yes, the facilities were excellent. But we were not taught to *question* much and few teachers encouraged us to think *out of the box* and examine the world from a wider perspective.

We had some engaging guest speakers. Kenneth Williams[38] performed for us in the Great Hall – the largest venue for an address and by all accounts was a great hit. Also addressing us in the Great Hall were Keith Joseph,[39] then Secretary of State for Education, who spoke about the ideological divide between East and West, and former GLC leader Ken Livingstone[40] who tried to convince us he had

---

[38] Kenneth Williams (1926-1988). British actor and comic performer.

[39] Sir Keith Joseph (1918-1994). Conservative MP and Secretary of State for Education from 1981 to 1986 – so during most of the period I was at Dulwich College.

[40] Ken Livingstone (b.1945). He later became a Labour MP and Mayor of

nothing against schools like Dulwich. Former Prime Minister Edward Heath[41] arrived looking grumpy and stayed so. None of these sermons encouraged us to look at the outside world with *compassion.*

One moving address was by a British ex-prisoner-of-war held by the Japanese in World War Two (I forget his name). He opened with dramatic rhetorical flashes, repeated for emphasis – "How vivid is your imagination? HOW vivid is your imagination? Can YOU imagine a field of yellow ...?" The gist was that he'd preserved his sanity by conjuring up an image of a heavenly spring-like meadow. But the speech, much of it ideational, soared above the heads of his audience. Mind you, that wouldn't have been difficult.

At the end, I heard some boys dismissing it as pretentious. But I'd appreciated it. Soon after, in the first days of spring, I went to Luz with my mother and enjoyed a solitary hillside walk above our villa and found the field laden with Mediterranean marigolds, oxalis, and mimosa. I was ecstatic because I'd found, in reality, this man's dream, *my* field of yellow. I was starting to appreciate nature. This was the upside of being an HSP. The downside was I could never have shared my delight with

London from 2000 to 2008.
[41] Sir Edward Heath (1916-2005). Conservative Prime Minister from 1970 to 1974.

anyone of my age. They'd have thought I was a pansy.

Dulwich College, at least *back then*, didn't furnish us with any sense of wonderment or "imagination". So when you read a book about the history of a school, or any institution, take it with a pinch of salt ... and pepper. It's like writing the history of a longstanding restaurant. You couldn't do it because you'd say that the staff has changed and if a restaurant is only as good as its chefs, so a school, likewise, is only as good as its teaching staff. Buildings don't make a school (although the sports grounds may sway you if your child is athletic) the people do, and something was missing at the top. Like sage advice that resonated.

Also, especially among the older staff, feelings were *verboten*. I've already said some of my family members were reluctant to discuss feelings. I'd be willing to bet you'd find this among many who went to single-sex schools, especially boarding schools. And it's not surprising when the top brass was so cold.

To those who say schooldays don't matter – well, why do well-heeled parents insist on spending a fortune on their children's education? And why are whole books – such as *Sad Little Men*[42] – written

---

[42] *Sad Little Men*, written by Richard Beard, is a powerful critique of the public school system and boarding schools. Although I was never a boarder myself, I agree with his arguments.

about schooldays and why is it the case that, yes, a discernible *type* is produced by these schools? I'm suspicious of people whose ties to their schooldays are over-strong and who revel in the memory of the closeted camaraderie. Excessive attachment to the "old school" often reveals emotional retardation.

In my first year at Dulwich we performed March Hares, a revue of sketches and gags, ostensibly in honour of the head of the Middle School, the legendary and long-serving David Knight.[43] One old Alleynian, a ravaged-looking, red-faced 60-year-old sports aficionado, recited a rugby marching song which resonated with the senior staff. At one point, he thumped his feet furiously on the dais while screaming out a mantra, part of a pep talk designed to motivate the first XV. He was boozed and battered, a heart attack waiting to happen, but as I looked at this relic reliving his golden era that never was I realised this display was comprehensible to the assembled audience. For him this was home, or more specifically the rugby pitch of Dulwich College was home. They understood him and he them. I saw the senior staff applauding him uproariously. I thought it was all pitiable.

I left Dulwich early. I usually leave *all* institutions early. I don't mean I caught the early train but that I

---

[43] David Knight's (1921-1999) ashes were scattered on the school grounds. It was his successor as head of the Middle School, Chris Rowe (Dulwich staff from 1981 to 1993), who made the "dichotomy" remark in my report.

left the College prematurely, before I was supposed to. I'd worked too hard at 4ᵗʰ term Oxbridge to the detriment of my A-levels and got hopelessly side-tracked.

One salutary lesson is that the characteristic that sets you apart at the time and maybe despise in yourself – in my case a certain heightened sensitivity, because I was *taught* to despise it – can be tapped to your advantage later on. And I do appreciate *some* of the good teachers I had there. But, although it may be ungallant of me to say so, it wasn't worth the substantial payment involved.[44]

And yet there was one tangible gain from Dulwich. My home bookshelves were stacked with textbooks from the school, partly because I was too disorganised to return them. Or too lazy. When my English teacher came over to stay one time I found him thumbing through them. "I see you've amassed a collection here."

Going back to reunions … 2019 saw the 400ᵗʰ anniversary of the foundation of the College. There were 11 attendees from the class of 1985. So if Emms's idea of a reunion of the class of 1985 had come to fruition, they could have all fitted around a couple of tables at the Crown and Greyhound pub in

---

[44] All this happened 40 years ago. I couldn't comment on the benefits of a Dulwich College education nowadays. It might have remedied the problems and omissions I have cited.

Dulwich village. By the way, Nigel Farage, not in the class of 1985, *did* attend.

7. It's All-Clear!

"The n…… in this woodpile is, has been, and always will be Daniel"

Gerard

By the early eighties, I was squeezing oranges so frantically that I felt my right wrist was developing repetitive strain injury. Gerard's guiding work had dried up. But he kept himself "busy". He signed up as a part-time handyman/driver to a wealthy London-based German businessman. The job involved buying materials from DIY stores. Gerard would keep the receipts and wait to be reimbursed. One day he called me into his "office" to offer a demonstration of his skills as a meticulous draughtsman.

"Now, watch this carefully while I do this because you won't have another opportunity."

I looked over his shoulder as he used a biro to make an invoice for 22 pounds into one for 32 pounds. As always with Gerard, he did every practical job well.

"I hope you're concentrating on this. Otherwise, I'm wasting my time." I now realised why Gerard had doctored my mother's passport that day in Luz. It was to shave three years off her age and so make her more appealing for guiding work.

***

The trips to Peter Dominic wine merchant were becoming more frequent, but also vaguely furtive towards the end. The transaction was like some young boy buying a pornographic magazine. The salesman would see Gerard coming, reach for the bottle of Gordon's gin and start wrapping it up in brown paper without waiting for the order. No eye contact and no jokes.

By then something was wrong not only in the household but with my racing anxiety levels. It wasn't just the fumbled key in the lock and the bad-tempered exchanges. I was losing spontaneity for fear of the next outburst and becoming accustomed to keywords and phrases heralding a long drinking session, such as "it's been a long day", "I need to calm down", "*you* need to calm down" and the ubiquitous joke, "I don't mind if I do". These were the obvious ones. But also there were subtler ones. "It's a dog's dinner" was one of Gerard's sayings that augured a long drinking session.

The rows between my mother and Gerard were deepening. One time, they were arguing so heatedly in the lounge that I accused them of both being "alcoholics".

She looked genuinely concerned. "How you can say such a thing?" she asked as she drained the last drop of gin and orange.

"If I'd spoken to my parents like that I'd have been beaten," said Gerard.

"You already did beat me," I replied.

I always knew when Gerard was hungover. The voice became gruffer and rougher, the face creased, even the bed linen was more ruffled. You'd have to be a drinker to understand. I dreaded the next drunken outburst. I had more and more trouble defending myself verbally but at the same time I was becoming more stubborn and less compliant. Conversation with Gerard was becoming pointless.

"You have the gall at 14 years old to contradict me. How dare you! I fought for my country." The routine varied in so much as I would be 14 or 15, and finally 16, but he'd say the same. He referred to my mother and myself as "you people" and "bleeding hearts" and the racist comments worsened.

I was relieved when, in the winter of 1982-3, Gerard went off to Praia da Luz on his own. I was ecstatic on several counts. First, because my mother wasn't leaving and also because it signalled their relationship was deteriorating. We travelled to Luz over Christmas straight into a tense atmosphere. One evening Gerard stormed out of the Fortaleza after yet another boozy bust-up. He must have cultivated some friends, in the looser sense of the word, because an acquaintance of ours, sitting at a nearby table, piped up: "Whatever this is about, I'm on Gerard's side." How anyone could have been "on Gerard's side" was beyond me.

When Gerard returned in March 1983 the tension got worse. His moods grew fouler. He would say I was "omnipresent", although I don't know where I was supposed to go. This was another euphemism for "cart him off to boarding school". He complained he could never find the right china and cutlery for his breakfast. His solution was to buy a plastic green breakfast set which we were never allowed to touch and which my mother abhorred. She hated everything that was not aesthetically pleasing.

Our final altercation, which now seems banal, centred on a shoe brush that he said I had laden with too much polish. He threw it at me and pounded the wall, screaming expletives in Spanish. I told him he was a "non-person", a word I had learned from my father to describe people he thought were insubstantial.

And that was our final exchange for a long time. Gerard retreated to his office at the top of the house where he wrote his diary. The next day, when Gerard was out, I read it. Perhaps he'd wanted me to see it because it was left open. His latest entry read: "The n..... in this woodpile is, has been, and always will be, Daniel." It was appropriate his final diary entry about me (as far as I'm aware) would contain a racist reference.

The next few weeks passed by without Gerard and me exchanging a single word. He'd brush past me on the stairs, knocking my shoulders. No "good morning", or "good night". Nothing. I had my meals separately from my mother and Gerard. Then, a month or so after our row, Gerard packed his bags.

I've already written that my dad had "divorced" Michael and Colin. Now, although they weren't married, history was repeating itself. Gerard was "divorcing" his 16-year-old "stepson" (me) ironically at a similar age to Michael and Colin when my dad had walked out. Gerard wanted my mother to himself, for sure, but also he'd lost interest in me now I was no longer a compliant, eager-to-please puppy dog.

I can't be sure it was our argument that propelled him to leave. But it was *wonderful*. Gerard relocated to a bedsit on Westbourne Park Road, the "grotto" as he called it, ironically not far from my father. I was *ecstatic* when he left. I'd imagined it would come down to a shooting or we'd have to expel him forcibly, prising his fingernails off the door. In the end, he had walked out. My mother said I'd done them all a service. It was April 1983. It felt like a new dawn had broken, as though celebrations would take place throughout Pimlico, commemorating Freedom Day.

My mother immediately improved. She shunned spirits and drank wine instead. She could no longer consider spending the whole winter in the Algarve. She got a second job to complement her guiding work and see her through the long, dreary winters. More importantly, the atmosphere was much better. During the eight years or so with Gerard every domestic activity had centred on drinking and I'd noticed that fewer friends were making contact.

Slowly, as they realised that Gerard had departed, old friends emerged, at first tentatively like a fox out of its hole. Is it safe? Dear Carlos was back in the picture with no one to belittle him about his fleeting screen appearances – "blink and he's gone", Gerard used to say, deliberately inverting his name to Douglas Carlos and making comments about his weight. (Maybe it was no coincidence that Carlos won a major recurring role in TV sitcom *Duty Free* at around this time!)

Carlos was another highly sensitive person, again long before the term was widely accepted. He told me how during spells of unemployment he'd become deeply depressed, seeing no one for days on end. He also confided in me that when he returned to his London bedsit from Andalusia, after filming his portrayal of Spanish poet Lorca in *Black Sound, Deep Song*, he'd cried.

He had a saintly character. Even at the height of his fame in *Duty Free*, when he was paid up to one thousand pounds to open a supermarket or post office, he'd donate his fee to charity. He also displayed some more difficult traits of being an HSP, for example reminiscing scathingly about some of his more famous co-stars, noting they hadn't been "nice" to him and had ignored him on-set. Now I recognise this reaction from my professional relationships, expecting others to enquire solicitously about my welfare when perhaps I was standoffish towards them.

But, as my mother once said about Carlos, other people wouldn't "understand" him. Carlos had no ego or vanity. So I was stunned one day when another London guide, Fiona, rang to offer him a job, only to be fobbed off. "I'm a star actor now!" he'd reportedly told her. When Fiona, who was one of my mother's friends, told us this story, I knew Carlos would *never* have said this. And I was right. It turned out to be his partner who was drunk when he answered.

Fiona was an attractive lady and now that Gerard was gone she could come over without fearing that Gerard would pinch her bottom or make inappropriate sexual innuendos. We could watch the news without one of his sick jokes about catastrophes being helpful because of population control. Kids could play more happily in the street, especially the boy who'd been prevented from retrieving his ball. The smoke had gone. I could ring dad more often now that Gerard was no longer there in the background, urging us to terminate an "expensive" conversation. My dad even came round after a school parents' evening. This was only the third or fourth occasion I'd seen my parents together.

My mum and I moved to a flat opposite Regent's Park. These were golden years for my mother, now in her fifties. She was popular once more and I was pleased that excessive drinking was behind her. Here again, I acted as a protector to a parent. I'd never told her about certain past events because I was nervous it would trigger a downfall in her. During her most abusive period she was so drunk I doubt she would have recalled the episodes concerned. So what would be the point of recalling something so unpleasant? But there was a paradox here. Because my mother had forgotten how abusive and derelict she'd been, she couldn't understand why I wasn't more accommodating towards her. And I didn't want to remind her of her drinking in case it triggered more drinking. How ironic is that? In addition, I was by now seeking solace in the bottle too, so what would be the point of the pot calling the kettle black?

And my mother never acknowledged she had a drink problem. For her, the menopause was a difficult period and she'd hit the bottle to help her through it. And so no remorse for that. Everyone thought she was wonderful, for example the way she presented dinner to me in front of the TV during this period. "Daniel has a tough life here," they'd say sarcastically, not realising what had preceded it.

Also, there was a massive mood swing between my mother sober and drunk. When she was sober, or even after a couple of glasses, she radiated gentleness. But when she was drunk she'd become catty. With alcoholics, the bigger the mood swing, the harder it is for those around them.

A holiday in Sri Lanka made me realise how my mother loathed confrontation. I was bitten by a sand-fly and endured a 13-hour agony on the return flight to London because I couldn't put my feet up. If I'd been able to put my foot horizontally the pain would have alleviated. But she refused to ask a couple, who were lying down on spare seats, to vacate them. I was surprised by her reluctance to approach strangers. When I challenged her about the flight she became defensive, citing the cost of the holiday. But I was similar – disliking confrontation. Hence we rarely talked about Gerard.

After a quiet period post-departure, Gerard started phoning again. I knew it was him because he'd hang up on me. I'd hear a hissing noise I recognised. Gradually he and my mother met again for the odd dinner, mostly outside the home. She kept me posted about Gerard's antics. He'd leave London around the time of the Notting Hill Carnival, to stay with affluent friends in the countryside. He was still as mean as ever – wrapping up old ashtrays to give away as gifts – still disparaging about everyone, still being rude to his son, and still lusting after young girls.

I once half-heartedly gave my mother an ultimatum about not seeing Gerard again. But I didn't really mean it. She still wanted "a man friend" (her phrase) to have a drink and meal with and there was no replacement. She also used him as a taxi driver when she had an early start to go to the airport to pick up tourists, and as a general handyman around the house.

After my mother moved to Albufeira, in 1994, she said she would never invite him there, as she had done to Luz. I knew she *would*, however, and I was proved right. Again, her destructive softness surfaced. She genuinely felt sorry for him because Gerard *was* hard-up by then. Her new Portuguese home was a two-bedroom flat, so this time there was no patio to work on. Gerard arrived out of season and I ensured we *never* overlapped.

In Albufeira, he antagonised people. His behaviour was worse than it had been in Praia da Luz. Maybe because he knew he was on borrowed time and there was little point in ingratiating himself. One day, sitting outside at my mother's local café in the square in Albufeira, he complained:

"We should be served first because we live here," he told the waiter who operated on a first-come, first-served basis.

"Excuse me, Gerard, but you don't live here," she said.

The waiter, a friend by now of my mother's, made the point. "I can't find out who's a resident and who's a holidaymaker and serve them like that."

Gerard also riled her friends, claiming a nice Chinese meal looked like something "a doggie had done".

My mother, in her early sixties, was still hoping to meet a man – a normal, nice man – but it didn't happen. She tended to attract some aggressive, "difficult" men. Was it because she came across as so soft and malleable? I too was surprised at the lack of suitors. Circa 1990, Robin Day,[45] Britain's irascible grand inquisitor-in-chief and *Question Time* presenter, drove her home one evening from a party in central London. I'm not sure he'd have proved any better. Perhaps her intelligence and linguistic versatility intimidated men. I know she was disappointed and so was I because I knew she would continue to see Gerard and, in a way, regard him as her boyfriend. She still bore his name and, from the gist of phone conversations I'd had with Gerard's

---

[45] Robin Day (1923-2000) British political interviewer and television presenter.

son, they'd never stated that the separation was permanent. They only said Gerard had moved out.

She continued to find excuses for him even in the wake of his bad behaviour in Albufeira. His father had died when he was young, he'd been bullied badly at school, his experience in the RAF during the war had left him unable to express feelings, the corner shop had run out of Chivers marmalade etc … She always tried to defend him while at the same time decrying some of his behaviour.

They met for the last time in 2001, having lunch together in Notting Hill. My mother came home looking deeply perturbed. Something was *very* wrong with Gerard. He had offered to *pay* for the lunch. He insisted on doing so even though she knew he was cash-strapped. He'd used his credit card.

He died in October of cancer, aged 80. I was in Lisbon at the time and walked back from evening class without feeling anything much. Gerard had said that if he were ever in hospital he'd refuse to be treated by black or Asian staff. A friend who visited him reported to my mother that she'd been in to find a black and Asian nurse holding each of his hands on either side of his bed.

I read a "tribute", penned by Gerard's daughter, for his funeral. She'd cited his love of photography but had also conceded: "You did not have an easy character." I thought of that football trapped in our basement because he wouldn't return it, and his extraordinary need to embarrass and humiliate people. I'd say this was an understatement. Oh … and his credit card bill ran to several thousand pounds.

But Gerard lives on. I'm reminded of him when I see Lee J Cobb in *12 Angry Men*, Paul Newman in *Hud* or Robert Duvall in *The Great Santini*. He believed that everyone would be 35 in heaven, mixing with Mozart or Beethoven or whoever. But would they want to mix with him?

My mother couldn't shake him off. He was her bit of rough. Were it not for him, she wouldn't have left me alone for three months every year, and probably wouldn't have become a problem drinker. My childhood would have been happier *but* provided me with less material for this book.

Some years after Gerard's departure I saw a play called *Orphans*[46] with Albert Finney. The gangster Harold (Finney) says "all you needed was a little encouragement" to one of the emotionally damaged, agoraphobic brothers who has abducted him. I cried, especially when I heard this line. Gerard's constant abuse of me reverberated in my head – "useless baggage", "peanut", "use what God gave you in place of a brain", "Jewish questions", "Jewish jerk",

---

[46] *Orphans*, by Lyle Kessler, had its London premiere in London at the Hampstead Theatre in 1986. A powerful and moving play.

and "n….. lover" … and the tears came. Yes, all you needed was a little encouragement.

But some people continued to enjoy Gerard's company. Even in his later years, when he was working as a police interpreter in the courts, he was still capable of provoking gales of laughter when telling stories to explain delicate nuances of translation. Years later, he apparently told my mother he gave me "the only laughs I ever had". His implication was this compensated for the rest. But it didn't. He had no self-insight whatsoever. He was only concerned about how something affected him. Earlier I wrote that, when I was 11 years old, I was similar. And this is my point. Gerard never grew up because he had a child's mind-set.

Several years after Gerard's departure I answered the phone and this time he didn't hang up. I reminded him of his infamous diary entry, the one about "the n….. in the woodpile". Gerard pretended not to know what I was talking about. But, fortunately, I knew the approximate date on which he had written it. He went off and came back to the phone. "Yes, I wrote that. I saw you as the obstacle standing between your mother and myself, the obstacle to my happiness." That's it from the bear's mouth, straight down the line.

In an alternative universe my mother would have married Carlos. He was intelligent, sensitive, and kind. My father would have married Jill. As for

Gerard – he was an obsessional Charles Aznavour [47] fan and used to play his songs on our cassette player endlessly. He once told me his favourite song was *Yesterday when I was Young*. I wonder if he digested the lyrics. "I never stopped to think what life was all about and every conversation I can now recall concerned itself with *me* and nothing else at all." That was Gerard too.

And, yet, here I have to make a concession. It's possible that *in his own way* Gerard *did* care for my mother. Apparently, he asked for her when he was nearing the end in hospital. As far as I know, he never hit her. Neither, again as far as I know, was he unfaithful to her during their eight years together. I never heard him declare his love as such *but* in as much as he was capable of it, I'd guess my mother was his "love". Nevertheless, he wasn't my type of person at all. But that's because on an emotional level we were antipodal. I am an HSP whereas he was an *in*sensitive person and never the twain shall meet.

I now see there was a conflict of values between my father and Gerard. On the rare occasions they did meet there was an uneasy stand-off. They never locked horns and Gerard had presented him with an attractive photo montage for his 60th birthday. But there was mutual suspicion. They never discussed what separated them because they knew where it would lead. Like when politicians of opposing factions meet in private, they traded pleasantries and small talk.

You couldn't find two people more different. I once heard Gerard say – "never give way to introspection; it's debilitating". If true, then my father was *severely* debilitated. But I never heard Gerard once question his own actions, rue any past misconduct, or admit he'd erred in any way. As a child, you look for role models and, at the earliest confluence of Gerard and my dad, I'd have veered towards Gerard because he seemed more fun. But now, when I look back, it's clearer than ever that my father had a far more upstanding character. But something bad was haunting him.

8. Gentle Men in a Rage

"I don't think we're on the same wavelength ..."

My dad

"There is no Beatitude for the lonesome.

The Book doesn't say they are blessed."

James Leo Herlihy, author of *Midnight Cowboy*

We usually carry several key memories around with us. In June 1986 I was re-taking a couple of A-levels. I walked back from the exam centre to my mother's flat near Regents Park. The following day I was due to sit my English exam.

I arrived back to find her sitting there ashen-faced. "Your father's dead. He's killed himself. He's taken an overdose of pills. But you must carry on as though nothing has happened."

She must have been insane to believe that was possible. This was her regressing to stiff upper lip. But she knew I had an exam the following day and, in a colossal miscalculation, she felt I could just about weather it ...

***

I'd always known my dad had emotional problems, what would now be diagnosed as anxiety and depression. I recall his caring nature, fastidiousness, his immaculate appearance ... and also his social awkwardness.

Many of us have famous doppelgangers. In my mother's case, it was Deborah Kerr.[48] They shared the same angular profile and radiance. Sometimes she would have to drop off American tourists at London theatres. My mother, who cared little for movies or plays because she dreaded an unpleasant plot line, would run some errands during the show and meet the group afterwards. If she caught a taxi and asked the driver to take her to the theatre, the routine was the same.

"Stage door?"

'No, the main entrance is fine."

"Whatever you like, Miss Kerr. I guess you've learned to dodge the fans at the stage door."

But I was struck by how flustered my dad became when people approached him about *his* doppelganger.

---

[48] Deborah Kerr (1921-2007). British stage and screen star, best known for *The King and I*.

One day in 1975 we were sitting in a café on Regent Street. I can date it accurately because Gerard had just moved in with us. My father, then in his mid-fifties, had a good head of hair, naturally long, greying at the temples, and a well-cropped moustache.

We sat opposite each other, my dad wearing a brown suede jacket and flared trousers. As usual, he had a pot of tea and cheesecake which he ate daintily – small mouthfuls. He took out a little silver box and put a sweetener into his tea. He'd stopped smoking when I was born and with each passing year he'd gained weight, not so much visible around his stomach but everywhere. His face grew fuller and his fingers broader. Eventually he would be considered obese but at this point the extra pounds became him because he'd been too thin when he was smoking.

I was woofing down American-style pancakes. My father, a solicitor, had a serious manner and the gravitas to match. He spoke deliberately and slowly, as if searching for the right word. It was an excessively ruminative process, like he was wary of saying something wrong. He was already showing signs of isolation. Apart from his office and seeing me on weekends he'd had little social contact in the three years since he had divorced my mother. I knew he loved me and cared for me but sometimes when he spoke it was like a lawyer counselling a client, or someone seeking clarification about a matter.

My father cleared his throat, the prelude to something serious. The situation with Gerard had rattled him. When he collected me on weekends, he'd taken to pulling up outside our house, never ringing the doorbell. He didn't want to see Gerard. So I guessed this exchange would be about the new arrival.

"I want you to promise me that you will always view me as your father, and not Gerard."

Although Gerard seemed convivial at this early stage, I'd never viewed him as a father figure.

"Of course, daddy," I said, truthfully.

Just then another couple with their son, a few years older than me, pointed to us from a nearby table.

"There's Graham Hill[49] having tea with his son. Go over and ask for his autograph. Take this serviette."

The boy sauntered over shyly.

"Mr. Hill, can you please sign your name?"

My dad looked at him sadly. He cleared his throat again and spoke loud enough for the other father to hear him.

---

[49] Graham Hill (1929-1975) British racing car driver, Formula One World Champion in 1962 and 1968.

"Oh dear, I'm sorry but I'm not Graham Hill." He was reddening as he said it. The boy crept away, looking disheartened.

His father spoke from the same table. "Are you sure you're not Graham Hill?"

"Yes, I'm sorry to disappoint you."

My dad had been taken for Britain's motor racing champion so often I thought he'd be used to it by now. But each occasion unnerved him. Later that year the autograph hunting ceased because, tragically, Graham Hill died in a private plane crash.

***

My parents met in 1963 when they were both volunteers at the Samaritans, the charity founded by Chad Varah[50] for those in emotional turmoil and at risk of suicide. They courted for a year or two before breaking up. From what my mother later told me (I never heard my dad's version) he felt guilty about dating a non-Jewish woman, knowing his late mother would have disapproved. They subsequently bumped into each other again at the Samaritans and this time they stayed together.

---

[50] Chad Varah (1911-2007) was a British Anglican priest. He founded the Samaritans in 1953.

I only have two photos of my parents together. One is of their wedding in 1966 at Kensington Registry Office, both smiling broadly and looking elegant. My mother was 35 and my father was 46. It was the second marriage for them both, my dad's first marriage to a Jewish woman having been childless.

My parents loved each other, I have no doubt about that. And I'm guessing, when I look at the photo, that this period was the nearest my father ever came to happiness. It was unusual for him to smile. Sadness and melancholy became him more. He had dark brown, doe eyes and he always looked mournful as though nursing some dreadful secret.

Another photograph of my parents is at Magaluf in about 1968. He still looks happy but the smile is not so wide here. Around two years after their marriage, it's more one of wry amusement. He was a handsome man but *distinguished-looking* is more apt. In this photo, he's wearing a light polo neck cashmere sweater and a dark jacket with a handkerchief. As ever, he looks immaculate. He'd say that a vital ingredient to a good holiday was a well-equipped bathroom.

A photo I like is of my father and myself in Praia da Luz. This was *long* before Gerard arrived and transformed the villa. I'm sitting on my dad's knee in the Luz Bay Club. But this time he's not smiling, but staring blankly, already looking burdened.

Nowadays psychologists talk about a highly sensitive person being a personality type. I'd say he was *not* a highly sensitive person (HSP) but, rather, an *extremely* sensitive person. (Maybe I should invent a new acronym for this – an ESP.)

My dad was out of sync with other people. I rarely saw him with others but, when I did, he'd say a strange thing if he thought there was a misunderstanding. "I don't think we're on the same wavelength." My dad was ahead of his time because HSPs *do* operate on a different wavelength from other people. Others might misunderstand us in communication because HSPs can get distracted by body posture, tone of voice, the comfort of the setting and the seating, the brightness of the light, the noise of traffic, a bird darting through the trees nearby, the proximity of another diner – a myriad of factors. You could say that reception, at least between an HSP and a non-HSP, is subject to interference, and so requires more fine-tuning to avoid putting the HSP out of sorts.

His voice had a slight tremor. Unlike me, he didn't stammer but you sensed that speaking was not a spontaneous act. He bridled easily and could detect offence behind a veneer of pleasantries. He radiated decency and dignity but also a certain excessive refinement and wariness that made others – particularly men – uncomfortable around him.

Everyone, by way of contrast, *liked* my mother. And perhaps the very quality that attracted him began to grate. People were drawn towards her. She gave people full eye contact, the broadest smile, a sincere show of interest, and a certain attractive energy. Everyone liked her *before* she did or said anything. Is it that other people sense an openness about someone before they've even engaged socially? An admirable quality for sure but it can also irritate others who never acquire it *no matter how hard they fucking try.* So her popularity and his own social timidity might have riled him. I can guess because I'm similar to my father.

One time, my mother organised a big party for the partners at his law firm. My father, who hated big social occasions, said they wouldn't come. But everyone had a great time and I'm sure it was down to her.

My dad was quite self-conscious, blushing in company, fingering his collar, his voice dry. Part of it was his Jewishness and his tentativeness among gentiles, bracing himself for some racist comment he, as a Jewish man, felt honour-bound to rebut. Then there were his experiences in the war and, he once told me, the instances where his fellow soldiers would get drunk and hurl anti-Semitic abuse at him.

The marriage ended acrimoniously but his poor relationship with Michael and Colin proved pivotal. I don't remember their marriage because they divorced when I was four. My mother said he spent a great deal of time sleeping. It must have been challenging for her because my dad was a depressive who thought happiness was a definition of idiocy, especially for Jews.

The period after their divorce was difficult for everyone. For a time my father rented a flat opposite our place in Porchester Terrace that gave him a vantage point into our living room. Sometimes he'd ring in an emotional state. "Can you move my son near the window, so I can see him?"

Dad gradually adjusted to divorced life, seeing me on weekends. Before Gerard arrived on the scene he'd still knock on the door and collect me, exchanging cool greetings with my mother. He'd bring a treat over, like a bag of Maltesers, and I'd run out to him. One rainy weekend he arrived with nothing and I was recalcitrant about joining him. Another time, my mother had an engagement with a friend in the country, a godmother figure whom I'd got to know well. I resisted seeing my father. This must have hurt his feelings but I was only eight. My dad was sitting in his Rover car (he always bought British) while she tried to push me into the back seat. It was a ridiculous spectacle but after some inducements I relented.

In the early days following their divorce, I'd stay the weekend at his one-bedroom flat in Bayswater. We'd play football on a Saturday afternoon and return in time for the wrestling. The biggest draws were Giant Haystacks and Big Daddy. Highlights of Saturday night viewing were *Sale of the Century* and *Hawaii Five-O*. I'd sleep on a pull-out bed in my father's room, listening to him snoring lightly in the background. He had a strange habit of holding his hand over the bridge of his nose as he drifted off. On a Sunday we'd have our lunch indoors, meatballs in gravy sauce out of a tin, which he'd wheel towards me on a portable table. I'd end up with *Black Beauty* on a Sunday afternoon and then he'd drive me home.

His flat was not a happy place. When the phone rang he'd usually say it's a wrong number. And it was. The books, with dark, dusty covers, were mostly by Jewish authors and focused heavily on the two world wars, especially the Holocaust and the atrocities. If I pulled out a book on the Somme or Gallipoli I'd find the pages heavily annotated, along with morbid attention to the death toll. My mother once said she took life fundamentally happily seriously and my dad took it *unhappily* seriously. These sweeping delineations of someone else's nature irritated me. Yet I couldn't disagree with her about that.

I liked his company because children do usually love their fathers and I could see his decency and dignity. But he was no laugh-a-minute person and had a pessimistic worldview. His work was his saviour, saving him from excessive introspection and warding off loneliness.

My dad was also unlucky. My mother told me how during their marriage he was undergoing a gruelling case at work involving an especially unscrupulous opposition lawyer. She suggested a holiday in Spain to escape. The first day, by the pool, my dad bumped into the same lawyer from whom he had fled!

My dad and I never went abroad together after my parents' divorce. In January or February he'd talk about taking me to Israel in the summer. Then by spring he was pondering somewhere in France, like La Baule. By June, he was planning a holiday in the Channel Islands, probably Jersey. Come the actual holiday, we'd go to Brighton, Eastbourne or Frinton.

The farthest we got, in the summer of 1975, was the Isle of Wight. And after the experience in Sandown I doubt he ever considered going abroad again. The holiday was a disaster. A virus spread through the resort and I got seriously ill, incapable of holding any food down. A doctor was called and my father had a meltdown. But worse followed. On the penultimate night we had to evacuate the hotel after a fire broke out. We fled in our dressing gowns, even though we were both unwell, and watched as fire crews arrived. A fireman was injured and the story made the news. When I arrived back in Pimlico I was severely weakened and had chronic diarrhoea for several days. Gerard thought it funny and, subsequently, whenever I had the runs, he'd call it "the Isle of Wights".

The first evening, before we got ill, was memorable. We were sitting around in a circle in the residents' lounge watching entertainment. Couples started dancing. The Master of Ceremonies had divined that certain ladies and gentlemen, generally of older years (55 and over as my father was), were holidaying alone because he said he would be pairing off singles. Sure enough, he grabbed a gentleman and introduced her to a lone lady. I looked at my dad and he was growing paler by the second. I knew he hated dancing and any forced group activity. He left.

"I don't feel well and I'll be going to my room."

My dad must have thought I had swallowed that excuse but I hadn't. When I came back to Pimlico, still ill, it perversely cheered up my father when my mother phoned him to say I'd been able to recall this. I'd have done the same, by the way. Like father, like son!

My mother did offer him the use of our villa in Praia da Luz, naturally at a time when she and Gerard weren't there. But I can understand why my dad refused. The villa would have been unrecognisable from his time. Also the local restaurateurs, used to seeing me with mum and Gerard, would have wondered who he was. And how would he have felt sleeping in the same bed as Mum and Gerard?

So I'd spend most of August in Luz and then go with my dad to the English seaside. One time we were in Frinton in the first days of September. I was as brown as a berry but it wasn't because of the British weather! So other holidaymakers looked at me strangely, puzzling over my magnificent tan. Typical weather for Frinton at that time of the year was 19 degrees and overcast. I don't know what my dad expected on the North Sea but he was disappointed if he hoped for wall-to-wall sunshine. One morning there was a downpour. My dad punched the wall. He was inclined to self-pity if luck turned against him. But that's the price you paid for a late summer holiday in the UK.

For all his qualities, he was *not* a charismatic man. He had presence but he wasn't charismatic. His whole instinct when he met people was to *draw in*. His veil of sadness was difficult for other men to penetrate. And this was enhanced when he met gentiles. He had a thin skin for anti-Semitism. One time he phoned up a London radio station to complain because a news story had referred to a "wealthy Jewish lawyer".

We were once in Hyde Park when one of the biggest National Front rallies of the era passed by. Assembled were all the bully boys of the far Right – plummy-voiced John Tyndall[51] bellowing on a megaphone side by side with Martin Webster,[52] his

---

[51] John Tyndall (1934-2005). British neo-Nazi leader.

gay, burly sidekick. And their legions of supporters, the jackbooted, tattooed dumb skinheads, some of whom were making Nazi salutes. My father looked on with such anger and hurt. Not only had he served in the war, he'd also participated in the battle of Cable Street against Oswald Mosley[53] in 1936. When he was angry there was a great physical transformation, his nostrils flared and his shoulders arched. And yet, perversely, he was at heart a mild man.

Some of his anti-German hatred was beyond the pale. If we were in a restaurant and he heard German being spoken at a nearby table, he'd become uppity. I wondered if he was showing off for my benefit. Now I realise he had persuaded himself. It was his obsession. One time we arrived in Eastbourne and the weather was glorious. This time, I thought, my dad could relax. We had just checked in at reception when the manager appeared.

"Good afternoon, and velcome to ze hotel. My name is Dietmar Schlieben."

My father hated Nazis – understandably – but also all Germans of a certain age because he believed they were complicit. He once charged into a bookshop looking for a memoir written by a

---

[52] Martin Webster (b.1943). British neo-Nazi and former ally of John Tyndall.
[53] Oswald Mosley (1896-1980). Leader of the British Union of Fascists in the 1930s. The Battle of Cable Street took place between fascist and anti-fascist groups in Cable Street in London's East End on 4 October 1936.

Holocaust survivor and started shouting when they didn't have it. He was a Jewish man of a certain type, spotting dog whistle anti-Semitism by populist politicians, and always alert to the word "Jew". It was a sensitive subject, *very* sensitive indeed.

It was just his luck that, at Sussex House, my first experience of anti-Semitism came from a boy with a German-sounding name who kicked me on the football pitch and said "Bloody Jews – I wish Hitler had killed more of you!" I made the cardinal mistake of telling my dad. It validated his view that most Germans, even kids, were closet Nazis.

"You tell this boy to meet you in the gym at 4pm after school for a boxing match. Then you punch him on the jaw," my dad told me over the phone, so angry he could barely speak.

I was puzzled by my dear dad's counsel. First, the gym of Sussex House School was in an annexe around the corner and locked after hours. Second, I'd never taken part in a boxing match. Third, I'd probably have missed if I'd tried to punch him. When our "fight" came, after a further exchange of insults, it was more of a wrestling match that saw us tumbling down the school back stairs. And it was best described as a draw.

***

My dad was a committed moviegoer, maybe because it was an escape into a different world, away from his private hell. When the Israelis rescued their hostages at Entebbe, this Jewish counter-punch, this body blow to those who said the Jews went too meekly to the gas chambers, gave rise to several movies. My father took me to see *Victory at Entebbe* at a fleapit cinema in Bayswater because he hated the vast West End venues.

Yaphet Kotto played Amin brilliantly, conveying the huge, bear-like menace behind the joviality. It was a clever performance but also, in a way, funny as Kotto (in character as Amin and posing for the Ugandan cameras) mock-befriended a young Orthodox Israeli boy, patting him like a benevolent uncle. It was chilling because we knew what had ensued. Amin, who was open about his Hitler-worship and dislike of Jews, later ordered the killing of Dora Bloch in retaliation for the successful Israeli raid.

When Kotto did his fake solicitousness with the Israel hostages, a black woman in the audience laughed uproariously.

"If you want to watch a comedy, go and see another film," my dad shouted at her.

I didn't fully appreciate how easily unsettled my father was by Nazis until one day we were in a hotel room in the New Forest. The movie, *The Passage*, starred Malcolm McDowell as a sadistic SS officer. It was a cartoon, psychopathic Nazi, even unintentionally funny. One movie critic called it "a campy performance that has to be seen to be disbelieved".

My father and I were lying side by side. An early scene had McDowell torturing a member of the French resistance in his kitchen. He'd tied the Frenchman's hands to a table. McDowell had an over-sized white chef's hat and was pretending to come up with a marvellous dish. But his culinary efforts, while chopping up onions, were interspersed with a clear threat to chop off the Frenchman's fingers. He poured the boiling contents of a frying pan over his captive's face, looking back and forth at the carving knife and the man's fingers. It was clear what was coming. My dad was rubbing his cheeks frantically, cursing at the screen. "This is nasty, very unpleasant," he kept saying, breathing heavily. But he was holding up.

More sadism ensued. McDowell threw a cigarette over a gypsy he'd tied to a tree and doused in petrol. I should have changed the channel but what was unfolding was so awful we both felt compelled to watch. McDowell subsequently abducted a young girl, brought her back to his quarters and lectured her on the wonders of the purported thousand-year Reich. He stripped and – lo and behold – he was wearing jockstraps emblazoned with a swastika. McDowell, in character, cackled before raping her. That was enough for my dad. He left the room. I turned the movie off, and found him in a helluva state, gripping the handrail in the bathroom.

It's only a film and at first I realised McDowell could only do what was scripted. (Well, no, because I read a subsequent interview with McDowell in which he said the SS jockstraps were *his* idea to make the character even more repulsive. He succeeded. And almost killed my dad off in the process!) Gerard, if he'd watched the scene, would have reacted differently, salivating over the violence and shouting "lovely jubberly" during the torture scenes.

I also found the movie unpleasant but because it was so wildly over-the-top, indeed "campy", I was better able to dismiss it. Fast forward to the present and now I see how wildly different reactions to films, especially violent or sadistic ones, separate the HSP from those of "normal" sensitivity and those, like Gerard, who are naturally *in*sensitive. Both my dad and I were repelled by stories of institutionalised brutality or bullying, especially when the bullied party was powerless to resist and the oppressor was backed up by the establishment.

I enjoyed movies that extended the boundaries of what was acceptable and depicted people moved to create or appreciate beauty, films like *Death in*

Venice and, especially, *Lust for Life*. Van Gogh was certainly an HSP, or an ESP, and I cried at various moments in the film, as I did – many years later – during *Saving Private Ryan* and *An English Patient*.

I spurned movies my peers at school liked. Even the Bond franchise, in those days starring Roger Moore, bored me. As a 15-year-old I was so impressed with *On Golden Pond* after watching it with my dad that I saw it again on my own. I watched a six-part TV series called *Plays for Pleasure*, generally about relationships, an older intellectual man romancing a young girl, or a schoolboy being reunited with a favourite schoolteacher. These were probably perceived as belonging to old fuddy-duddy land but I found them heart-warming. I favoured gentler films that made me reflect on the human condition.

Later, as I entered my twenties, I preferred going to the theatre and watching theatrical giants – actors like Albert Finney, Peter O'Toole, and Anthony Hopkins – to attending a pop concert. The theatrical experience afforded extraordinary memories. I can still recall sections of dialogue, whereas a concert was like a fairground thrill, intoxicating but instantly forgotten. I disliked loud music anyway. I wasn't cut out for the modern era, preferring as I did the music of Aznavour, Piaf or Sinatra. Yes, I was a "sensitive squaggy" and, yes, I was like my father. I'm not saying all this to make you think how mature I was but for you to understand my *isolation*. I was a laughing stock at school on account of my strange tastes. A total nerd.

My dad and I both enjoyed thought-provoking entertainment. We saw great films together, sensitive dramas such as *Kramer versus Kramer*, *Terms of Endearment*, *Ordinary People*, and *Chariots of Fire*. We also enjoyed television series like *To Serve Them All My Days* about inter-war life in a fictional boys' boarding school. When he died I missed his insights into such dramas, his perceptive dissection of the characterisations, and his ability to pick up a sub-text.

***

Anxiety and obsession dogged my dad. And then a self-loathing crept in when he realised he was in their grip. We used to laugh at my father's timekeeping. He was usually early for any appointment. This was great when I was put on early report at school (you had to be there an hour beforehand) on account of my mother's habitual failure to get me there on time. So my dad took over and drove me there by 8am as the punishment demanded, every time.

In other instances, however, I realised dad's excessive punctuality sprang from nervousness.

We'd visit someone, arrive early, leave the car and walk around the block while he checked his watch every minute. Even on holiday the watch-gazing was compulsory – "it's ten to four", then "it's five past four", betraying an anxiety disorder.

Yet he had gravitas, he was a respected lawyer and it was important to him to be fastidious in his work. His neurosis must have pained him, especially when it led to exhaustion and forgetfulness. And, boy, was he absent-minded, comically so. He was always getting lost and asking the way, especially if we had a new route. But I wonder if he listened to directions because he was in such a state.

He'd park his car while it was still light, say on an autumn day, and forget where he'd left it. One time we came out of a tea place in Kensington High Street and it escaped him where he'd left the car. He got his keys out and we must have tried a hundred different locks when three burly guys appeared. They were ready to wrestle him to the ground. They turned out to be plainclothes policemen. Then they saw me and backed off.

"Wait a minute, I don't like this at all," said my father who chewed them out good. "I'll be taking this up with your superiors. You'll be hearing from me."

"We're very sorry, sir. We had no idea you were out with your son."

"See you in court," said my father in what became a famous parting salvo of his. The idea of my dad as a car thief made me laugh. If he found a 20-pound note on the ground he'd hand it in at a police station!

My dad disliked the brutality of the world, the intense competition. He was kind and hated to see people suffering, but at the same time, and in some way contrarily, he believed people were too flippant and too dismissive of other people's tragedies. He wanted people to exhibit the same sensitivity he did but, deep down, he must have known that few would.

He did go too far sometimes but now I see some of his behaviour stemmed from deep depression. One time he heard about a Jewish guy, maybe a Holocaust survivor, who'd relocated near Auschwitz. My father said he sympathised with him and was minded to follow suit. This was ironic; most Jews would have wanted to escape from Auschwitz but my dad – forever contrary – was trying to get *near the place*! He also told me he was minded to travel to South America to lynch arch-war criminal Josef Mengele. Doubtless, many would have approved of the goal. But, as I look back, I doubt he'd have made it to Sao Paulo considering the furthest south he'd been with me after the divorce was, as I have already mentioned, the Isle of Wight.[54]

---

[54] In any case we now know that by the time my dad starting sharing this fantasy with me (in the early 1980s) Mengele (1911-1979) was already

All this may have an ever so slight touch of self-flagellation but I bet it's not *that* uncommon among Jews of his generation. But my dad was always attentive, unsparingly so to my concerns, and I understand him because I'm from the same flesh and blood. He was not a sunshine spreader but he had deeper qualities.

He disliked excessive frivolity if he thought it inappropriate. On the day of President Kennedy's assassination in 1963 he and my mother were dining out in a London restaurant called Shangri-La. She told me he berated some fellow diners for laughing too loudly. I had similar feelings after Princess Diana died in 1997 when I saw a couple of girls laughing over their takeaway pizzas in my block. I felt like telling them to behave with more decorum.

My dad had old-fashioned courtesies and values that now, sadly, seem outdated. (He'd be 104 if he were alive today.) If the news related an egregious crime, or a politician had behaved dishonourably, he'd shout "shame, shame" at the TV. Always twice and with sincerity. The concept of "shame" is no longer part of public life anywhere in the West. Even when people do behave dishonourably, they're reluctant to acknowledge it, let alone suffer embarrassment on account of it. People may say "it's a shame I couldn't get to the meeting" or "what a shame he got

---

dead, having drowned off the coast of Brazil.

ill" but "shame" in the sense of dishonour is seldom mentioned.

After my dad died I met a friend's mother whom he would meet at those weekly Sussex House coffee mornings. She said to me "he was a real gentleman". He was a dignified man beaten down by neurosis and, yes, an extremely cruel era. His extreme sensitivity aligned with a mentally taxing job meant he tired easily. It's well known that HSPs need more down time to recover because their nervous system is more vulnerable to external stimuli and stresses. And my father – as I have pointed out – was an *extremely* sensitive man.

Perhaps he felt he could only cope with being a father and a lawyer. The commitment and sacrifice involved in being in a relationship was too much. But by shunning a relationship he was now on a dangerously introspective journey because he was a lone traveller and without close friends. My dad became lonelier and sadder than ever.

There may be temporary relief in ceasing to strive for happiness. If you believe it's no longer attainable – as my dad concluded – then sadness, which requires no front and no effort (in someone who self-identifies as a chronic depressive) is a more natural state. But extreme sadness, if it continues indefinitely, breaks social rules, brooks no intrusion, and repels others. So the "sufferer" becomes ever more tentative when meeting people.

The chronic depressive will react bitterly if he sees over-joyousness in others. He certainly won't be comfortable in a group of men, at a sporting event, or in the pub, where there's mutual ribbing and banter. The larger the group, the more the merriment. The gathering becomes a social test and the depressed person is rooted out and deemed socially unacceptable. It's a form of natural selection; the "group" excludes the perpetually sad person, and the rejected one feels his "otherness" more strongly than ever.

Not that my dad would have had much in common with other men. Men are aggressive, dirty, lustful, coarse and ambitious. They have dirt under their fingernails and wear their imperfections with pride. They act like pigs when they're in locker rooms . . . I jest but *many* men have *some* of these attributes. But my dad wasn't like that and he shunned male company.

The depressed person becomes wary of anyone pricking his private hell. Every social "threat" is magnified. Extreme sadness feeds on itself. He who cries, cries alone and all that, and the lonely city (to cite a book I liked by Olivia Laing) becomes lonelier. In time the isolated person loses the knack of social chit-chat, so any attempt at it – even on a good day when a spark of optimism remains – flounders.

My dad took sadness to an extreme. After his death I found a tape on which he recorded the funeral of Princess Grace of Monaco off the TV in 1982. It was a solemn and emotional event, especially because she'd died prematurely. My dad had punctuated the recording by commenting on the "broken" picture of Prince Rainier, epitomising, as he put it, "all that is sad in the world today". It was a heart-breaking spectacle but my dad was already broken-hearted anyway.

Extreme sadness is not the most convivial quality but we should beware of the toxic masculinity that defines male bonding. The sensitive will shun this initiation and feel excluded. No wonder depression and suicide rates are so high among young men because what's socially unacceptable becomes ever more implosive.

Others probably perceived my father as morose. My mother once observed that he made others miserable. But what Jewish man of that war generation was happy-go-lucky? They don't exist. Blame it on Hitler. My dad was a tragic victim of his times. In a different world, minus World War Two, and with more understanding of mental health issues, he might have flourished.

He was also prescribed anti-depressants because when he died the coroner's report noted a "massive" amount of tablets in his flat. My dad's addiction to these pills must have also contributed to his downfall. He was withdrawn from them in a London clinic, and went through hell. He had a nurse who looked after him towards the end, "a paid companion" as he once said with a tinge of self-disgust. He hoped to continue working after 1984, the year of his purported retirement, and for a while he continued part-time. He complained about his chosen profession but his job gave his life structure and purpose.

One day in 1985 there was a meeting with a bumptious senior partner from his law practice. This partner insisted on letting him go. Dad pleaded for his name to at least be kept on the notepaper as a consultant. But this was rejected. It was his death knell.

Dad, stripped of his routine, disintegrated. He became highly vulnerable to suggestion. If he saw a programme on television about Parkinson's he would mysteriously develop the symptoms, an exact replica of manifestations of the illness. He was convinced he had heart trouble despite repeated medical reassurances. Loneliness proved his undoing.

***

What "ailed" my father? Labels can be tricky but he certainly had anxiety and depression. He was a broken man, obsessing over the past. My dad's problem was also one of *concealment*. I found it difficult to find help for my anxiety about 30 years ago. So for my dad, half a century ago, forget it! Men soldiered on and kept everything inside. He did go to see psychiatrists and psychotherapists but perhaps they didn't probe. Instead they handed out pills like sweets.

I shouldn't have been surprised by his suicide. He'd had longstanding mental health issues. I now see there's no such thing as "a typical suicide" and it's ludicrous to pretend such. Each person may have different reasons. So never believe it when people say "he/she isn't the type". It's a dangerous statement. Some may have serious financial problems, others a debilitating and painful physical illness, others might believe they have perpetrated something "shameful". Others can see no way out of a serious dilemma. Sometimes the person might be generally coping but, underneath, life is too much. Then there's a mishap and the dam bursts. It could be something mundane like missing an appointment or being late for a plane. And they suddenly think – what's the point? This could be a *spontaneous* suicide.

Sometimes the person might have been considering suicide for a long time and this, I conclude, was the case with my father. I never saw his suicide note but he left recordings mentioning depression and suicidal feelings. In the tapes he said it was the "sensitive, kind and caring who go under" and "the beasts who survive". A generalisation and one born out of despair, but there's some truth in that.

I had therapy after his suicide and one or two counsellors (foolishly) argued with me when I said I didn't feel angry towards my dad about what had happened. True, his suicide *was* badly timed because the following day I had an exam. But my father was so far gone I doubt he was aware of it. I don't feel angry because we have the same genes. My dad did well to carry on working as long as he did given his longstanding demons.

He was of artistic temperament. He should have been in the music business because he loved opera and, by all accounts, had been a talented singer. Although he loved classical music he said he could no longer listen to it because, he said, it pulled at his heartstrings. "It's best not to stir unfulfilled longings," he'd say. So even the pleasure of listening to music was denied him.

My father once told me his parents had hoped he'd enter one of the three "great professions", medicine, accountancy, or law. I never had the self-discipline to hold down such a job. I might have lasted six months but no more. He was crucified on the cross of respectability and spent 40 years in the law. And it exhausted him.

He was unusual in that if he asked someone how they were, he'd wait for the answer. But the reverse also applied. If my mother – once the acrimony of their divorce had subsided – asked him how he was, he'd reply: "How long have you got?"

It would be silly to pretend I don't have regrets. There were things I would/should have said. But I was only 19. In particular, I would have thanked him for compensating for my mother's absences, especially during those winters away.

Even now, 37 years on from my father's death, whenever I read of a suicide of a famous person or an acquaintance, it brings it all back. My dad lived his later years like a shadow, a ghost. No one could permeate or cut through the inner hell he inhabited. He once told me that the years after 1971 were all a blur. The charitable view would be he was working hard to pay for my education. But, yes, these years must have been lonely for him.

Sometimes when someone of fine character dies prematurely, we hear people paying tribute by saying "they were too good for this world". Perhaps, in certain cases, "too good for this world" means "too sensitive for this world". Or that the world can be a cruel and *insensitive* place.

It's a paradox that lonely people don't attract people because their neediness can be off-putting. I was once walking down Queensway when I saw my dad marching purposefully up to the top on the other side of the road, his hands lunging forward. It may seem ridiculous that I didn't run up to him to speak. Yet something in his demeanour stopped me. It was as though he was being attacked by an inner demon, and he was retaliating. Angry. Not violent, just angry. I now recognise him in me because I sometimes have a similar way of walking.

My mother once said my dad couldn't live with people but couldn't live without them either. He couldn't function well with people because in some ways he got their vibes too strongly. But he also found it difficult being alone. I know my dad as an HSP, or even an ESP, because I'm one.

A few weeks before he died my dad asked my mother if she would have him back. She equivocated. I don't blame her at all for this because my dad was – for all his lovable ways – a difficult man requiring considerable care. We compromised, a flat 200 metres away from us in Regent's Park. This would have been the best solution, enabling us to monitor him without a full-time cohabitation. (She also had Colin and Michael to consider and their relationship with my dad, as I have already outlined, was not good.)

We inspected the flat in question and found it suitable. So I was genuinely surprised when one day, over the phone, my dad announced he was staying where he was. This should have triggered alarm bells. The last time I saw him he bore a look of dolorous goodness but also pained resignation. I tried to encourage him. He laughed in a strange, defeated way. He'd already decided ...

I coped with the funeral fairly "well" – by which I mean I was not overcome. The rabbi described my dad as a *sensitive*, caring man who expected too much of himself and other people. There's that word again.

I was less stoical a couple of weeks later when my mother and I went to his flat to collect his clothes. We were leaving, locking the door, when a neighbour on the same landing approached us and asked me if I was Mr. Kupfermann's son. I nodded.

"I'm a bit hurt he didn't say goodbye, you know," she said.

I said nothing.

"He told me he was moving to Scotland. It would have been nice if he'd said goodbye at least."

My dad was such a quintessentially urban creature, the last person to have *ever* contemplated such a move. But apparently, this neighbour explained, he'd told her he was moving to Scotland to a cottage near a stream. It was so sad and solitary, and this far-fetched, far-flung fantasy opened the floodgates to my grief ...

... My mother was excellent in the immediate aftermath of dad's death and gave total support. I just wanted to get drunk but that had been going on for a long time *before* my father's death. I was to be a champion drinker. Ironically, my dad hated drink, even spitting out a chocolate the final Christmas he spent with us because it contained a trace of alcohol.

But I'd always liked booze, not for the taste but for the effect. It made me less shy and more combative. I also liked how it made me more spontaneous because for years I'd had to monitor my words. So I had all the ingredients for a troubled time. A perfect storm? A hurricane, more like.

9. Clean Hands

"A little something you inherited"

My mother

"But if the drinking is habitual, the brain begins to compensate for these calming effects by producing an increase in excitatory neurotransmitters. What this means in practice is that when one stops drinking, even for a day or two, the increased activity manifests itself by way of an eruption of anxiety, more severe than anything that came before. This neuroadaptation is what drives addiction in the susceptible, eventually making the drinker require alcohol to function at all."

Olivia Laing in *The Trip to Echo Spring*

I wish I'd read those words 35 years ago …

My life didn't disintegrate because of a speech impediment, although for several years I had dreaded talking, especially in large groups. It didn't fall apart because I was a lost half-Jew, trying to fit into gentile society. Or because of my weakness for alcohol. Neither did it fall apart exclusively on the back of a dysfunctional and isolated childhood and a sadistic "stepfather". And I can't pin my decline on my father's suicide because I'd been suffering from anxiety and depression *before* his death. Rather, it was a combination of *all* the above. Also, I now had an inheritance enabling me to withdraw from normal life. My twenties were to be an unbelievable car crash.

But it was true that my speech deteriorated further after my dad's death. I worried about it more. I'd never encountered other people with speech impediments and could only conclude it was symptomatic of a deep-rooted deficiency. With enough drink in me I could hide my stammer.

Incredibly, like the cripple drawn to the athletics track, I had fantasised about becoming an actor. I didn't stammer when I was reciting verse to myself. So I'd managed to convince myself all it would require to gain fluency would be a supreme effort. I did an audition for a one-year drama course in the London suburbs and – lo and behold – I hardly stammered at all and got a place.

I soon found out once I was interacting with other drama students and dealing with the pressure of having to say my cue *immediately* that the dreaded stammer was *still* there. I think it's true of sensitive people that just because you can do something in private *doesn't mean you can do it in public*. Our senses and our nervous system are overwhelmed too. And the more I tried to force fluency, the worse it got.

You often hear it said about people who stammer, that they are supposedly fluent when they sing or act. If you ever attended a karaoke event for stammerers, you'd know it isn't necessarily so! I quickly realised a career as an actor was not for me. But I didn't want to withdraw from the course, and so I drank more and persevered in small parts.

But even saying a few lines was a problem. One day my drama teacher pulled me up and said. "Look, I must be honest with you. I don't want everyone on opening night to be focused on you and asking themselves – 'who is THAT'?"

My mind went back to stories of how theatrical greats had been discovered. Audiences had focused on them and asked precisely that question. "Who is THAT?" but I realised my drama teacher didn't mean it in the sense of standout success. But, rather, standout stammering. He was a kind man and so it must have pained him to be so honest. He continued. "I did hear something odd in your audition but I hadn't realised it was *that* bad."

I didn't know what to say. But, for the rest of the course, I drank more and more and found it enabled me to say my few lines. Some fellow students thought my speech was improving but this wasn't so. I became more fluent with drink. My mother later commented that the drama course had done me good but, in reality, it reinforced my sense of inadequacy.

Many speech courses and therapies focus on how to talk fluently, taking your time, and not capitulating to speed pressures. But one of the consequences of severe stammering, apart from the obvious frustration of not being able to articulate normally, is that feelings are trapped. I found it difficult to express annoyance and anger. I'd spent my childhood bottling up feelings of neglect and loneliness.

My drinking reached epic levels. I was once discussing plans with someone of my age, looking ahead 10 years. This guy told me, almost as a matter of fact: "You won't be here in 10 years." I couldn't disagree.

One morning in autumn 1987 I woke up after another bender to find I'd sprained my ankle. I took a taxi to St Mary's Hospital where my foot was put in a plaster. A nurse questioned me about my accident and I admitted that the night before I'd drunk at least eight pints of strong lager.

"You'll have no liver left by the time you're thirty. You know, all this is self-inflicted and we could really do without this. We're so busy this morning, taking care of more people than usual."

"What do you mean?"

"The *fire* at King's Cross. We've been treating some of the injured all through the night."

"What fire?"

The nurse glared at me. I'd been so pissed that I was oblivious to the fire that was to claim 31 lives. In my drunken stupor I hadn't heard any news for 16 hours.

Other memoirists often contrast the disparity between others' perceptions of their outward life and the inner reality. They write something like "to all ostensive purposes I was a successful professional (insert esteemed occupation) whereas I was crumbling inside". In my own case too there was a disparity. But not like the one above. Outwardly, especially after this accident, I'd have come across as a hobbling disaster. Inwardly, I wasn't even hobbling, I was more like a catatonic catastrophe!

After the drama course I went to university but dropped out after one year. No degree. Meanwhile, my drinking was getting worse. I'd go out to a pub, drink myself insensible and wake up the following morning, always in my bed, but with little recollection of the night before. Usually, all I had left on me was "boozer's change", small bits of copper and silver, either because I'd spent everything or been robbed. I lost so many bank cards that my local branch got tired of seeing me.

I had some money from my father's estate but this was a mixed blessing because, normally, a young jobless man without qualifications would be broke and forced to confront his problems. But I ignored them and got drunk. The hangovers were so bad that they were a continuation of drunkenness; possibly I derived some masochistic pleasure in the experience. My eyes were usually bloodshot and my head throbbed permanently.

On another windswept autumn day I was sitting on a station platform in London when a nice girl came up to me and struck up a conversation. She mentioned pubs in Hampstead I'd frequented, so we should have had common ground. I looked at her and couldn't say a word. You could say I'd lost confidence but I'm not sure I'd ever acquired it. Gerard's criticisms had eroded my self-esteem. Also, pointedly, my life had been secluded from girls. I had two half-brothers and went to all-boys' schools and my mother had few friends who had children because her job tended to take her into contact with other singles.

***

One day I went to the job centre in London and asked a member of staff what employment would suit me. I must have stammered badly because he drew my attention to an advert for a gallery attendant. I visited the offices of a security firm and a lady interviewed me.

"You do realise what you will be doing, don't you? You'll be walking up and down an art gallery. It's sad for someone with your good qualifications."

Thirty-three years ago, 10 O levels and 3 A levels would have been "good qualifications".

She continued. "You won't have to do much talking".

Perfect! I could pace up and down an art gallery and continue drinking. I could disappear into the nothingness I was sure awaited me. I wouldn't be noticed.

Wrong! I didn't know I'd be posted to the Hayward Gallery, one of the South Bank's most popular exhibition sites. And at the end of 1990 anybody who was anybody, and anybody who wanted to be somebody, came to see the exhibition on Jasper Johns. For movie fans out there, I felt like the character at the end of *The Tenant* who imagines everyone is there to witness his downfall.

Michael Foot (the man who haunted the nightmares of David Emms) visited as did John Cleese, Lauren Bacall, and Jacqueline Bisset. That there were so many distinguished guests was not a problem for me. The only communication was directing visitors to the cloakroom, occasionally reminding them not to take pictures, and reprimanding school kids for sticking chewing gum on the exhibits.

It felt like everyone I'd ever met – from my great uncle Alan to old classmates and my history teacher, nearly all my mother's middle-class friends, even a British friend I recognised from Praia da Luz – came to these exhibitions. I loathed meeting people who knew me from school. It must have been comical because, in my position as a gallery attendant, there was nowhere to go. Upstairs was a café for the outside public. One day I sheltered in there from my old head of history at Dulwich College. But he found me and recognised me.

I spent a year at the Hayward Gallery. The biggest events surrounded the opening day of a new exhibition when the director of the gallery would welcome luminaries, even the arts minister and the artist themselves if they were still alive. Then they'd swan off to the Ivy in Covent Garden for canapés and champagne, leaving me and my mates rat-arsed in the guards' quarter downstairs or in a pub near Waterloo Station.

One day, after several exhibitions, our company lost the contract. I could have left the security firm, but it would have meant being voluntarily unemployed, and that I didn't want. I fell into conversation with another guard.

"They're going to offer us all kinds of jobs," he told me. "But be careful what you agree to. Don't work in Tesco in Leyton High Road."

"Why?"

"You ain't the type, you're too middle-class, too white, and too soft."

I had to admit it was a perceptive thumbnail portrait.

"Take my advice, it ain't for people like you," he added.

The following day the phone rang and it was the head office of the security firm.

"Daniel, we don't want you to be dossin' – so we'd like you to go Tesco, Leyton High Road, near the Bakers Arms pub. Be there at 10am. You'll be on shift with another guard. He'll show you the ropes."

"But I've been told I'm too m– m– m …"

"Be there at 10 am, ok?"

I arrived at Tesco supermarket to find the other guard in place, a short black fellow. He nodded in my direction and the first thing he said was "I just caught a guy stealin' a bottle of Remy Martin".

This was an early indication he took the job seriously because I hadn't reckoned for *arresting* people. Most security guards I'd met, at the Hayward Gallery at least, were sleeping on the job. And my immediate reaction was – if you want to steal a bottle of Remy Martin, I mean if you're desperate for it, if you're an alcoholic, or a drunk, well, you're welcome to it …

"This is a rough area and we're expected to get results. Professional thieves stake out the whole street," he told me, pointing to a couple of girls walking past.

It was the run-up to the 1992 general election, a period of economic crisis. One day a battered-looking bloke – the kind who frequents pubs where you need three previous convictions before you're allowed in – beckoned me from the door and put a couple of coins in my hand.

"Get us a lemon, mate. I've been banned from this place so many times."

A white establishment figure was seen as the enemy. And my timing was impeccable. A few weeks in and the LA riots fired off and even here, in this faraway corner of London's East End, there was tension. Once I vaguely scanned a black guy as I was pacing the aisle. He turned around and gazed at me contemptuously. "You ought to be shot," he said.

I was once admiring a black family, impeccably attired in white clothes, at the checkout.

"Hey man, why are you staring at me? Not all black people are thieves! I have a university education!"

Around this time a white guy came in, picked up what turned out to be a leg of lamb and fled with it. The other guard and I called out to him. But he ran off with it. "There's a recession on, mate!" he shouted.

I could see the funny side but the other security guard didn't, chased after him and brought him crashing to the ground. As he lay on the floor, trying to shake off the guard, the would-be shoplifter screamed. "Get off me, you gorilla!"

Yes, racism was widespread but under the surface and sometimes manifesting itself in one side misconstruing the other's intentions.

My fellow security guard would bang fists with his black mates and they'd say "black power!" So, one day, I (jocularly) banged fists and said "Jewish Power!" One of the guys said Jews had power anyway, so why would I say such a thing? I couldn't pull off being an oppressed minority. What did they see? A well-spoken, affluent white guy.

It *was* a useful learning exercise about life on the street and so, to all young people doing dive jobs, learn what you can from them. You'd be surprised how much information you can pick up and how many skills you can add to your toolbox.

At least none of my mother's middle-class friends would see me in Leyton High Road, a troubled area but beyond the pale for them. Neither would she ever come near this place. It wasn't her cup of … rosé wine.

***

Some of my behaviour was appalling, ricocheting from bar to bar, so drunk I could barely stand. I was ready for rehab and wouldn't have resisted. Instead, it was all downhill for me. Ironically, my mother improved after Gerard's departure. If you see addiction as an illness, she was in remission. Now that she didn't have a boyfriend, she looked to me for company and companionship.

She had sold Praia da Luz in 1986, so there were no bolt holes. I regret the sale. Luz was, and is, a special place. The only person Mum kept in touch with in Luz was Alison. You leave a place and that's it. People move on. But this was a happy time for my mother; she was fulfilled at work and popular once more.

Meanwhile, I spiralled into decline. Depression and dread dogged me. I'd screwed up my chances of a career and in your twenties if you don't catch the train you think you're finished. An anxiety attack came when I concluded that the meaningless path I'd taken couldn't be reversed. It's the November sleepless night again. You stare at the ceiling. There seems no way forward or back. Nothing will change. But that sensation, real enough at the time, is, thankfully, wrong. Because even while you're feeling this way the length of the day is shifting, the sun will rise and set at different times, and new people can enter your social circle. Just as nature gradually changes, life itself also brings changes, albeit indiscernibly. I'm sounding like Master Kan in *Kung Fu* now.

My mother could see I was in a bad way and tried to help. But my father's suicide and preceding "illnesses", and, yes, my whole point is that anxiety and depression *are* illnesses, meant she saw my behaviour through the prism of *his* condition.

Yet now I see his advice had been sound on many issues. He'd warned me against drinking alcohol from a young age. "You could be setting yourself up for trouble." He'd also suggested I might find a greater "affinity" (his word) with Jewish people. This wasn't inverted racism but a recognition that I had some typical Jewish traits: neuroticism, urban angst, and introspection etc. He'd also warned me against spending too much time on my own as a child. And, true to his word, he'd never used me as a ping pong ball against my mother. He'd always behaved in a gentlemanly fashion even when angry. On that dreadful night in Pimlico he'd even had the good grace to walk away out of my earshot when he'd castigated my mother.

Granted, his suicide had not helped me. It would be ludicrous to deny it was anything other than a tragedy. But I was gradually understanding that my dad's undeniable mental health issues had enabled my mother to dismiss him as a "nutter". She responded to everything he said with an eye roll – as if to say, "You know what he's like".

So whenever my dad had protested about those winters, she could always say or infer, "well, this over-the-top reaction is typical of your father; he has trouble coping with some everyday situations, so who's he to give advice?"

After his suicide, my mother, while acknowledging his finer points, his good character and compassionate nature, could define him further. She once said to me: "He couldn't cope with very much" and "life was a struggle for him".

I was now wrestling with anxiety and depression but some of it (although I don't deny the *possibility* of a hereditary dimension) was down to the instability and separations of my childhood. So I decided to go into therapy. My mother was not against it *per se* but she assumed I'd be talking about my father's suicide and *his* problems, *not* the period preceding it. She was issuing a tacit disclaimer, refusing to concede any of my psychological problems stemmed from my childhood.

I hated her sweeping delineation of my problems, uttered in a throwaway gentle voice. One time she said to me when I was depressed that "it's a little something you've inherited". The clear implication was I was ill, like my dad, so there was little I could do. This loaded phrase cleared her of any responsibility, and "blamed" my late father, who was no longer there to answer back, for my problems. In a way, it also killed off my recovery for I was starting to realise my displaced childhood had destabilised me. But my mother's catch-all statement haunted me. *"It's a little something you've inherited."*

So there were many other implications stemming from that. If what she said was true then I'd *always* have emotional problems. Maybe there *was* a chemical imbalance in the brain. Perhaps my mother really believed my dad had been ill and that I *had* inherited something. Is it possible she thought she was helping me to understand why I felt so bad?

My half-brothers also thought ruminating over feelings was pointless. But a good therapist may help you to block repeat patterns of self-destructive behaviour. They will not necessarily "cure" anxiety or depression, or stop addictive behaviour. But greater self-insight can help you handle emotional problems better and help you counsel others when they are troubled.

I didn't find my mother's advice constructive. She had this stock of set phrases. "Life isn't a bed of roses." "Think of life as a picture – with darkness and light." Many years later, after her death, I was looking through some of her albums and correspondence. I found the last letters her father, (my grandfather whom I had never met) had sent her. This was from 1960. The same trite phrase, the one about "life isn't a bed of roses", was included in every letter. This banal advice is passed down the generations, a sticking plaster wielded out during times of despair. But they do little good. Break the chain, folks, break the chain …

Even at school when I had complained about anti-Semitism she merely replied "there will always be something about you people don't like". Nowadays, hopefully, racism at school would be a disciplinary matter. Yet, 40 years ago, it was normal. Fatally, here too, my mother's advice on Jewish issues was flawed. She viewed Jewishness as a religion. Although I had a Jewish name she believed it was something I could divest myself of, rather like undressing at night.

None of this helped my anxiety and depression or my drinking. And here again my mother was silent. It was clear by now (1990) that all her sons had drinking problems, but this was seldom broached. And now I see she didn't want to acknowledge her advice had been wrong, or, God forbid, that she'd set a poor example and we'd inherited some weakness for alcohol from *her*! Even though she could see all three of us were going on massive benders, she refused to call out our excesses.

At rock bottom, around the time I'd dropped out of university, I might have agreed to go to rehab. But she never suggested it. She only mentioned the money I was spending on booze, but not the scale of my addiction. This was a role reversal of everything we normally hear. It's usually the sufferer who's in denial and another family member who comes to them, offers them so-called tough love, and urges them to seek help. In the movies, it's always like "we love you but we've seen you do this and that …" If someone had suggested this to me I might have agreed. And the root causes of my drinking, i.e. the anxiety and depression and my speech problem, would have been uncovered. If so, I might not have wasted a decade.

Also, although terms like anxiety and depression are now commonplace, 30 years ago, especially among men, they were rarely discussed or tolerated. My mother, on one occasion when I was especially despondent, had accused me of self-pity. I got even *more* depressed after that. One time she came back with some pills, saying someone selling herbal remedies had told her they would help. Of course, pills to cure depression, pills to cure an earthquake.

My mother could also offer little help with my speech problem. Her usual recourse was to claim I didn't have one. Yet, whenever I spoke at length, and especially when someone else was present, she'd start clicking her fingernails ferociously, avert her eyes, and even leave the room while I was blocking. One time she referred to it as "a silly habit". It was the worst thing she could say. My speech problem underlay much of my anxiety. I didn't know anyone else who stammered. Knowing the great Winston Churchill had a similar problem didn't help because when I played tapes of his speeches I couldn't hear a trace of it.

The fact I could speak to my mother, one to one, largely without stammering, genuinely confounded her. She didn't realise stammering is an anxiety-related condition. But this doesn't mean it's controllable. Imagine you're walking on a tightrope and you have a drop of a mere foot. You wouldn't feel nervous about falling. But if you were walking across the same tightrope and it straddled the Grand Canyon then most people would feel differently.

One Christmas there were too many family members present, including Michael and his new young wife, and the social demands did my head in. I got drunk and became rude. When we returned home, the two of us, my mother said. "I suppose you wanted me to yourself."

"Why do you always think everything is about you?" I asked. "I couldn't cope with the speech involved."

"But you're not stammering now."

"You don't understand how stammering works."

"Don't be so sensitive about it all!"

If all this makes my mother seem like an idiot, I should stress she was not. Quite the reverse. Everyone misses her greatly now she's gone. She also, and this has been confirmed to me many times, dispensed wise advice to *others*. But she was too close to me to offer *me* wise counsel. The person closest to you is not necessarily best equipped to help. In addition, the confluence of afflictions – anxiety, depression, addiction, and my speech problem – were precisely those that were *never* broached 35 years ago. Not only did my mother not understand them but there was little help on offer for *any* of these afflictions.

My mother, born in 1931, was also a victim of her time and her upbringing when many "heavy" topics were ignored. So she refused to confront depression and drink addiction. Just as she seldom watched movies or read novels – in case they contained upsetting plotlines – so she refused to acknowledge the growing problems in her family. She was an escapist. Going to Praia da Luz every winter had been the most obvious manifestation. But I now realise her refusal to confront unpleasantness was a serious flaw.

All her books were wonderful travel tomes, replete with beautiful photographs and tales of journeys in Provence or Tuscany. If she saw an upsetting news story, she'd leave the room. She never watched the news voluntarily. If she bought a newspaper she'd turn to the crossword page. I doubt she read the top stories.

When I reflect on her furnishings, the exquisite fans in her lounge, the frilled lace curtains and antiques, the crystal glasses and solid silver cutlery, I realise it was an attempt to cocoon herself in an exquisite doll's house. She loved shopping in Harrods and Fortnum and Mason. Here, in these magnificent stores, she never had to countenance ugliness. She must have felt the same way in the peaceful patio in Praia da Luz. Keep anything unappealing out. Even biros were not allowed in her home. She "l-o-a-t-h-e-d" them, she would say with emphasis.

One time, my mother, later a tour director, was guiding tourists around Poland and they visited Auschwitz. She stayed outside.

"I know your father wouldn't have wanted me to see it," she subsequently told me. This reasoning, explaining *her* decision by pretending it contravened someone else's wishes, was typical of her. If she'd said, "I couldn't stomach something so dreadful," this would have been more accurate.

She couldn't accept unpleasantness invading her life because it was emotionally and aesthetically displeasing. She *could* accept that my father had had mental health problems. But this had no direct link to her. Her friends would be surprised that a lady they remembered as infinitely generous so hated unpleasantness. After all, she would have been the first to help if one of her friends needed something, if someone was ill or bereaved.

But the key thing was that *her* hands had to be clean. And weren't they just, always impeccably manicured with beautiful soft skin. "Look at your lovely hands," friends would say. After all, she'd wear gloves to wash a few bits of cutlery. I can also understand her reluctance to witness unpleasantness because I'm part of her skin.

She couldn't acknowledge things were amiss in case they reflected badly on her. She would rather have me quiet in a corner, like a zipped-up teddy bear. Stammering, drinking problems, anxiety, depression and dirty clothes, all were to be handled some other time.

Colin was also complicit because he over-praised me for menial jobs. He'd been jealous of me because at least I'd had a hands-on father whereas his had disappeared. Perhaps he'd also resented my early academic success in school. So if I did well in a menial job it was an extended "g-o-o-d" – the way a psychiatric nurse addresses a mental patient who manages to draw a straight line!

If you'd asked me what I wanted to do when I was a teenager, I'd have said "journalism". But this looked a world away in my twenties. My speech impediment grew worse; just checking in by phone to my security firm from a supermarket was a problem. Most of the time they merely anticipated what I was saying and hung up on me.

***

I went to Albufeira in Portugal and distributed flyers from restaurants but this wasn't enough to pay the rent and fund my binge drinking. I was living off my father's inheritance. By the end of 1993 I'd reached rock bottom. In the summer at least I could have kidded myself I was in some (menial) occupation. But as the season ended, and the tourists disappeared, and the heavens opened, I was drinking by myself.

My mother visited me several times in Albufeira during the six months I was there. Full credit to her for doing so because she could see I was increasingly self-destructive. Perhaps also part of me was looking to sabotage relationships so I could retreat further into my abyss. Her visits gave me the incentive to sober up, at least temporarily.

I'd spent the summer and autumn trying to woo a Scandinavian girl who worked in one of the bars. She was the blonde princess of my dreams, like my childhood unattainable goddess. There's a reason why Jewish guys often lust after the fair-haired goddess. First, the obvious aesthetic appeal but also the belief that to be blonde, blue-eyed and beautiful is the antithesis of the Jewish experience. As a Jew, you soon become used to being hated and scorned. Whereas the blonde film star beauty never has to endure racism, everyone loves her and so – from a Jewish perspective – her life is enviably *uncomplicated.* She needn't be intelligent, she need not have the refined sensibilities and vulnerability of the HSP, in my case a highly sensitive Jew. She is what she is and the world is at her feet. At least that's how it looked to me. The rosy-cheeked, pink-skinned Swede with a voluptuous figure must be happy, right?

My efforts in talking to the Scandinavian beauty came to naught. One evening I found out she was leaving the next day, driving back to the UK with friends to see her British boyfriend. I too was due to fly back to the UK the following day. God knows what I was thinking because it was too late. Nevertheless, with my impeccable timing, I decided to intercept her and declare my love. I went to the bar where she worked and saw that this late in the season there were few customers and it was effectively a closed event. She was already tipsy, surrounded by friends. I didn't bother trying to join the party. I climbed back up the hill, bought a green bottle of *Aldeia Velha* aguardente, and retreated to my bedroom. This time I drank it all. And I'd already been drinking beforehand.

At this point I was like a homeless drug addict. If I'd died in this rented room in Albufeira that night I doubt my body would have been discovered. The landlady had gone back to Lisbon now that the season had ended. I'd paid my rent for the month and so she wouldn't bother me. My mother was in London (albeit concerned about my welfare when we spoke on the phone) and I was alone, apart from my *Aldeia Velha*.

Yes, I'd fancied the Scandinavian girl but … to be honest … that green bottle had a *greater* hold over me. By now I felt so ill that the only thing I thought would make it better was the aguardente, just to forget … When drinking reaches this point, and you realise your life is a total mess, what's the point in being sober?

I drank purely for the effect. Sometimes the first taste of liquor made me want to throw up. But a second swig got me through. When I was drinking spirits I imagined a syringe with a powerful tranquilliser being injected directly into my brain, anesthetising all the self-hatred, the conflicting emotions, the fear of speaking, the self-hatred, and, above all, all those excessive *feelings* I'd been chastised for. That wretched *sensitivity* which made me so easily "got at", a target for derision. Time for another injection, another shot of triple aguardente, to put you to sleep … any other shit could be handled tomorrow. I blamed everything for what was troubling me except the drink itself which was the one thing I thought was making me feel better.

Many years later, when I was living in Portugal, our family befriended a great guy named Dermot Staveacre,[55] a recovered alcoholic turned counsellor to other alcoholics. Back in 2002, I'd interviewed him wearing my journalist's hat and he told me about his own rock bottom. When he was still living in the UK, he'd had the chance to go on a date with film star Julie Christie.[56] At this (late) stage in his condition he'd spurned the opportunity in favour of spending his evening alone with a bottle of brandy! Imagine, he'd turned down the chance to be with one of Britain's most beautiful women for the sake of booze! I feigned disbelief when he told me. Shock and horror! But, in reality, you see, I *could* understand his attitude all too well.

The day after my massive bender in Albufeira, I woke up and realised I had to get to the airport. The whites of my eyes were not pretty conjunctivitis pink but scarlet red. My hair stood up on end no matter what I did. I drank some coke because I had a raging

---

[55] Dermot received an appreciation in *The Guardian*, penned by his brother, when he died in 2017.
https://www.theguardian.com/society/2017/jun/21/dermot-staveacre-obituary
[56] Julie Christie (b.1940). British actress most famous for *Billy Liar*, *Darling*, *Dr Zhivago* and *Don't Look Now*.

thirst, brushed my teeth twice, sucked on strong mints and aired the room because it reeked like a liquor distillery. I was so hungover I could barely move, let alone drag my case around. I was still drunk from the night before. I'd have failed any breathalyser test, even 10 hours after my last drink.

I'd got used to feeling terrible the following day but this "morning after" was so severe it was like I had taken another hallucinogenic drug. I staggered outside. When the December sun appeared from behind a cloud, it blinded me. All I could think about was a yoghurt or strawberry milkshake trickling down my throat.

When I eventually got on the plane – and I'd even wondered if they might stop me at the check-in given my condition   I felt my head was going to sever voluntarily from my body, like I'd be self-decapitating. My nose felt weird too; I had the recurring sensation that my septum would burst and my nostrils would be blown away. I picked up a complimentary tabloid, pulled down the table, and left a sweaty imprint. An attractive girl at my side turned away from me. The stench of brandy must have been overpowering. I was already exhausted, even though it was barely noon, just from the strain of moving around when I felt like three sacks of potatoes were balanced on top of my head.

Momentarily, I felt sleep overtaking me. But when you're deeply hungover, sleep arrives not as a caressing tug but as a knockout drug shooting up your body and thumping your brain. You feel the exact moment your cortex shuts down but, cruelly, you fail to go under because the headache is too ferocious. You're then propelled back into bright lights, more dazed than ever, like you've stirred from an anaesthetic and you find yourself in an operating theatre. So I reconciled to staying awake.

Headlined in the newspaper that day in December 1993 was the Scott inquiry about arms to Iraq. The previous day, former Prime Minister Margaret Thatcher had been grilled by a silver-tongued barrister named Presiley Baxendale. The writer praised the QC for wrong-footing the self-possessed "Iron Lady". The article carried a photo of the bewigged Baxendale. Staring at this photo, as we sat there, flying over the Bay of Biscay, I felt her eyes drilling through me. I'd committed a heinous crime. I was on trial for my life.

"What have I done?" I asked the judge out loud.

"YOU'VE WASTED YOUR LIFE!"

***

My love affair with drink stemmed in part from my fear of speaking. Sober or hungover, my dirty secret was getting worse than ever. It was time for the dirty secret to come out … my stammer was so bad, the more I avoided situations, the worse it became. I was spending too much time alone, reliving old conversations. I'd stammered so severely I couldn't defend myself from those seeking to criticise me. Becoming more assertive is difficult when you have a speech impediment.

Loneliness became a habit. If you add up everything besetting me – lost Jew syndrome, the speech problem, anxiety, panic attacks, depression, heightened sensitivity – there seemed little point in being with people. They wouldn't understand me. So I was on my own most of the time. I walked a lot, sometimes to Heathrow Airport from my home near Baker Street. I couldn't sit still or stay in one place.

The more time you spend on your own, the harder it is to break out of it and adjust to being with people again, especially groups of people. You lose touch with people's everyday concerns and your conversation becomes awkward. I was struck by something Brian Keenan said after his excruciating and lengthy solitary confinement as a hostage in Lebanon. Ironically, after his release, he said he'd spent a period alone on the west coast of Ireland.

I was using booze to calm down. But drinking heavily to alleviate anxiety doesn't work. Only in the immediate short-term does it have any effect. The following day, the anxiety is worse than ever, requiring heavier doses of liquor to extinguish it, as

Olivia Laing pointed out so eloquently. Treating an anxiety disorder with a massive intake of spirits is like pouring oil on a fire. To regain your equilibrium from the anxiety-ridden hungover you need more liquor. So soon you're drinking to feel "normal" in the conventional sense.

One question perplexed me. Did my stammer cause my anxiety or did my anxiety cause my stammer? I genuinely have no answer. But, back in 1993, I knew I had to find support for the problem.

10. Obstruction

"That sad sack of an interiorised stammerer is lost in the moose trap of constant inhibition."

Speech pathologist Charles Van Riper

In the mid-Nineties there used to be a Chinese restaurant in London's Soho district called Wonki's which was renowned for the rudeness of its staff. And so it was that a group of stammerers, including myself, would visit for Sunday lunch as part of our "desensitisation" programming.

'I'd like chicken, er …s…s'

"Come on – point to the menu and tell me what you want. I don't have all day. Just say it!"

"Sweet ….."

"Sweet and sour chicken? Ok!"

"And to drink, a f..f…f..Fanta orange"

"Is there anything else? I've got others to serve."

"And ..p…p…p"

"A punch in the face? I'll give it to you in a minute. Now come on."

"PRAWN CRACKERS"

Back in 1993 I'd joined the British Stammering Association, based in Bethnal Green. In those days it was called the Association for Stammerers, or AFS for short. I'd go in a couple of days a week, dealing with post and answering the phone. For the first time I encountered other stammerers and felt more comfortable (read slightly less uncomfortable) answering the phone without feeling under time pressure.

Like many stammerers, the phone was my worst nightmare and to be avoided. The reason is simple; no one can see you and notice if you have a silent block, or you're struggling to speak, so they interrupt you or hang up. The old-fashioned handsets (this was still pre-the internet, smartphone era) made it worse. You never knew who was calling and the recipient didn't either, meaning you had to announce yourself and the purpose of your call, things most people take for granted but which stammerers find hard. There was a propensity to talk over each other. And also the urgency of making a rapid response that depends exclusively on oral communication, unlike in a face-to-face conversation where you can gesture instead of talking.

It was a shock at first to find how severely others stammered at the BSA. Yes, there were people worse than me because some of my stammer was covert, and also my speech tended to fluctuate. In this sense, a severe stammerer fares better because at least people know what to expect. But I was still taken aback by some of the worst cases. I wondered how they managed in their everyday lives and, sadly, some didn't. A severe stammerer worked in the dark room of a chemist and was effectively struck dumb if he had to speak in a group. It took 30 seconds for him to articulate one word, his jaw locked as he dribbled.

The association was run by a great guy called Peter Cartwright, a non-stammerer who nonetheless showed exemplary patience and understanding in his dealings with us and never betrayed irritation with our (sometimes long) blocks. But Peter once let out he didn't see why stammerers experienced such extreme variation in their speech depending on *who* were they talking to. He might not have realised it but he had hit the proverbial nail on the head. Because this, for me, was the "x factor" that triggered the severity of stammering. The "x factor" is the occasion. It's all about the audience (whether one person or more) and one's *feeling* towards the audience, and the self-fulfilling prophesy we give ourselves, especially our apprehension at facing a particular speaking occasion.

Fact is, the *vast majority* of stammerers can speak perfectly fluently when they're on their own or, for example, when talking to their dog. Yes, I have met some stammerers who claim this *isn't* true for them, that they still, for example, experience blocks and hesitations and struggle when speaking to themselves, or to a pet. Perhaps these people have come to associate/equate speaking with anxiety to such an extent that even speaking to themselves triggers struggle. But, in *most* cases, I'm sure there's nothing wrong with our speaking mechanism or our brain function. We have come to associate speaking with nervousness and the fear of blocking has triggered an inner struggle to avoid stammering. *In other words, stammering is what we're doing when we try not to stammer.* It's a cruel trick we play on ourselves.

But even the most severe sufferers, those who stammered on every consonant of every word, will occasionally forget their disability and speak normally. I know because I once counted myself as one of them. So it's the other person or group that triggers the anxiety associated with stammering.

Therefore, from the outset, I was suspicious of any treatment claiming to "cure" stammering because I saw it as embedded psychological self-programming. If you could forget you stammered, you probably wouldn't stammer. But how can we develop such a *"forgettery"*?

Various speech therapy courses proved popular for a time, especially one involving intense diaphragmatic breathing, usually at the behest of a charismatic therapist "guru". It was easy to make progress surrounded by the solidarity inherent in group speech therapy. An integral part of stammering is the sufferer's self-perception of his own solitariness, or the hostility of the "other". The "guru" works within a supportive atmosphere and this inevitably helps people to become more fluent.

The stammer normally returned once the effect of the "gimmick" – the chosen therapy in question – had worn off and everyday speech pressures resurrected themselves, i.e. your typical office situation where someone has their back to you and walks away when you're in mid-stammer! Sadly, I have seen many cases of this whereby people emerged from therapy fluent only to regress to square one after a few weeks.

Even some speech and language therapists showed remarkable ignorance about stammering. In 1994 I attended an open day in which one therapist claimed stammering varied according to whether we were standing up or sitting down! This reminds me of the classic exchange in the great movie *The King's Speech* in which King George VI tells his speech therapist, Lionel Logue, that physicians have told him smoking relaxes the throat.

"They're idiots," replies Logue.

"They've all been knighted," says the king.

"Makes it official, then," says Logue.

The feared "x factor" was entirely subjective. It could be something as mundane as asking for a drink from an air hostess. I knew one guy who told me this induced such a panic attack that he pretended to be asleep on a plane rather than request anything. Or it could be asking for something at the post office. Or talking to that girl you liked. Or making a crucial presentation at the workplace. It all depends on your apprehension beforehand. And here is the link between stammering and anxiety and, yes, *sensitivity*. For, although there may be some stammerers who have developed a stammer as a result of a traumatic brain injury I'd say that *in most cases* it is an emotional reaction, springing from heightened sensitivity to a particular interaction.

Anxiety and stress do not cause stammering, by which I mean there is no direct link because if that were the case then all people would be struggling to speak in stressful situations. But among those who do develop a stammer, I'd say that anxiety and stress nearly always compound the problem and exacerbate the blocks.

Most stammering develops during childhood and, in the UK for example, affects around two per cent of the population. Stammering is *not* just occasionally repeating, or stumbling over, words. This is something that everyone does occasionally and has nothing to do with the struggle of stammering, one accompanied by anxiety and fear.

Stammering is a disorder of social interaction that, in the majority of cases, has little basis in any deficiency of the speech mechanism. No more than anyone who has a persistent blushing problem has a problem with their cheeks. It arises from an excess of delicacy to the presence of one's fellow beings and therefore, is usually found in HSPs. The stammerer is not a worthless person, but one who is excessively mindful of others' reactions. And here we must reiterate that what HSPs can do in private – in this case talking – is harder in a face-to-face situation. Not that all HSPs will stammer. But I'd venture to say that their nervous system is often over-stimulated at a public rendition and they may fall short of what they know they could do, i.e. below their potential, and they may compensate by resorting to alcohol or tranquillisers.

My speech varies according to whom I'm talking to. Do I feel comfortable with that person? This is the key factor. Not that my stammer will disappear completely when I'm talking to someone with whom I feel comfortable. But it gets markedly better. For example, I was more fluent with my mother because I sensed any dysfluency on my part, any struggle, would be more *acceptable* to her. By contrast, my speech with Gerard, or anyone who has ever laughed at my stammer, was horrendous. In addition, my speech in front of a large group where one is inevitably interrupted and under greater time constraints, is always worse.

Since I believe that stammering is a disorder of social interaction, one signified by struggle, I don't like the term "stammering" because much of the time a stammerer won't even *stammer*. Many times I've tried to explain that I wish I *could* stammer. You'd hear or witness silent blocks as I tried to speak, manifesting inner struggle. So I prefer the word "obstruction" to convey the condition.

***

What causes stammering? I have a hunch. The power of speech separates the human race from the animal kingdom. It's something most people take for granted. But stammerers don't. In the more severe cases, it can take a minute or so to say one's name. Imagine breathing was no longer an automatic function but one requiring constant effort and you begin to get a feel for what severe stammerers face.

Speech reveals a person's character, with timbre and projection conveying a great deal beyond the content of the words themselves. It's only natural that trauma would affect speech, that when someone is paralysed with fear, words don't come. Even in fluent speakers, nervousness can be detected in speech not only through stammering but a tremor at a particular juncture which betrays that the speaker is on uncertain ground. I bet a lie detector test, which traditionally measures skin conductivity, respiration, and blood pressure, could also detect subtle deviations in a person's voice when they're lying.

Equally, the human voice, apart from the content, conveys someone's personality through its depth, timbre, pitch and speed. Highly Sensitive People (HSPs) "betray" their nature as soon as they speak. Their speech may contain a hint of delicacy, and even the voice emanates not from deep in the chest but from higher up – as if the speaker is engaging his thoughts more studiously. Sensitive people also flush more easily when speaking and touch their faces more frequently. If an HSP shouted "taxi" it would sound different from a conventionally macho alpha male. The "command" from the HSP would be milder in tone, containing a hint of uncertainty.

In western culture, the highly sensitive man is still frowned upon. In America, which has a more macho culture than Europe, where males learn from an early age that the slightest mannerism matters, the highly sensitive man would still probably be (incorrectly) equated with effeminacy. It's not strange that most stammerers are males, precisely because they're the ones whom traditional society calls on to be authoritative. Hence depression, sadness, and tentativeness are not regarded as admirable attributes; they're viewed as unacceptable. Therefore the young boy becomes wary of expressing them and this blocks normal communication. And if you approach every display of "vulnerable" emotion with trepidation you'd also approach speaking in the same vein. Something inside you views human expression as dangerous.

This excessive wariness about speaking – and in the broader sense expressing emotions – is central to understanding stammering. I've met stammerers who have said they have never been able to convey anger; others have told me they feel trapped in themselves. Tentativeness is the key. Most stammerers are gatekeepers of their own words as if something is unacceptable about some aspect of their nature. This is strange if we assume there isn't anything especially "deviant" about their behaviour. If I had to guess, I'd say our high sensitivity means we are wary of, in some way, offending others. So we keep everything bottled up and one day it either implodes or explodes. Extroverted people, often those of charismatic nature, speak freely.

It's difficult to explain to normal speakers, for whom speech is automatic, the exact nature of stammering. In particular, *please*, parents and siblings of the afflicted, don't mock the sufferer or belittle him. In such cases, you will only feed the anxiety and therefore the avoidance behaviour which characterises the stammerer. The sufferer inevitably will feel insecure in every speaking situation where he feels he could be derided. That way you fuel the problem.

Most stammerers were men and made up most attendees at self-help groups at London's Michael Palin[57] Centre and the City Lit where I'd do evening courses with titles like "stammering the workplace", "assertiveness for people who stammer" and "drama for people who stammer". There were no miracle cures but there was strength in solidarity.

Naturally, there were some funny moments. Especially in the self-help group when more than one stammerer tried to start talking at the same time, all accompanied by head jerking, rocking and foot tapping, all "tricks" to get out of a block. But I never laughed. It's important *not* to. At the City Lit I encountered a severe stammerer, an intelligent Oxbridge graduate, who always held eye contact through some long blocks. Averting the eyes was a hallmark of stammerers during extended blocks, stemming from self-consciousness and embarrassment. So this guy was trying not to shift his eyes.

During one evening class, I gave my new friend a chocolate near the end of a break. We re-assembled.

"Would you like some chocolate?"

"Oh yes, th..th…th…th…th …"

In stammering therapy, and dealing with other stammerers in general, we are told *not* to finish the

---

[57] Named after actor and comedian Michael Palin (b.1943) whose father stammered. He starred in the movie *A Fish Called Wanda*.

other person's words even if we know what they're going to say. So I stood there while he maintained rigid eye contact and tried to convey his appreciation. By now everyone was taking their places and our speech therapist took her seat (therapists were usually women) and prepared to address us.

Meanwhile, my friend and I were still locked together, eyeball to eyeball, while he tried to say what I knew he was trying to say. It lasted some time, long after the class had reconvened.

We should learn to laugh at ourselves a bit because part of the problem was that we were over-sensitive to people's reactions. That definitely didn't mean laughing at each other when we spoke. *No way* because we were supposed to support each other. But it did mean not bridling when storylines in movies depicted us. There was a crucial difference between the *general* and the *personal* when it came to humour.

A classic example was the movie *A Fish Called Wanda* which divided the stammering community. Some people found it grossly insensitive. But certain people do find stammering funny precisely because speaking is something most of us do automatically. So to hear stammerers spending a minute trying to say their name (and this was no exaggeration in certain cases I knew) must be incomprehensible to most people. Just like it's funny when we see someone struggling with anything most of us do naturally, like climbing a staircase or doing our tie.

If you look at Laurel and Hardy, they milk everyday situations for all their worth precisely because they know these are the ones inducing laughter. So we laugh when we see Herbert Lom as Inspector Dreyfus accidentally falling out of his window. But we wouldn't laugh in real life if we were to witness something similar. But that's my point – *A Fish Called Wanda* was a public spectacle involving a fictitious character, not the singling out of a real person for derision.

I've always been unforgiving about anyone who laughed at me *personally* on account of my stammering. One or two youthful friendships went by the wayside because the "friend" in question couldn't contain his natural bumptiousness and couldn't, or *wouldn't*, stop imitating my stammer or laughing at it.

Stammering also had its tragic side. While in my early days as a volunteer at the AFS (as it was then called) a young guy, same age as me, 27, committed suicide. He had two degrees but had been told at job interviews –"get rid of that stammer and we'll give you the job". So don't believe those who ever tell you a speech impediment, specifically a stammer, is ever trivial.

Hence I was disappointed in Esther Rantzen[58] when she was guest speaker at an open day for the BSA (it became known as the British Stammering Association) in 1995. I'm sure she meant well but, alluding to the young man who died, she used the word "minor" to describe the problem of stammering. Since human beings are defined through their speech, anything interfering with it is hardly "minor". Her husband, documentary filmmaker Desmond Wilcox, had had a stammer when he was younger but had "overcome" it. So she thought it was a problem that could be conquered.

Jonathan Miller,[59] a patron of the BSA, was surprisingly dismissive of stammering when I bumped into him in the late 1990s near his home in North London. He said he was more interested in campaigning for Alzheimer's because it was "much more important". Perhaps he'd acquired such self-confidence over the years that he had come to downplay stammering. But that didn't necessarily apply to others. He had "broken out of the box", as they say. Similarly, Nicholas Parsons,[60] arriving at a BSA event in around 1995, privately expressed impatience with those who had "mild stammers" because, he said, they should be able to overcome their problem. Again, his remarks were silly because

---

[58] Esther Rantzen, born 1940, British television personality and presenter.
[59] Jonathan Miller (1934-2019) British theatre and opera director, actor, author and television presenter.
[60] Nicholas Parsons (1923-2020) British actor and radio and television presenter.

stammering is under the surface, characterised by word and situation avoidance. Famous people should be careful what they say.

In addition, too much time was given to the stammerer's presumed inability to impart one crucial piece of information. People think stammering is about being able to say *one thing*, i.e. a destination. That's a problem for some people, and for me too in the past, but more importantly it's an ongoing disorder of interaction. Can you tell a story to a group of people, one where timing is crucial? Will they listen or will they become restless when you struggle over a word? Will they start talking to themselves as you approach the punch line?

A flaw in the otherwise excellent *The King's Speech* was the children (Princess Margaret and the future Queen) listening to the King attentively with good eye contact as he told them a funny story. A *major* misconception of the BSA back in the mid-1990s was that people will listen to you while you're blocking. That *doesn't* happen outside a support group.

Stammering varies from person to person but it's like a fingerprint. I know of cases where men can't state what they want in a shop. In other cases it tends to come out more as people form deeper relationships. In other words, intimacy creates more fears. Stammering can undermine one's ability to hold down relationships because it gets in the way of assertiveness.

Many young male stammerers were lonely. We were rooting for each other to break out – find a good, decent job and a girlfriend. But it was also human nature that, when someone did "break out", we got jealous. One volunteer at our office stayed with an old guy in Florida, an author who'd written a book about stammering. While there he met an American girl and within a short time he'd moved over to the "sunshine state" and got married. He had broken out of the cage so many stammerers found themselves in.

Isolation was a persistent problem I could recognise because if you're unemployed and on your own it can be crucifying. Again, this was before the arrival of social media which, to a certain extent, helped connect people. So we'd find pen pals among other stammerers. I exchanged letters with people from all over the UK. One unemployed guy, who lived near me, wrote regularly to me, pouring out his heart about loneliness, and how he'd visit the gym just to have somewhere to go. In one of his letters he suggested we meet. At the end of the letter, he asked me to enclose a photo. He added. "I'm sure you're very beautiful." We'd been writing at cross purposes. He thought my name was Danielle. I felt awful because I'd been his ticket to happiness.

Many courses were on offer for stammerers, employing various methods, notably the diaphragmatic breathing technique I have already cited. I didn't go on this course but I did accompany several of them to Wonki's and Speakers Corner in Hyde Park where they braved sceptical crowds by speaking about stammering. I'd spent years trying not to stammer. So it took some time to accept that fighting my dysfluency was exacerbating it. I needed to speak more spontaneously, with or without stammering, to grow more relaxed about speaking.

One day I was writing a piece on stammering for the association's quarterly magazine when I found a great quote by renowned speech therapist Charles Van Riper.[61] "That sad sack of an interiorised stammerer is caught in the moose trap of constant inhibition. He needs to let rip and speak and act spontaneously." Some of that could have applied to me. My behaviour had become too self-vigilant and self-conscious. And part of the reason sprang from being too careful not to betray secrets and offend someone – and not to provoke a scene. Ironically, that was one of the reasons for me to sink into several years of drunken oblivion. It was a way of letting it all out when I was drunk. I had to re-learn how to be spontaneous when I was sober and not to shun speaking situations because as Van Riper put it, "avoidance is the pump in the reservoir of fear".

---

[61] Charles Van Riper, renowned American speech therapist (1905-1994).

Yet to this day I can still stammer badly when anxiety grips me. I'm not saying stammerers can never improve. Not at all. Improved self-confidence ushers in greater fluency. But talk of a "cure" can be self-defeating because it places too great a self-expectation. I've met so many stammerers over the years and sometimes they would say: "I'm stammering less than I used to" and I'd think "don't worry about stammering less, focus on speaking more".

Some stammerers reject speech therapy altogether, advocating a more holistic approach. They believe, rather like I do, that stammering stems from a frightening experience, perhaps one buried in the subconscious. I'd say stammerers suffer higher levels of anxiety than other people. If we could develop greater indifference to others' reactions – a "fuck 'em" attitude – then this would render improvement. I'd found drink made me fluent, at least in the short term. That's why it proved such an insidious problem.

We're still in the dark ages because, three decades on from the events I describe, stammering remains a largely hidden disability. And when you do hear people stammering it's always within the context of *stammerers discussing stammering*. If the subject is stammering and the atmosphere is supportive, then it's within the comfort zone. But when do you hear people who stammer discussing other topics on TV?

When, if *ever*, will you ever hear someone with a stammer debating issues on a programme like *Question Time*?

One of the heroes of my youth was the late Patrick Campbell,[62] a regular panellist on *Call My Bluff*. The subject was never stammering, so it would have been tough for him, surrounded as he was by articulate speakers. I'd watch as he struggled through long blocks. The others to their credit (and even more so since this was the prehistoric era as far as stammering was concerned) waited patiently for him to say his piece. We need more people like Campbell on TV nowadays.

Stammering proved so insidious for me because I loved the English language. I enjoyed listening to those with a masterly vocal instrument such as Richard Burton. The perfectionist in me, the one who knew the recital depended on the right emphasis and intonation, hated stammering so much that it created the avoidance which fuelled the problem.

Fortunately, stammering usually eases with age. The key enabler for the disability is trying to "force" fluency because you feel the speaking occasion demands it. You feel you mustn't stammer in front of that girl or at a job interview. And the tension triggers the opposite. All these kinds of challenges, the ones giving so many young stammerers terrible

[62] Patrick Campbell (1913-1980). Irish journalist, humourist and television personality. A regular panelist on *Call My Bluff* alongside Frank Muir.

anxiety, ease as one ages. And if you were using booze to cope with the accompanying anxiety (and you don't develop into a full-blown addict) then chances are that drinking will also fall into abeyance.

***

What turned me round from the drinking? There was no epiphany, no moment of illumination, *but* I did have a moment of "clarity" in the communal toilet of a girlfriend's bedsit one winter's evening. Just a gradual realisation that this way of existing made no sense. Another time, an elderly couple looked horrified when I opened a half bottle of scotch one night on the tube and drank most of it. Going to the Association for Stammerers helped me. A graphic account of Peter Cook's death in January 1995 from liver failure further swayed me.

During the week I stopped drinking. Most days I was now sober. Given my huge consumption to date this was an achievement. But nobody noticed. There were no headlines proclaiming my sobriety, no TV programmes given over to my week-time abstinence, no guard of honour at the entrance to my workplace, no 10-gun salute. One of the problems in taking such a step, especially without the camaraderie of AA, is that no one really cares. Yet it's momentous for the person making the decision.

In sobriety I noticed deficiencies that had eluded me: the dirt, dust, the cobwebs, the door off its hinges, the greasy compartments in the fridge, holes in my socks, and torn curtains. It was all a shock. But these were the tentative first steps of sobriety, me just poking my nose out of my drunken stupor.

A line in *Macbeth* came to mind. "I am in blood / Stepped in so far, that, should I wade no more, / Returning were as tedious as go o'er." I now saw how some drunks, I mean those who have lost *everything*, could tell themselves they might as well carry on drinking because there's little left to play for anyway. All I had achieved at this stage, in achieving sobriety most of the time, was to slowly come to terms with reality.

Most movies about drinking problems also imply that once you stop, the road to happiness beckons. Or at least abstinence will herald a dramatic improvement. But it was going to be a long haul. Many jerks are still jerks when they stop drinking. Gerard had once called me "a Jewish jerk". Hopefully, I *wasn't* a jerk. But the constant drunkenness had rendered me apathetic, and I was gradually realising that the dysfunctional, lonely childhood I'd led, seeking to protect people, living in fear of the next drunken outburst, had robbed me of other skills. I wasn't even a dry-knuckle drunk, counting days of sobriety every week. I'd never had a normal life and I'd go further – never seen a normal relationship.

Much of day-to-day living had bypassed me. Yes, I had started to allow myself certain feelings, to realise they were valid because I had experienced them. But this was step one out of ten. I did find a job at the Home Office. But by then I was also suffering from depression. I'd been living in a fantasy world for several years, getting drunk in front of the TV. But watching so many movies had made me forget that some people were ugly, that they had snot, and that most people led, to cite Thoreau, lives of quiet desperation.

Most offices were large and open-plan, so you'd be beavering away alongside, say, 20 other colleagues. Here is where my sensitivity had a bad effect. I'd pick up vibes too easily, so if I felt one person in a room didn't like me, it tended to affect my dealing with that person and undermine my performance. And, also, because I'd had little experience with these kinds of jobs, if an attractive girl smiled at me during some menial or routine interaction, I'd misinterpret it as meaning she liked me.

Looking back, I was coming to terms with being an HSP but, again, before the term gained currency. I'd always felt different to other people. True to type for all HSPs, a majestic sunset could keep me entranced, likewise falling leaves on a golden autumn day or the waves rolling in on a beach or, yes, for sure, a good-looking girl sitting opposite me on the underground. Nothing strange about that – they are all the hallmarks of the HSP, easily beaten down but easily buoyed, feeling slights but also praise more acutely, disliking confrontation and noise and crowds. I was also strangely skilled at detecting illnesses in other people, often being able to tell who had, for example, a migraine or heart condition.

The list of characteristics of your classic HSP is well known, or at least easily found on the internet. So I won't regale you with all of them here. Except to say I ticked almost *every* box, especially that I am easily startled, tend to tire easily if I'm in a group of loud people, need more time to myself to recuperate after a busy day, dislike violent entertainment and am deeply moved by beauty in every (perceived) form. In addition, there are things I do well in private but would find extremely difficult to do in public or if under close scrutiny. (I even dislike it if I'm frying eggs and someone is looking over my shoulder.) I was always being told not to "over-think" things and yes, of course, subjected to the constant and wearisome admonition "don't be so sensitive".

HSPs quickly notice idiosyncrasies about other people that others might not, for example recurrent catchphrases and patterns of speech. I was also affected by the resonance and rhythm of other people's voices. If someone's voice was too shrill or irritating I found it difficult to be in their company.

Contrarily, and in this respect being an HSP might be advantageous, I'd notice an attractive timbre.

My search for "beauty" in whatever form could backfire. One day, circa 1991, I was watching a TV documentary about South African white supremacist Eugene Terreblanche,[63] even then a spent force as he sought to fend off majority rule in apartheid's dying days. I had no time for Terreblanche's politics which were Nazi in all but name. Also, as a person, he came across as a swaggering bully. But what a voice he had! The documentary entitled *The Leader, His Driver and the Driver's Wife* opened with narration by Nick Broomfield. He might have been a talented filmmaker, pioneering the type of documentary later made more famous by Michael Moore, but (sorry Mr. Broomfield!) he delivered his narration in a quick-fire, flat, high-pitched monotone. The contrast with Terreblanche couldn't have been greater. Aside from an imposing physical presence, ET (as he was popularly known) had a deep, rich, earthy baritone voice and an uncanny ability to convey something with a grunt.

---

[63] Eugene Terreblanche, South African neo-Nazi, (1941-2010). Nick Broomfield (b.1948) later made a follow-up documentary in 2006, featuring Terreblanche, called *His Big White Self.* Terreblanche was murdered by his farm workers in 2010.

[64] Journalist Jani Allen described Terreblanche's voice thus: "It's a rich, earth-brown voice. Sometimes it has the loamy texture of a newly ploughed mealie field. Sometimes it's a caress of worn corduroy."

Terreblanche's voice was penetrating, loud when he wanted it to be, but at other times seductively caressing.[64] Many years later, when I heard a poetry rendition by Terreblanche on a news segment on the BBC, albeit in Afrikaans, it gave me goose pimples. The same cadences, majesty, and melodiousness Terreblanche invested in his oratory were also present in his poetry. Politically, Terreblanche proved a poor strategist who played right into the hands of his opponents. Yet listening to him made me realise how great orators (because he *was* one in spite of his buffoonery) can influence people not only through content but by *technique*.

***

My working life at the Home Office contained little sense of beauty. One day I was so depressed I couldn't move. It was strange because I was in a decent office overlooking St James's Park. But the lack of creativity involved in the work was getting to me. I was no longer drunk, merely dejected and apathetic about the flow of my life. I couldn't see myself climbing up the greasy pole of the Home Office ladder either. It seemed a herculean task to start again at the age of 28 and, so for a while I drifted. Occasionally I applied for a higher grade job but with no deep hunger.

Something else accounted for the severity of my depression and this was the gradual realisation that all my feelings had been invalidated. I'd felt I couldn't express how I felt without it being contradicted. I wasn't allowed to say I was "pissed off" in my family – it was unacceptable. A "depression day" on the weekend meant sleeping late, curled up in the foetal position. Sometimes I was so down that even keeping my eyelids open was a stretch. So I found a way of walking around with them halfway open. I would be too depressed to read articles about depression. Game over.

For those who don't suffer depression, well, lucky you! When you're at your worst, everything is insurmountable. The laundry piles up and smirks at you accusingly. The terrace needs to be swept but you can't summon up the energy. In extreme cases, the depressed person takes to his bed while his life falls apart. In my case, depression meant *carelessness*, a sense of merely going through the motions but functioning at 20 per cent capacity. Nowadays, I try to snap out of it by doing one thing properly, even if it's just changing the bed, no matter how long it takes. If I can do something well, I can re-focus and recover.

My career didn't progress much at the Home Office. A decade earlier I'd been a candidate for Oxford entry but I'd floundered badly at the interview and my exam result was uneven. As my mother once said: "I should imagine you would interview badly". This was another of her euphemisms for "you have a bad stammer". But being up for Oxford entry showed my potential. Now one of my reports at the Home Office said I was "a slow learner".

I survived the drudgery by trying to look at the funny side. I worked primarily in the Publications Unit, taking calls from the public about Home Office journals and sending them off. But we had the usual nutty inquiries from some people who thought the Home Office had something to do with home improvement. "Can I build an extension to my loft?"

I still had problems answering phones. One day I answered and all my techniques came to nothing. A female member of staff played amateur psychologist. "Some bastard frightened you when you were a child," she said to me. To paraphrase what prime ministers used to say – "I refer readers to the events I described in chapter one".

My anxiety and sensitivity were always there and my confidence was easily deflated. One time, in the autumn of 1997, I found two invitations to a London event attended by various famous authors organised by the international PEN foundation. (The invitations were intended for more senior civil servants but I conveniently ignored that!) I, a humble aspiring author, could mix with the bigwigs. I took a friend with me, an extrovert black guy with a naïve, child-like sense of wonderment, and an infectious laugh.

I'd never seen so many distinguished guests in the same room but I was too shy to engage any of them. Not so my friend. It was not that he was determined not to be fazed by any supposed VIP but that he was *never* fazed by anyone. He sidled up to Lady Antonia Fraser,[65] addressed her as "Antonia", and commented he was the only black guy there. Antonia Fraser looked down at him (my friend was short), half-smiled benignly as if to say she understood and pretended to be comfortable with the conversation.

My friend next spotted Frank Muir[66] (famous comedy writer and raconteur) and reminded him of the pinnacle of his distinguished career. Yes, you've got it, his legendary participation in the Fruit and Nut adverts! He did a Gene Kelly-like dance and reminded Mr. Muir of that jingle, complete with a slight Woy Jenkins-like mispronunciation of the consonant 'r' "Fwank" had brought to the part, "Evewyone's a fwuit and nut case ..., cwazy for those Cadbuwy's nuts and waisons, what a combination, Cadbuwy's fwuit and nut ..."

Mr. Muir, dressed in a striped jacked and trademark bowtie, nodded appreciatively while looking over

---

[65] Lady Antonia Fraser (b.1932). British author of history, novels, biographies and detective fiction, widow of Harold Pinter.
[66] Frank Muir (1920-1998). Muir was also a regular panelist on *Call My Bluff*, alongside Patrick Campbell who was mentioned in the previous chapter.

my friend's shoulder. He beckoned to an acquaintance, trying not to make it too obvious he was pleading to be rescued. I wonder if this incident killed him off because, sadly, the illustrious Mr. Muir died a couple of months later.

Meanwhile, at our side, two famous and well-heeled authors were deep in conversation, Frederick Forsyth and Jeffrey Archer.[67] My friend sidled up to them. "Why don't us three start our own business?"

I'd never liked Archer. He had a rat-like, English-cold face, deeply lined on his forehead, curiously (aptly as we shall see) forming the letter "W". For "wanker"? Mr. Forsyth gradually withdrew and I was left facing the former Conservative MP, party chairman, best-selling author and – in the happy and not too distant future – proven perjurer. I'd only read one of his books, *Shall we Tell the President?* And I tried to tell him so.

'I've read 'shall we tell the …p…p' I began. A combination of self-consciousness and tension gripped me as I struggled to say the word.

"Yes, yes, PRESIDENT," said Archer, glaring up at me disdainfully through his piggy, accusing eyes. He must have seen me struggling but his tone carried not only impatience but derision.

---

[67] Jeffrey Archer (b.1940), described on Wikipedia as "English novelist, life peer, convicted criminal, and former politician".

I tried to tell him I was writing a novel but again got stuck.

Archer pointed to a famous agent standing a few feet away and said: "Go and introduce yourself." He caught the eye of the agent concerned and bellowed so that everyone could hear. "This wimp will talk to you about his book." My friend turned and looked at me, stunned at Archer's rudeness. Everyone had heard him. I was left struck dumb, my dignity eroded. Meanwhile, Archer strode off, dumping his glass of champagne. Later, I thought of the names I could have called him, "you whore-chasing, insider share dealing, pathological liar". He'd even brought the great Wendy Craig and Frank Finlay to a career-low when they starred in his (over-obvious) murder mystery *Beyond Reasonable Doubt*. But that's all with hindsight. Rather like Ken battling his tormentor Otto in *A Fish Called Wanda*, the words wouldn't come. But I was glad several years down the line when he got his comeuppance.

Highly sensitive people, even those who don't stammer, often have difficulty delivering the riposte, the rejoinder, the *bon mot* at the time. What one should have said comes afterward and that's why HSPs tend to dwell on the past, and relive past injustices.

***

I'd covered it all up with drink and this was my most ostensible problem. It was a camouflage for my inner self. While I was in the pub, or watching television, I could forget it all. But the downside of becoming sober, or at least reverting to normal social drinking, was that now my problems were still stark and real.

Was drinking my primary problem? A symptom or a cause? I ask this because in classic alcoholism the sufferer is normally in denial, at least certainly in the early stages. In the treatment of alcoholism they say the person has to acknowledge their addiction before they can recover. And this means they have to accept they have no control over their drinking. In such instances the only logical next step is abstention. But a question bothers me. Many alcoholics out there won't admit their addiction. Hence they deceive themselves they're not alcoholics despite their progressive loss of control. So can the reverse apply? Maybe some people are falsely labelled alcoholics when they are merely self-medicating for anxiety and depression, or another primary disorder. I now believe I fell into the latter category.

Another reason leads me to conclude this. Back in the era to which I'm referring there was less understanding or discussion of mental health issues. So there was a tendency only to discuss the manifestation of a problem. In other words, someone is drinking heavily, therefore their primary problem must be their abuse of alcohol when, in reality, "experts" failed to examine what lay behind it. Of course, my drinking was severely detrimental to my health – and even exacerbated my anxiety and depression – but what was causing me to self-medicate? It could be that there are many others like me who have been incorrectly labelled as alcoholics as if it were their primary disorder when it was really an (inadequate) tranquilliser for other medical issues. *Problem drinking is not just for alcoholics.*

From now on, as soon as I started at the Home Office, I would gradually regain control of my drinking. As I turned 30 I no longer felt the compulsion to get drunk whenever something bad happened. But my anxiety and depression were still there. I needed to find something to give my life meaning before the stammer, the drink, and the instability had hit. I had to go back to reading and writing, to enjoyable pursuits.

Also, they say there's nothing like seeing other drinkers in trouble to concentrate the mind. My mother's drinking was still under control. But my two half-brothers were in deep trouble with drink. Back in Pimlico days, Colin had made home-made beer, storing it in tubs at the top of the house. How innocent all that seemed by the late Nineties. Towards the end he was on four to six bottles of wine day, going out to Sainsbury's and buying huge cartons of cheap wine home which he'd consume for most of the day. In *his* case, I was convinced he'd have to stop drinking entirely. He was too far gone for any attempts at controlled drinking to work.

One of my last severe binges occurred around the year 2000. I woke up near Highgate School with no recollection of how I'd arrived there. I wonder if God was trying to tell me something! I got a cab back home and the driver, seeing my alarming state, said something that resonated. "You don't love yourself enough." He was right. The benders became rarer and in my last years in London I spent less time in pubs. I even declined some invitations because I knew where they would lead.

Once I'd curbed my intake – by which I mean the "what the hell happened last night?" sprees that marked my twenties – I saw our family's drinking history afresh. Big boozing sessions had always been billed as "fun time". Like, "hey, we deserve to have a good time and a laugh".

If really heavy drinking was so convivial, how come we'd all ended up in dire straits? My mother was now on her own and in reduced circumstances. My two half-brothers were usually drunk when I saw them. Michael's marriage was a violent mess and one day, circa 1999, I'd found Colin lying on the floor of his lounge, drunk and crying. And me? I'd lost a decade to (mostly) solitary drunken stupor. But even with friends I couldn't say the times were especially *fun*. I'd stagger back from some pub crawl in Camden on a Saturday night, get a bit lippy in the chippy, and waste my Sunday holding my head. Exciting, eh?

Around this time I watched a documentary on the life of British actor Oliver Reed[68] who'd died in 1999. I wasn't interested in watching a catalogue of all his hellraising. All the "Ollie got pissed and climbed down the chimney" stories bored me. But I *was* vaguely curious to see how his family and friends had dealt with his alcoholism. Because Reed's name, more than any other British actor of his era, was synonymous with marathon boozing sessions. Sadly, he'd become more famous for his drunkenness than for his acting.

The programme revealed that family members *had* made a concerted attempt to help Reed. They'd even written a letter to him, which would now be classified as an "intervention". But this had received short shrift. More striking was an account by one of Reed's friends, Stephen Ford, of a visit to Guernsey where the actor had lived for several years. Ford described how, after a "wild" New Year's Eve party, he and Reed had taken a coastal walk. Ford had recorded it all.

---

[68] Oliver Reed (1938-1999). British film star known for movies like *Oliver! Women in Love*, and *Castaway*. He died in Malta in a pub after a long drinking session during a break from filming *Gladiator*. The documentary was called *The Real Oliver Reed*.

Reed, looking sober and clad in wellies, was filmed ambling around cliffs and caves. Ford recalled this time fondly. "It was one of the nicest times *ever* because it was so nice and gentle and it was just walking along and Oliver describing the things he saw …" This was Ford's favourite memory of their friendship, *not* Reed paralytic in a pub, but the two of them walking along the Guernsey shore of a winter's day.

As I looked back at my life – I saw the same. What were the best times? They were with my mother in Praia da Luz *before* she met Gerard and the spirits flowed, picking shells off the beach at Luz with Michael *before* he dived into the bottle, travelling through Dorset with Jill, swimming with my dad at Dolphin Square, or playing football with him in the park. All my happy memories were of sober times. *Drunks kid themselves they're cultivating great memories.* Instead, boozing had ushered in anger, guilt, anxiety, self-loathing and recriminations.

Problem drinkers should see people in the grip of alcoholism. I subscribe to the deep immersion theory. See patients who have liver cirrhosis and witness at first hand their agony. Seeing drunks up close was a reminder of what I wanted to leave behind.

Back in Portugal in 2003 I was caretaking a friend's house in Albufeira when the owner's friend came to stay. Julian, a former school teacher, had decided to leave the profession from an early age; I'm told it was on account of his drinking. He stored his belongings in a garage and spent the years travelling. His intake grew, usually beer and wine, but continuously throughout the day. At 8am one hot summer's day I espied from my lounge Julian downing a bottle of Sagres beer in one gulp. He'd reach for the beer as soon as he woke up. I never saw him eat anything more than little bits of cheese. When my friend's house was occupied with summer guests, Julian took to sleeping in a secluded corner at the back of the garden. He thought he'd managed to avoid their scrutiny. But they soon noticed him peeing in the garden and demanded his removal. As the house caretaker, I was summoned to explain the situation.

The guests took me down to see Julian, who was dishevelled, dirty, sweating, wearing only shorts and broken sandals. They pointed to him like a museum object. The man jabbed his finger at Julian's distended stomach, poking him in his buttonhole.

"That is all liquid bloat," he said in front of Julian, who looked away sheepishly. "This is a sick man who should be in hospital."

I couldn't disagree. Julian departed the house and moved to the beach where, one night, he was attacked. Probably too drunk to defend himself.

Irrespective of the countries Julian was able to visit thanks to his "freedom" – he'd boasted he'd retired at the age of 32 – I couldn't see his existence as anything but pitiable, with its constant uncertainty about where to sleep, and eternal celibacy. And the cause of it all was booze. Julian staggered on and died a few years later after a stroke.

For those struggling with a drinking problem or addiction – do go to AA meetings if you can, but don't *depend* on self-help books if you're expecting to stumble on a moment of illumination. These books – and, yes, even this one! – may help but it's better to go down to skid row and mix with homeless drunks and smell the blood, vomit, and shit first-hand.

Recently, I was on a morning bus from Sofia to Vratsa in Bulgaria. We were finding our seats when an overweight guy, around 40, staggered aboard. Straight away there was an almighty blast of liquor and on a cold day, with the windows closed, the whole rear of the bus quickly reeked like a distillery. I'd have travelled on the roof, at least to breathe fresh air! It was unbearable, so bad that no one wanted to sit by him. He began talking to himself in English, in a breathy, self-pitying whining lament, repeating the same negative mantra – "I hate my life, I hate Bulgaria, I hate Vratsa," even (curiously) "I hate white people" – which conveniently included everyone on the bus! He'd fall silent for a while, take another gulp from his vodka bottle only to start again as if talking to an imaginary foe. "Alright, you win, I'm a loser, I've failed, I hate my life."

I tried to remonstrate with him but when I looked at his puffy, elephantine face and vacant eyes, I knew it was useless. You can't reason with drunks. Within a couple of minutes, the refrain resumed: "I'm a loser, I hate Vratsa, I hate my life…you win." We made a toilet stop at a café and our friend staggered off, not just to urinate but to replenish supplies. He returned with another half-bottle of vodka only to start all over again. "I'm a loser, I failed in my life" and even "I'm an alcoholic".

When we arrived at Vratsa I had a soft drink with my lunch.

11. Seagulls and Sunsets

"Why worry? I'll be dead soon!"

My mother

My mother moved permanently to the Algarve in 1994, this time to Albufeira. As in Luz, she never swam, went to the beach, or exercised. The Algarve was not first choice. She'd wanted to live in the South of France but she was priced out. Also I'd spent six months in Albufeira the previous year.

It was probably a mistake because the Algarve is a transient region. It's a place for established couples; if one person dies, or meets someone else, their partner would generally return to their country of origin. The prospect of growing old in a foreign country, where you could be separated from extended family members, and especially the clarion call of the *grandchildren*, meant that few people lasted the course. Business people moved on if their venture failed – only to reinvent themselves somewhere else. And the Portuguese, although cordial and welcoming, kept Brits at a distance, maybe figuring the cultural divide was too great. Lurking under the surface was the constant threat of abandonment.

At first, my mother was still working as a tour director around Europe. She was still in demand in the business, even past retirement age. In 2000, when she was one year off 70, I accompanied her to Nice where she had a group of Americans. Again, I looked on in awe as she, with infinite patience, dealt with their complaints: the hotel room was too small, the pillows too hard, the mini bar had no ice cubes, the air conditioning blew too cold, the bedside light wasn't working properly etc.

In the hotel foyer I watched as one spoiled tourist wagged her finger at my mother and beckoned her towards him. Only she could deal with their ludicrous questions – "can we get to Switzerland and back again in a day?" without losing her cool. Even more galling was the behaviour of the younger tourists who'd spurn the wonderful set meals provided by the city's finest restaurateurs – tomatoes with mozzarella cheese, or a delectable Provençal salad – in favour of McDonalds. Her patience and charm were as strong as ever.

My mother slowed down in the early noughties. I could see that as she was spending more time in the Algarve she was becoming depressed. During the late 1990s, while I was still based in the UK, I took frequent holidays in Albufeira. But, in between, I had frequent phone chats that revealed her bizarre character. She couldn't say anything directly. She had the strangest habit of passing off what was her inquiry as someone else's.

"I was speaking to Gloria the other day and she said to me: 'You know, I haven't seen Daniel for some time, I wonder when he's going to visit.'"

If I didn't take the bait she'd continue.

"Gloria asked me how long it had been since you were last here. I said I didn't know and added that you were probably busy in London."

This was tantamount to my mother asking me when I was next coming out. But she would never phrase it that way. By passing it off as someone else's query she could say, truthfully if you accepted her version of the conversation, that *she* was putting me under no pressure at all. It was *other people* being solicitous about my welfare and movements.

I usually went to Albufeira three times a year. If the gap was longer than usual, and I showed no sign of indicating my next trip, her tone would become more urgent. But, again, she'd only express it through comments allegedly uttered by others.

"I went to scc my doctor the other day," she'd tell me. "Nothing to worry about. But he noted I was living alone and said I needed some help around the flat. He asked me how many sons I had and I said I had three. I told him you lived in London and were busy and had a girlfriend ..." (there she'd pause for a few seconds to see if I would confirm or deny) "but you'd probably be over soon". (Another long pause.) "But I told him I wouldn't press it because I'm not the possessive type."

I've never met anyone with my mother's speech pattern before or since. A psychologist would classify it as a devious ploy to express her innermost feelings through other people, or extract information by pretending others were doing the asking. I didn't notice it when I was young because kids don't. But as I grew older, and she grew more isolated, this strange habit of reported conversation accelerated.

"Someone bumped into me in the square and said to me: 'You do look pale, are you alright?' I told her I don't sunbathe, and that's why I'm pale, it's just she's comparing me to people who fry in the sun. (A little muffled laugh.) But then she added: 'No, I think you should see a doctor and find out what's going on.' I told her: 'Oh, come on, don't be so absurd, what have I got to go to the doctor for? And, besides, even if I am ill and coming to the end of my life, I can't complain. After all, I'm 70-odd now, so that's it, isn't it"?

I was not used to this style of speaking and not deft enough to know how to respond. I wondered if these exchanges really *had* occurred. I didn't want to accuse her of lying but they seemed unlikely. I was gradually coming to understand my mother as Miss Manipulative but I'd sometimes ask myself if I was becoming too cynical and she *did* need to go to the doctor, after all. Many of her reported conversations were intended to sow worry. But she could issue a disclaimer. It was not her who had weaved them but a (perhaps mythical) third party.

Her fear of confrontation was so great that she refused to tackle my half-brother, Colin, about his chain smoking when she knew Colin and I were planning to fly out one Christmas. Again, I had a phone call.

"I told Fred the other day that you and Colin were coming over for the holidays. He said: 'Oh it's so nice Daniel's coming. How long is he coming over for?'" (I hadn't yet booked the trip.) A pause. "And then she said: 'But I do notice you have a tendency to cough and Colin's chain-smoking won't do you any good. I said, 'how perceptive of you to notice that. I do wish someone would have a word with him about it'. Fred said: 'You should ask Colin to smoke outside'. I said: 'I wouldn't like to suggest it myself but maybe someone else can'." This was my cue to tell Colin not to smoke indoors.

In 2001 I moved to Portugal. My idea was to settle and work in Lisbon for a while. I knew the language and I liked the city. Also my mother had no one to keep an eye on her and I had no close family in the UK. She never forced me to come to live in Portugal but the odd reported conversation syndrome made clear she thought it would be a good idea.

"I spoke to Carlos the other day on the phone and he sent his best to you. He said: 'I can't imagine Daniel living too far away from you.' I said: 'I wouldn't dream of being too needy. After all, he's an adult now and must make his own life. Just because I'm getting old and not as mobile as I used to be shouldn't influence him in *any* way whatsoever.'"

When my mother said something shouldn't be an issue, you knew it *was*. One day I'd arrived on holiday for a week and only just put my case down when she said sweetly: "I think I have breast cancer but I won't bother getting it looked at. How was your flight? You've only had a sandwich? I bet you're hungry." I spent a good few days accompanying her back and forth to doctors and all for nothing.

I again noticed her refusal to look unpleasantness in the eye. On the rare occasion she watched a movie at home (in those days a VHS recording) she chose *Death in Venice* because she liked Dirk Bogarde's memoirs, and Gustav Mahler's music. The plot concerned an older man who becomes besotted with a beautiful-looking boy.

After the film ended my mother looked perplexed.

"The relationship between the Bogarde character and the boy – I mean he was admiring him as an object of beauty, like an exquisite painting, isn't that so? I mean that … there was no sexual undertone to all this, surely?"

I coughed. "I think there just, conceivably, might have been."

***

My mother's early old age or late middle age, between her sixties and seventies, passed off uneventfully. She came to see my dad as the love of her life and no longer criticised him, although she still felt (correctly) that he'd had serious emotional issues. She grew wiser and more thoughtful in her guidance, often mentoring others. After she died I was told by several young people in Albufeira how she'd befriended them and offered sensible advice. She left generous tips, she sat at the bedside of the elderly, regularly visited a terminally ill acquaintance, taught French to a young girl, and made her new home in Albufeira into a pretty and, yes, a happy place. She wrote down recipes complete with idiot-proof instructions for me. "The best red peppers are in our local supermarket. They are down the aisle on the right hand side. You'll be able to spot them. They look like misshapen apples but their stems are longer."

I looked forward to seeing her, first as a visitor from the UK and later from my flat in Lisbon, although I knew it was pointless attempting anything resembling a joke in her company and that still grated. Because she didn't have a partner, she was intense in wanting me to bestow affection. If she thought I was being standoffish I was subjected to her strange double-speak again, not reported conversations this time, but recollections that I knew carried a hidden admonition.

"You know, I loved my dad. I used to do *so* much for him. When I knew he was coming home I'd have his drink and slippers ready."

I just sat there.

"Would you say you're an affectionate son? What do you think? Do you think you are? I think you are .... most of the time."

I felt a transference was taking place. Because my mother had no companion she was hoping I would fill in for a boyfriend. But she was also intense in her friendships. They were like miniature love affairs. In Albufeira there was this great restaurant run by a French gay proprietor and his partner. She loved talking to Jean-Pierre in her flawless French. One day a young Moroccan waiter with a dazzling smile started working there and eventually Jean-Pierre's partner dallied with him and took off back to France. Jean-Pierre was devastated, sold the restaurant and left. She was heartbroken to say goodbye to a close friend she'd known for 8 years, whose restaurant she had frequented daily.

When I read about highly sensitive people, with all the revelations that came my way – and the multitude, in my case, of ticked boxes – I realised that not only was my father an HSP, but, yes, *also my mother*. The depths of her friendships, her arousal at the beauty of nature, her love of artwork, her extreme restlessness in sleeping – all marked her out as such. She was not as sensitive as my father (*no one was!*) but she was an HSP nonetheless and in her case one manifestation was her persistent refusal to countenance unpleasantness, her tendency to flee trouble (both literally and figuratively), her dislike of conflict and her need to be around other people. So when Jean-Pierre left, she was devastated.

My mother, once she moved to a studio flat when she turned 71, gradually returned to drinking heavily, starting at 11.30am with two or three glasses of wine and then three or four in the evening. After dinner, the whisky would flow. Plenty of people may over-drink in the sun but the key factor is not so much the consumption but the reaction to it. Her balance was becoming precarious but it didn't stop her drinking. Far from it – her intake increased which made her even more unstable on her feet.

She went to Nice for an extended stay and took her dog, Fleur, with her, renting a flat near the port. She took exemplary care of Fleur, taking her to cafes and restaurants and inside shopping malls. When my girlfriend and I travelled to see her over Christmas we dined out on the first night at an exquisite restaurant, my mother feeding Fleur duck à l'orange under the table. Back at her apartment she casually asked us to go out and buy a box of 10 bottles of wine from a corner shop. She said "this will last me the week". My Bulgarian girlfriend, later my wife, found it incredible that a lady in her seventies would be drinking so much. "Shouldn't she be on juice?"

My mother returned to Albufeira in 2005 because, she claimed, the damp climate of Nice didn't help her health. Now fully retired, she would never travel again. My girlfriend and I were now based in Lisbon but we were frequent weekend visitors. Both my half-brothers were living in the UK, and both in big trouble with drink. I knew she was worried about them. I tried to support her by continuing to curb my intake.

One time I came down on my own to Albufeira and slept on the sofa in her studio. My mother, now 74, looked frail and worn out after the trip to Nice. It was a spring evening and there was a lovely pink sunset. It was only 9pm but she went to sleep early, always after another generous helping of wine. I brought her some face cream and a hot water bottle which she needed even on a mild night.

She was in her dressing gown and sitting on the end of the bed. I opened her kitchen cupboard and noticed many of her favourite sauces and condiments had expired, which was unusual for her. It was a demarcation point. Yes, she had entered old age. Her studio flat overlooked a square which had an Indian restaurant and a launderette. She'd got into the habit of dropping her laundry from the French windows and they'd pick it up for her. If she wanted an Indian takeaway she'd call out her order from the window and they'd bring it to her.

She was in the mood for a heart-to-heart on this visit. "You know, I didn't envisage things ending this way with Michael and Colin. And I didn't think *I* would end up like this. I'm tired of living and feel I'm coming to the end. I'd like to see my parents in heaven." She pointed to a photo of her father by the bed. "He knows what I mean."

My mother's voice sounded so weary and listless. She lay down on the bed and I tucked her in with her "hotty" as she called her hot water bottle. She continued. "I hope I've been a good mother to you … most of the time."

I became tearful at seeing her so jaded. The most gorgeous sunset I'd ever seen was now fading. A few seagulls were cooing on the roofs opposite.

"I couldn't have loved you more," she said. I kissed her on the forehead and she looked so frail and pale, ready for her next journey …

"Good night, mama. Love you too."

I prepared to go to sleep. But occasionally, on the way to the bathroom, I'd check on my mother. Her delicate appearance, her sweet, resigned air, the faraway look in her eyes, and her pallid complexion, led me to conclude her end was near. As I looked at her sleeping she was so incredibly still. I bent down closer to her and this time I could barely hear her breathing. And then … closer still … until our cheeks almost touched.

"Would you pour me another half glass of wine?" she suddenly said.

I'd seen far too many movies. And also I'd never had grandparents or been around old people. This same scene was to be repeated *so* many times – the majestic sunset, my mother looking spent, the birds flying over … and many "half glasses" of wine … and me imagining Sinatra singing *My Way* in the background.

The next morning she was up as usual, heading down to the coffee shop. She'd had trouble walking on the calçada (Portuguese cobbled pavement) that made the little hill down her street perilous, especially if it was raining. So the condominium generously built a handrail. Nevertheless, on a couple of occasions, it didn't prevent her ending up in the bushes after a fall.

As she grew older she had a private doctor, "an absolutely c-h-a-r-m-i-n-g" man, with whom she had regular consultations at Albufeira's International Health Centre. When she eventually left, the staff there said they'd miss her. "She was one of our best patients," the receptionist told me. By "best" they meant "most prolific".

And she still captivated people. Several years later we took her to another doctor in Albufeira, in preparation for a potential colostomy. My mother used a stick by then. I could tell that the doctor who examined her was tired. He glanced up at her and there she was, looking as sweet-faced and benevolent as ever, and the doctor warmed to her instantly as everyone did.

My mother still loved her jewellery, especially her gold bracelet and broach. She liked to dress up before going down to the café that was next door to a charity shop where they sold second-hand clothes and books. She'd sit at the cafe and "play" with her gold bracelet, gazing at it affectionately as she flicked her wrists. Many frequent habitués of the charity shop were hard-up gypsies hunting bargains. She couldn't go to an ATM and apparently, if we weren't there to help her, she gave her card to other "trustworthy" people, together with the PIN.

I told her to be careful about security. But she brushed it all aside.

"Oh, why worry?" she once said as she guzzled another glass of wine. "I'll be dead soon."

The prospect of her imminent demise became a recurrent joke in the family. Every Christmas was her "last" and since she thought the end was nigh, she'd have all her meals out, leave generous tips, have her hair done and fingernails manicured regularly. "Living on a budget" was not a phrase she understood.

My mother deteriorated after I moved to Bulgaria in 2007. People reported she would drink too much in the bar at the bottom of the hill and the proprietor would have to drive her the short distance back. I still visited her at least twice a year. But no matter how long I spent there, as soon as I got back to Sofia and I checked on her, she'd start up again.

"I wish I had you here with me. I miss you so much."

One time I visited and she had a bad infection. I decided to delay my flight back to Sofia to look after her. As she sat by the French bay window overlooking the square, she again sought to be contrary.

"I want you to go home. Don't worry about me. I've had my life. If I die, so what? You should go home to your family and prioritise them."

Every exchange with her was, I felt, a strange psychological game. It was as though she was testing my love for her. But also the way she talked carried the underlying message, "I'm ill but don't worry about it." The constant self-delineations continued. "I think I was the ideal mother for you." And "you'll miss me after I've gone." Or "people tell me how brave I am living on my own at my age but I tell them – 'what can I do'"?

One day she phoned me with yet another reported conversation. "I got talking to a lady in the doctor's waiting room the other day. She said to me: 'You're not living on your own, surely?' I said: 'yes I am'. And she said: 'But don't you have any children to look after you?' I said: 'No, my children live in the UK and Bulgaria.' She then said: 'Don't you have any sisters, brothers, nieces or nephews?' I said: 'No, I don't.'"

My mother had probably hoped I'd be living nearby to take care of her.

When she turned 80 she was hospitalised with pneumonia. She was never the same again. A succession of carers were brought in but seldom lasted long because she accused them of stealing (a recurrent problem when she had lost something) and also because her hygiene and incontinence deteriorated to the point she needed full-time care. No nurse would stay with her in the studio because they demanded their own room.

She still had Fleur but my mother's immobility was such that getting up to open the door was becoming difficult. So while she was in hospital we decided to build a dog flap in the door, in tune with Fleur's specifications. But when she returned she found the flap aesthetically displeasing (typical for her) and had it filled in. Fleur had a penchant for chasing anyone who looked scruffy, especially men in overalls. Sometimes she'd go for their ankles, so we fitted her with a muzzle. But my mother thought it looked bad and Fleur was uncomfortable, so she had it removed.

Colin and I were now only seeing my mother on occasional visits. We tried to get her a mobile phone because she found it difficult to reach her landline. But her long fingernails proved cumbersome. Or did they? We also tried to connect her up to Skype which would have enabled her to see us and her grandchildren. But she refused to countenance it. We also provided a walker, a Zimmer frame on wheels. But she hated the look of it and wouldn't use it. In any case, she was never a dextrous person and probably would have ended up careering down the little hill where she lived.

With Michael living in the UK and me living in Bulgaria – that made five grandchildren in absentia. So many people said to me: "What a shame your mother can't see her grandchildren. She must regret that." I wasn't so sure. In reality, she'd never had much interest in any of them. Nevertheless, I took my 7-year-old daughter to Albufeira in 2012 when my mother was 81. She took us out to a great restaurant, walking slowly with a stick, where we sat and enjoyed avocado and prawns. But they didn't talk much. She wanted *me* there, not her grandchildren.

Something was odd about our relationship and it stemmed from the events I described earlier. Whenever we met, and it was just the two of us, she'd tell me she loved me every 10 minutes. Nothing wrong with that but the needy, pleading look in her eyes demanded instant reciprocity. She was probably feeling guilty for her past behaviour and, rather than apologise, she thought she could atone by constant affirmations of devotion.

My mother was clearly suffering from dementia as she passed eighty. She talked of the distant past with clarity but she was forgetting more and more important dates, such as our birthdays. We signed up a couple of neighbours in Albufeira to come in several times a day to check on her. But now I wonder if her dementia, which is a slow-moving condition, hadn't taken hold of her earlier. Her obsession with thefts had started many years before. Even in her old flat, where she lived until she was 71, she had complained that cleaners were taking items from her, including a pair of gold scissors and some expensive travel books. I found them all behind, or under, sofas and wardrobes. She also burned through bundles of money. Small wonder because after her death, I learned she'd "loaned" her bank card to people wanting to withdraw cash. I doubt many of the sums were re-paid.

Although I'd never wanted to live with her into adulthood, I worried about her living alone. When I did visit I found crates of wine delivered to the door, always the ones with screw caps because she could no longer uncork a bottle. When she went out 20 euro notes were visible in her handbag, fluttering away in the wind. I was constantly getting calls from worried helpers, neighbours and friends. Burglaries were increasing in Albufeira and she was having problems shutting the door. When Fleur died in 2015 there was no guard dog left to ward off strangers. She was still drinking heavily and, when I curled up for the night in Sofia, I used to wonder if she had fallen out of bed or whether she'd managed to close the door.

My mother couldn't continue to live alone. Her incontinence and forgetfulness were getting worse. Helpers were just doing patch-up jobs. Many relatives must be in the same position. But she wouldn't budge. And the central problem remained. No one would agree to stay with her unless they had their own room. The situation deteriorated. A British lady of roughly her age (but more clear-headed) had offered to have her to live in her large house. Whenever I visited she had the TV on, usually on UK Gold, showing comedy classics from the 1970s.

"I couldn't live with her because she'd want to watch *The Two Ronnies*," my mother told me.

"But you can't stay here, Mum, it's too dangerous for you."

"But why do you worry? I'll be dead soon anyway," she'd say, draining her glass of rose wine.

"Well, that's irresponsible."

Our conversations went in circles. She wouldn't leave the flat.

***

More and more people reported passing by my mother's flat to find the front door ajar, the television blasting away, and her collapsed on the sofa in an inebriated condition. We signed up another neighbour to also check on her several times a day and this, besides the regular nurse, we hoped, would be sufficient. But we reckoned without that dangling gold bracelet. It had clearly impressed certain opportunists. The sharks were circling. A flurry of fruit vendors appeared near the charity shop. My mother would buy some raspberries and they'd accompany her back home, ostensibly to help her carry the trays. But I wondered if the real motive wasn't to look around …

One night in spring 2016 a neighbour heard a noise outside her door. He came out to find a young guy, with a scarf wrapped around his face, trying to dismantle the grill on her bathroom window. With the grill removed someone of slim build could just squeeze through the window. Our neighbour managed to intercept him and he ran off. We assumed that was the end of it. After all, our burglar had been caught in the act and was unlikely to return. Or so we thought …

For years my mother had complained of thefts and being exploited. Naturally, it didn't help when she was cavalier about her personal possessions and security. But this was all part of dementia. So many well-meaning people had been dismissed because they were supposedly stealing. But the reverse also applied. Maybe she'd trusted people who didn't deserve it. We learned to dismiss certain things she said. Certain grandiose beliefs must be delusions, weren't they?

She once claimed she was queuing in a supermarket near Albufeira – back when Fleur was still alive and

when my mother could still walk reasonably well –
when she met a French couple who apparently
ferried themselves between the Algarve and the
South of France on a private jet. She mentioned to
this couple how she'd enjoyed living in Nice. They
said they travelled to Nice from Faro regularly on
their plane, sometimes going for the day if they had
errands to run. They promised to call her when they
planned to go. Who would look after Fleur? Bring
her with you, they supposedly told her. She claimed
this couple called her several times and sure enough,
she and Fleur would go to Nice for the day, flying
time an hour and a quarter, no need to queue up with
hoi polloi. They'd be in Nice by mid-morning, have
lunch in the Cours Saleya, walk around the port, and
be back in Albufeira by evening.

Several times I'd call and get no answer during the
day and she would pass off her absences by
explaining this French couple had called and she'd
accompanied them to Nice. One time she told me she
and Fleur had also flown to Barcelona with her
wealthy friends. It sounded like a tall story,
especially since the people in the local charity shop
reported that Fleur came in to see them every day
without fail. Was it all in her imagination? We
tended to pass it off as an exercise in wish-fulfilment
from someone who claimed to be bored in Albufeira.
I hope it *was* true. I'll never know.

Likewise, my mother's suspicions of constant thefts seemed over-egged. Yes, she was in danger of living alone and we were constantly trying to persuade her to move. But we didn't believe her when she told us that at night she could hear the same sounds outside her door, as if someone was trying to tamper with her bathroom window *again*. I dismissed it. I was sure this would-be burglar wouldn't be as brazen as to return – would he?

I was woken one day with terrible news. A man had "broken into" my mother's apartment. I put "broken into" in inverted commas because from what I could see there was no actual break-in. It wasn't needed. The front door had either been left open or … more likely in view of what ensued … she had let in an intruder at 2am. We know it was 2am because that was when her neighbour heard shouting.

Her neighbour rushed round to the flat. It was a warm May evening. He was dressed only in pyjamas bottoms. The light was on in the hallway. The door was open. He found my mother lying on the floor with a hooded figure over her, threatening her. The neighbour shouted something in Portuguese. He couldn't remember what he said because in the lightning fog of war, everything is blurred and yet so quick.

"When I tried to enter, the burglar flung the door into me and stabbed me. It wasn't an act of self-defence. His thrust was meant to kill," this neighbour later told me.

The intruder was armed with a long sabre, with a sharp knife at the end. He fled but her neighbour sustained injuries to the arm and chest requiring 20 stitches. He recovered but her assailant was never caught and my mother was left traumatised. A nurse took her in the following day, the same one who'd been looking after her part-time.

My mother left her home willingly and *never* set foot in her flat again. Neither did she *ever* mention the incident that ultimately enabled her eviction. If "eviction" sounds like an over-strong word, it's because I thought it would require that to get her out of there. She'd resisted for years, ignoring all our entreaties. In a perverse, terrible way, the incident, which was all over within a minute, had finally secured the help she needed.

The nurse wrote down a detailed assessment of my mother's state. She had to because I explained, for financial reasons, the likeliest scenario would be that I'd have to take her with me to Bulgaria. So she wrote down on a card how she, as a nurse, viewed her illnesses. Among them were "Alzheimer's" and "alcoholism". It was funny because she was now 85 and – you think – alcoholics are people who died long before old age. If you were British you might picture George Best languishing in hospital with liver failure, or Oliver Reed paralytic on a chat show, or Jeffrey Bernard propping up the bar looking like a Biafra. But all these guys had died young. It was the first time someone other than myself had specified her problem.

But there it was written down. The fire brigade had picked her up off the floor so often (30-40 times) that they said if they came around again they would put her into a state-run dormitory for homeless and elderly people. A care service, which equipped my mother with an emergency bracelet, complained of her extreme intoxication. They also mentioned her "abusive behaviour" when she was drunk.

Alcoholism, when you reach the age of 80, isn't taken seriously. People tended to laugh about her intake – unless they were the fire brigade or helpers – and just say "good for her". But her drinking made her a sitting duck.

My mother's nurse did drive her back to the flat in Albufeira, so she could collect some of her favourite clothes. But she sat in the car, shaking. A couple of months later I took her with me to Bulgaria, although she had no recollection of the trip. She was happy to be with me. I put her in a care home in Sofia. Her 22-year sojourn in Portugal was over.

I stayed with her in the home for the first three days or so because I figured the relocation would disorientate her. I doubt she knew where she was. After a couple of days I returned to our apartment in

Sofia. I'd just walked through the door when I got a phone call from the head of the care home.

"Your mother has managed to find her way down to the garden. And she's demanding a taxi take her to Harrods."

I went back to the care home and told her she was in Bulgaria, *not* Belgravia! How typical of her to ask to be taken to Harrods! Over the next couple of years the delusions continued. She claimed to have rung Fortnum and Mason to ask for Christmas hampers. And she *hated* the woolly jumpers, scarves and hats she had to wear if she was to venture outside in a Bulgarian winter. She refused to put them on because she didn't like the look of them.

I visited her as often as I could in the care home before the dreaded Covid scuppered all my best intentions. I'd take her down to the garden in her wheelchair, draw up a chair at her side and hold her hand. She still loved flowers and she still charmed everyone she met. Even the grumpier Bulgarian residents of the home, nearly all ladies, would greet her warmly, take her hand and offer to help.

She died in November 2020 in a hospice in Sofia. By an extraordinary coincidence her funeral took place on what would have been Gerard's 100th birthday. And she still bore his surname. Even in death she was still tied to the man I wish she'd never met.

***

"I couldn't have loved you more."

My mother *did* love me profoundly. And, out of her three sons, I was her favourite. But at the end she was so lonely that there was a transference, shifting all her needs onto me. One time I'd visited her in the care home. When I left a couple of hours later she was bereft. "But surely, it's till death us do part," she said.

She shirked some responsibilities in her time and was too proud or too non-confrontational to help me in any constructive way. But I do miss her tremendously, her intrinsic gentleness of tone and her (sometimes destructive) softness.

She once told me some stories of her childhood, involving isolation and neglect that reminded me of my experience. I listened mesmerised as she described being on her own far too much after her mother died when she was nine. Ironically, as I've intimated, she'd done the same to me when I was the same age. But she couldn't see it. Break the chain, folks!

She couldn't convict anyone on a jury. So, if she couldn't convict a serious criminal, how could she have convicted Gerard who, after all, was not a killer? And he'd had a bad childhood ...

A major scandal once affected my father's legal practice. One of his partners had embezzled some money and fled to South America. Until the theft, which hit my dad hard, the partner concerned was to be my guardian if my parents died. I don't know what the legal consequences were for the offending solicitor. But I do remember my mother phoning my father with the news of his passing in 1982. From the gist of the conversation I gathered she was telling my dad we should "forgive and forget" and pass condolences to his widow. My dad would do no such thing.

Yet again she couldn't convict ...

***

It was sad that my mother died in Bulgaria. I wish she had popped off in her local pub in Albufeira, a glass of rose wine in her hand, five years earlier. But it wasn't to be. At least, I had consoled myself, when she comes to Bulgaria I'd be able to see her regularly.

But Covid jettisoned all our good intentions and, in any case, she had been so deaf and so confused that any conversation was becoming difficult. Sometimes she thought she was still in Portugal, at other times in her childhood home near Liverpool.

We had a simple funeral service conducted by a Bulgarian priest. I knew how my mother loved flowers and so we picked some wonderful bouquets to adorn the coffin before the cremation.

We'd been expecting her death for years. Every Christmas was her last, every ache was the prelude to terminal cancer, every parting goodnight accompanied by glorious sunsets and "curtain music" in the background … and yet, *and yet* I was overcome at the funeral. I looked at her in the coffin and her intrinsic goodness still radiated from her. Her whole life had been a bid to ward off pain. But I realise where this defensiveness came from. And, yes, I realised I was similar in some ways.

Her own mother's death was the key event. It must have been momentous. Subsequently, she was desperate to keep anything hurtful out of her orbit. Sadly, this meant, despite her intrinsic kindness, she was unable to deal effectively with other people's emotional problems, especially those near her.

She had a terror of loneliness and, intrinsically, a low self-worth. So when her first husband came along and then Gerard, neither of whom had good characters, she felt she was lucky to have found *anyone*. I realised that lengthy chapters in my mother's life fell short of what she deserved or could have achieved. Her own low self-esteem became a tyranny that she inflicted on others.

She had chosen me to "partner" her in later years. While I didn't have a permanent girlfriend it was a lingering hope. But when I married and moved to Bulgaria the hope was crushed. She couldn't see she'd done parenting back to front. The possessive mother of later years had been absent too often during my childhood. But, towards the end of her life, she was depressed by *my* absences.

I often think of her in the middle of the night. She was such a restless sleeper...

12. Being an HSP and the 13 (Mis)steps

"There's something wrong with a society that shames males who do not act in a tough, aggressive, and emotionally repressed manner—especially when such a significant portion of the population simply isn't cut out for, or comfortable with, these behaviours."

Ted Zeff. From his book *The Strong, Sensitive Boy*[69]

"Three passions, simple but overwhelmingly strong, have governed my life: the longing for love, the search for knowledge, and unbearable pity for the suffering of mankind."

Bertrand Russell[70]

Discovering and reading material about HSPs opened so many doors for me. For years I wondered why I felt so different from others. The more obvious criteria for "membership", for example, an aversion to loud noise and violent films and a love of nature, a heightened sense of perceived beauty and

---

[69] Ted Zeff (d.2019) was a pioneer in the HSP field. He was especially known for his work helping highly sensitive boys and men.

[70] Bertrand Russell (1872-1970) won the Nobel Prize for literature for his *History of Western Philosophy*. He wrote the words cited above in the prelude to his autobiography.

ugliness, are now well documented and characteristics that I've already mentioned. But I also realised other aspects of my behaviour also stemmed from being an HSP.

Some examples: I've always disliked being touched by strangers, whether it's being frisked at airport security or having my hair cut. I'm fussier than most about beds because, like my mother, I'm a restless sleeper which, in turn, stems from over-vivid dreams. I scratch myself more when I have a minor irritation, and a mosquito circling near me can keep me awake for hours. I feel more self-conscious in social situations and I have fewer friendships than the average person but, like my mother's, they tend to be more intense – while they last. Also, HSPs like meaningful conversation, not mere banter. How many times have I been lonely in company? How many times have I said to myself: "What the hell am I doing here?"

I've tended to avoid run-of-the-mill soap operas and spurned populism, whether in politics or broad popular culture. Like most other HSPs, I'm no daredevil. It's unlikely you'll ever find me or my fellow HSPs as fighter pilots, spies, stuntmen, or hang gliders. Society should be a balance of different types of people. Your HSP is unlikely to be James Bond. *So I make no claim of innate superiority for HSPs. And I know that many non-HSPs can be kind, caring and compassionate individuals. I'm also not insisting that non-HSPs should tread on eggshells around us for fear of upsetting our "refined" nervous system.* I only ask others to accept us as *different.* But that is the whole point. HSPs, especially men, have *not* hitherto been accepted by society.

As far as careers are concerned, I'd wager it's relatively unlikely you'll find HSPs in prominent public roles, such as leading politicians. We usually over-think, see the other person's point of view too much and therefore equivocate in decision-making. Also, we'd find it stressful leading from the front and being perpetually scrutinised. *But* that's based on current expectations; we value toughness more than sensitivity in our leaders, a situation that could change as the public tires of narcissists and self-publicists.

People may say it's not good to be a sensitive politician. You always hear that you need a thick skin. But is this the sole criteria? Do we *really* want more leaders like Putin, Trump, Berlusconi, Erdogan and Orban? Or do we need more leaders like New Zealand's Jacinda Ardern[71] who stressed in her farewell speech in April 2023 that you can be "anxious, sensitive, kind and wear your heart on your sleeve" and still become a successful leader? Yes, she is definitely an HSP, a self-described "precious petal"!

---

[71] Jacinda Ardern, Prime Minister of New Zealand from 2017 to 2023.

In British politics I'd wager that Shirley Williams, my mother's perennial favourite, was an HSP, as was conservative politician Keith Joseph. But I'd say a smaller share of politicians, and fewer than the oft-cited 20 per cent of the population at large, are HSPs.

A disproportionate number of HSPs are in the creative arts, because, by definition, a great artist feels more than the average person. My mother once gave me "a tour" of her paintings. An alarming number of the artists were "mad" (her word but I understand the context) the description embracing sufferers of severe depression of which, sadly, a number became alcoholics and suicides. For example, my mother had a painting by Mark Gertler[72] who had several spells in sanatoriums and committed suicide in 1939.

Another of her favourites was Alan Lowndes,[73] a British painter known for his depictions of modern northern life and atmospheric seascapes. He was unfairly ignored at the time of his death, overshadowed by L.S. Lowry whose works covered similar subjects. But Lowndes's reputation has subsequently grown. I read a subsequent appreciation of Lowndes in the *Daily Telegraph* from 1984. Headlined "he could paint but couldn't live", it mentioned he had died of liver cirrhosis.

[72] Mark Gertler (1891-1939).
[73] Alan Lowndes (1921-1978).

Another appreciation on the blog of Peter James Field, noted of Lowndes: "Affected by a stammer that seriously affected his communication, he had succumbed to alcoholism. I wasn't surprised. I had always sensed the sadness and awkward isolation of a man who'd devoted his life to those strange, clunky observations."

The most famous example of an HSP painter was Vincent van Gogh. His tormented life has been well chronicled, not only his slavish devotion to work but his anguish over his unrequited love for his cousin, his loneliness and his depressions and breakdowns. In his need for love but also his isolation (which stemmed from a need to retreat when he knew his senses were being overwhelmed) we see classic HSP behaviour. We also know of his mental exhaustion when he was in the "manic" phase of creativity. I was also struck by something Kirk Douglas,[74] who played Van Gogh in *Lust for Life*, said of the artist, namely that "he needed people so much he couldn't admit it, even to himself." This was also true of my father.

Many writers and poets were HSPs, most notably Tennessee Williams and Malcom Lowry,[75] whose

---

[74] Kirk Douglas (1916-2020). Douglas later recounted how John Wayne chastised him for playing such a "weakling" in *Lust for Life*.

[75] Malcolm Lowry (1909-1957). Alcoholic writer whose most famous novel *Under the Volcano* was a semi-autobiographical account of a drunken consul in Mexico. It was later made into a film with Albert Finney. Lowry also suffered from severe anxiety and depression.

works featured tortured characters. Likewise, great musicians, Nick Drake, Amy Winehouse and Jim Morrison, and countless others. And although being an HSP is manifestly *not* a mental illness, it would be foolish to deny that being highly sensitive makes one prone to anxiety, depression and addiction.

Painting and writing involve less interaction with other people. So these would attract a disproportionate number of HSPs who would find other performing arts too draining. It's well-known that HSPs can do things in private they might be unable to do in public because their nervous system gets over-stimulated. So regular participation in a grand spectacle could be too demanding. Hence fewer successful actors are HSPs precisely because performing demands perpetual scrutiny even in rehearsal. And, after all, the actor is nothing without an audience.

Acting also, unless the performer is in a one-man show, demands constant interaction with others. It also requires a certain equanimity so that you're not fazed by the proximity of a camera or the audience's reactions. Self-consciousness and anxiety could lead to skewed timing. For many HSPs the stress of live performance, the sheer toll it takes on one's nervous system and the self-possession required to keep in character, would be too taxing.

Naturally, exceptions exist. Peter Sellers[76] was a clear example, a man noted (like my father) for taking offence easily. Dudley Moore[77] certainly was an HSP, a performer with many insecurities and who, according to his biographer, was often exhausted by the day's end on account of his anxiety. Montgomery Clift[78] was all too obviously an HSP. I'd also say Dirk Bogarde[79] was an HSP; his interviews and writings betray a certain touchiness, a wariness of intrusion and a degree of introspection uncommon among film stars.

You will notice I've referenced highly sensitive *men* in the creative arts. Men will find it harder to admit being HSPs as long as society demands they shun introspection and be sparse of feeling and fast to action – a Hemingwayesque dream that many men (probably not even Hemingway himself!) can live down to. So it is that male HSPs may be especially prone, as I was, to self-medicating with alcohol to numb feelings of anxiety and depression.

When I was young I bridled at being described as "sensitive". I adopted a ghost personality to disguise my sensitivity, pretending to, for example, like pubs. Now I'm not so keen on pubs unless I'm in the company of a close friend or two. Restaurants, nature trails, and seaside walks are more my mark.

---

[76] Peter Sellers (1925-1980). Most famous for the Pink Panther movies.

[77] Dudley Moore (1935-2002), known for films such as *10* and *Arthur*, also former comedy partner of Peter Cook.

[78] Montgomery Clift (1920-1965).

[79] Dirk Bogarde (1921-1999). His landmark films included *Victim*, *The Servant* and *Death in Venice*.

It's a breakthrough, albeit in one's fifties (!), to admit to being a sensitive male. I can now see my entire life through that lens. Alcohol, at the beginning, quashed these feelings but became a problem in itself. Above all, I do see how being a highly sensitive man can make one lonely. It's harder to make friends because most men are not like that. My mother's words about Carlos resonate – "most people wouldn't understand him." And there will always be those who don't like you because you are sensitive – but you have to be sufficiently *insensitive* not to worry about them.

I failed to fulfil my potential when I was young because I was an HSP and developed anxiety and depression. But, hopefully, some good aspects of being an HSP, namely intuition and empathy, are in my makeup too. My father had it tougher 50 years or so ago and, in a way, although it pains me to say so, he never had a chance. My mother, also an HSP, had a happier life but shunned unpalatable realities.

The passage of time, and also penning this memoir, has led me to a greater understanding of my parents. It's all part of ageing. Sometimes I catch myself walking home after a bad day, head bowed and disconsolate, and … whoosh, I remember my dad had a similar posture when he returned from his office. I now see his frustrated fury at a world that didn't understand him.

Similarly, now that I have reached my late fifties and lost some friends because they either moved on or died, I can empathise more with my mother. She would stop in her tracks when she passed her favourite French restaurant in Albufeira, where her great friend Jean-Pierre worked, close her eyes, and say "memories".

I see how lonely her final years were in Albufeira, as one friend after another died or moved on. I can understand the allure of that lovely bottle of sparkling wine. What better way to celebrate Portugal than with a fruity pink *Mateus Rosé*? And a double whisky nightcap just … to forget it all.

Yes, as you get older, you feel your parents' anguish.

Many of my life choices have been guided, unconsciously, by being an HSP, although it's a term I wouldn't have recognised 25 or 30 years ago. HSPs need more downtime because they get more easily overwhelmed by their work. For this reason, I'd say the European model of work versus leisure time is far more appropriate for HSPs than, for example, the American one.

Above all, I've come to accept who I am. Part of my father's problem – apart from the emotional problems afflicting him – was that he lived feeling he could not *come out* as an HSP. Yes, in private conversation, and on the tapes he left behind on his death, he referred to himself as "sensitive". But the wider notion of being an HSP was not in the public domain. My mother once found a piece of paper in which my dad had listed some of his troubles. He noted, amongst others, "obsessional thoughts", "feelings of unreality", "vulnerability to suggestion", "persistent fatigue" and "inability to reach decisions". But he couldn't "admit" to being an HSP in public. Even 30 years ago, when I was in the acme of my youth, it would have been difficult.

Most of my childhood was dysfunctional and disruptive. It was a brutish era in which young boys were taught not to express emotions – other than anger – but rather to actively suppress them. When I reflect on my formative years and its combustible framework it would have been surprising had I *not* developed low self-esteem and problems with depression and addiction.

I accept one is likely to inherit a certain temperamental disposition from one's parents. As such, you are, for sure, liable to be sensitive if your parents were. But I draw the line at saying one has *inherited* a mental disorder from a parent.

HSPs also need more sleep than the average person but sleep is more likely to be interrupted. If you've had a dysfunctional life, especially one involving so much subterranean secrecy, then you do ruminate when darkness comes. I'm reminded of the words of F Scott Fitzgerald (undoubtedly another HSP) on the subject of insomnia in *The Crack-up*. "I could have acted thus, refrained from this, and been bold where I was timid, cautious where I was rash. I need not have hurt her like that. Nor said this to him."

At the beginning, I mentioned sudden "spasms" when I first go to sleep. This could be a legacy of childhood trauma. And although, at the beginning of this memoir, I was reluctant to use the word "trauma" to describe my early experiences, I now realise the term *does* apply to me. That's a breakthrough in itself because if I'd ever said this to my family it would have been invalidated immediately.

Writing this memoir made me realise it wasn't only feelings of anxiety and loneliness I'd internalised. I'd also bottled up a great deal of anger and, no, I'm *not* referring to my father's suicide, but rather to the period preceding it. What good is it being angry when you're alone in a house? To whom do you rightfully express it? Especially, what good does it do to be angry when you're being unfairly punished but coming up against an immovable object? Scream and pound the walls all you like. No one was ever going to hear me. As I grew older I occasionally avoided confrontation for fear of unleashing the anger in me and also in someone else. Such locked-in behaviour is typical of stammerers and sensitive people. My anger towards my mother – and I had some – has also abated. I understand it was difficult for her because my father did have a depressive condition and anxiety neurosis. Given the context of the time it would have been hard for her to know what to do.

Now, in my mid-fifties, I accept I'm an HSP, with all the advantages and the drawbacks. At times I'd have wished for fewer troughs. But, as President Richard Nixon once said, "only if you've been in the deepest valley can you know how magnificent it is to be on the highest mountain". Maybe he was an HSP too?

***

Some would say there's little point in looking back half a century ago. What's done is done, they say. If you agree you're unlikely to have progressed beyond chapter one. When people say there's little point in looking back, they usually mean they don't believe in analysing what happened. I'd say you can *look* back, as long as you don't *live* back.

The main point of reviewing the past, aside from re-living happy memories, is to break a damaging chain of behaviour. Also, through understanding why loved ones made mistakes, we can hopefully avoid repeating them. We may well commit *other* mistakes, of course, but that's inevitable.

I seldom saw my parents together. What would I say to them if I could turn back the clock to, say, 40 years ago, to a period when they were both compos mentis? I'd say that I loved them. But I'd make clear there were times when I felt lonely and abandoned. And I'd have liked to have spent more time with them. Ironically, my dad handled litigation in his role as a solicitor, including dealing with bitter divorces. He always used to say: "It's the children who suffer." Too true.

I have learned certain tough lessons and here are a few of them.

1. I'd have benefited from more care and less love. Don't misunderstand me, I do believe that love is a human need. The reality is most children know their parents love them. But love and care are **very** different. Saying "I love you" from 1500 miles away isn't good enough. Loneliness isn't assuaged by someone loving you from a distance but by company over the dinner table and a chat here and there.

2. Respect a disability – by which I mean don't ridicule it but acknowledge it and present it openly to would-be interviewers and school authorities. Factor it in; don't become a prisoner to it but ignoring it, or laughing at it, will backfire. A speech impediment is especially difficult to treat because of its "here one moment, gone the next" manifestation. Stammering tends to be like a fingerprint. Don't assume that if a person is fluent in a certain situation

that it is in some way controllable. Remember the old axiom about being struck dumb? How did this originate? What happens when people are traumatised?

3. Neglect is as bad as abuse. Just because you weren't raped, or you weren't in a paedophile ring, doesn't mean your early years were great. If your clothes are dirty, your diet poor and you're alone too much, that can be as destructive as abuse. Don't leave children unattended. Solitary confinement is the worst torture. Boarding schools are awful institutions but it's just as bad to leave your children with siblings, half-siblings and friends *too often*, no matter how well-intentioned they may be.

4. Don't introduce children to alcohol too early. Children who start drinking alcohol at a young age are more likely to get into trouble. If your son or daughter is in the throes of a serious drinking problem, focus on the damage to their health, not the money they're spending. Drinking problems don't respond to an itemised list of expenses. But if you tell your child they may choke on their own vomit that could sink in. It would have made me think because, despite my problems, I didn't want to die. Or that no girl will fall for a drunkard – unless perhaps you're famous.

The destructiveness of alcohol, the way it decimated our family, haunts me. There's an old saying – a fool and his money are easily parted. Maybe, but not nearly as fast as the alcoholic and his money. My mother died broke, and my half-brother Michael was sleeping rough for a time before being crippled by strokes in his mid-sixties. Colin was left with only 18 per cent liver function at the age of 50, although he later succeeded in stopping drinking. I never knew my two half-brothers well because drink stood in the way. In addition, so much of my mother's weird behaviour can only be attributed to booze.

But there is a difference between a drinking problem and alcoholism. Not that the two are always mutually exclusive but they can be different afflictions. Alcoholism is signified by progressive loss of control, obsession with "the next drink" and withdrawal symptoms on cessation. Sometimes, however, someone can be drinking heavily to cope with an unbearable situation, or a hidden emotional (undiagnosed, perhaps) condition. Once the person's circumstances improve, then one should leave open the option that they may regain control over their intake.

5. Don't use your children as a sponge for your feelings or as a go-between with your divorced partner. You can't talk to them as if they're your therapist. Go to a close friend instead or a counsellor, or record your thoughts, or talk to the mirror. Children aren't there to soak up all your frustrations. Certain secrets are best kept forever.

Also, don't drink too much if you know you're likely to spill all the family skeletons.

6. Extreme racism is never justified, never something you have to learn to live with. Anti-Semitism is not about religion but *race*, the dislike of the unlike. My dad was right when he said I might find that Jewish people would understand me better. My nature was urban Jewish geeky when you consider my morbidity, neuroticism, introspection, and tendency to depression.

Does being Jewish mean you're more likely to suffer from anxiety and depression? I'd say, yes, because Jews feel fundamentally insecure, irrespective of the wealth or power they might have acquired. It's a paradox that most gentile anti-Semitism is built on the notion that Jews are part of the Establishment and wielders of great power and (shadowy) influence. And yet, I suspect, that the same anti-Semite, in particular the jackbooted skinhead, knows how meek the individual Jew is, how unlikely he is to fight back. It's the confluence of (perceived) group power and individual powerlessness that make the Jew such an attractive target.

7. Don't belittle mental health difficulties or jump to conclusions based on false suppositions. We've made progress in the past 40 years. Yet, even now, when I talk of mental health issues, even some surprisingly open people (otherwise) clam up or change the subject.

We judge people on how we *frame* them. My mother once said apropos of my father: "He had more problems than anyone I knew who tried to lead a normal life." She didn't know many people who had mental health problems anyway, so I've never taken that statement seriously. But if he wasn't leading a "normal" life, the perception might have been different. People might then say "your dad has shown enormous courage in battling on through these mental health problems".

Another important caveat. My dad suffered from anxiety and depression, which was self-evident. But this *did not* mean he was nuts. He spoke sense on major issues of the day. Yet, on account of his inner demons, his sage advice was rejected.

In recent decades it's become fashionable for addicts to introduce themselves thus – "my name is David and I'm an alcoholic." It would be good if one day people, especially men, were able to introduce themselves and say: "My name is David and I suffer from anxiety and depression." Concealment, suppression, and denial feed mental health problems. Men, in particular, should be encouraged to be franker about feelings. But, sadly, few men feel able to come "out" as HSPs.

8. The suffering at British boarding schools, which I've witnessed in my family, makes me shudder. The Battle of Waterloo was won on the playing fields of Eton, ran the old saying. And this attitude referred to

all the country's top and most prestigious boarding schools. If you have to refer to a battle fought more than two centuries ago to justify the existence of these strange institutions, then God help us! These schools, I'm now convinced, teach people to suppress feelings, not to confront them. Also, many who undergo this "rite of passage" are unlikely to be able to offer good advice to others. I look forward to the day when these wretched institutions are abolished.

Even single sex schools, without the boarding component, are not healthy institutions, especially for sensitive boys. A muscular, aggressive, outgoing "sporty" type may thrive but for a more bookish, introspective person it's liable to be hell.

9. From everywhere nowadays you see the advice to "be positive". No sooner has someone received the news that they are gravely ill, than they're being pressured to "be positive". If that means be grateful for the good in your life – your relationship etc. – I agree. If by "positive", you mean go to bed with happy thoughts, dwelling on the good, not the bad, I agree again. But if being "positive" means never having the right to be angry, even bitter, that you were treated badly, or never telling yourself you deserved better, I *disagree*. You have to own your feelings and accept them before moving on. You can't get better unless you admit what's ailing you in the first place.

10. Low self-esteem carries dangers for the bearer. Others detect it and exploit it. Although my mother was a London Blue Badge guide, and a linguist of repute who gathered wonderful testimonials, she had fundamental insecurities. She was convinced she was plain (untrue) but also she felt she was unlikely to meet anyone after she divorced my dad because she had three boys. I didn't see it that way and, what's more, I had an ideal partner for her – our actor friend Carlos! Sadly, people who have low self-esteem *can* attract unsuitable partners. She spent too many years with two awful men, *not* my father, I hasten to add!

11. Beware of "baggage-laden" advice from your parents. They may offer you perfectly sensible advice. But their advice may also be suffused with self-justifications. They don't want to concede they created an unstable, dysfunctional background for you because they'd be admitting culpability for the very problems they're advising you about. A parent is unlikely to say – "some of this was all my fault".

Especially in families where the parents are divorced and have little contact with each other, they may seek to blame the other partner or say "you're like your mother/father". This acquits them of all responsibility and passes the buck on to someone else. If the problem plaguing you "links" you to the same condition that afflicted a deceased parent, e.g. alcoholism or severe depression, the implication is clear. You can't do much to improve your situation. But you shouldn't take that at face value.

Don't let other people explain away the source of your depressions. You're entitled to explain it yourself without being told you shouldn't feel that way or you only feel a certain way because you are weak-willed or, worse still, you inherited defects from family members. Certainly I felt angry about aspects of my childhood. Self-pity can be dangerous but burying negative feelings doesn't work either.

12. Be careful not to use your holiday home (if you have one) as an exit clause from responsibility and a convenient way to abscond. Not everyone wants to move to Spain or Portugal to drown in alcohol. But it could be an unconscious motivation for those with a latent drinking problem. If you're spending a few months of every year in your dream second home – and are living for that "escape" – try not to neglect the first one.

13. Beware of your children inheriting money at 20. By the time they're 30, they will have hopefully made a life and become more responsible. So if you have teenagers and you fear for your health, it's better to allocate your money to a trust fund in your will. This was not my mother's fault. Neither my dad's – well, only in so far as he died.

***

My greatest achievement was as a protector. I nearly used this as a title for this book. My father never found out how bad my mother's drinking was, or how rampant anti-Semitism was in our household and at my school. He never found out about her drunken abuse of him. I protected them both from the repercussions of their own words. This was never my role – and it shouldn't have been *any* child's role – but this is how it panned out.

My mother never knew the privations and humiliations I'd endured during those winters away. She'd forgotten how wayward her behaviour was. And looking at her in the docility of old age I was never going to remind her. A terrible irony here – when she had reduced her drinking I was reluctant to remind her of her drunken indiscretions in case she reverted to booze.

I internalised too much and ended up damaged as a consequence. So my "achievement" in protecting them could have been my downfall.

Afterword

The Doll's House

Shakespeare has a wonderful line about us all being passing players with our entrances and exits. Most of us are semi-forgotten whether we like it or not. Type in the names of the key players in this drama and nothing will come up on You Tube. They live on only in the memory of survivors. And what happens when they go too?

Our house in Praia da Luz was the stage for *all* the players in my story. I don't regret its purchase at all. But, I have to say, I *never* thought my mother would spend up to five months a year there, as she was doing in the late 1970s. Everything I have described here was enabled by its acquisition. Without it, there wouldn't have been so many extreme highs and lows, and my childhood would have been less dysfunctional but also – for sure – less enjoyable at times because I *loved* being by the sea in a warm climate.

***

It's 2022. I'm now 55, I still have bouts of anxiety and depression and I still drink a couple of glasses of wine every day because I never really wanted to renounce it completely. *But* – and this is the crucial point – if you gave me a bottle of whisky I no longer feel the need to drink most of it in a single session. I'm now happily married with two children aged 12 and 18 and a loving and supportive wife. I don't talk much about the past and don't believe in deluging my children with "heavy" details from it. There's an old saying in journalism: "if in doubt, leave it out!" The same applies to delicate aspects of family history.

But I do encourage my children to vent their emotions. I'd rather that they kicked the door in than internalise anger the way I did. Hopefully, too, there's none of the cloak and dagger subterfuge that characterised my childhood. It's early days yet but – fingers and toes crossed(!) – neither child seems to have the apprehension and sense of dread that dogged my early years.

I have enjoyed robust physical health. I haven't lived in the UK for over 20 years. I've been based in Sofia, Bulgaria for 15 years. And I'm making my first trip back to the Algarve since my mother's death two year ago. I'm in Praia da Luz and – what luck! – it's a glorious late autumn day, so different to those dreary November days in London I described earlier.

The Luz Bay Club, once just containing a restaurant and bar and a couple of pools, is now a fully-fledged hotel, rising to a couple of storeys. Our former holiday home has been re-christened *Casa das Bonecas* (the Doll's House). The new owners may never know how apt that is. Now I see it was a small villa. As always, our recollections from childhood are that places were bigger than they were. My mother tried to make it her little exquisite corner of paradise and, in many ways, she succeeded.

The patio contains far fewer flowers and plants than in Gerard's day. The lounge has been shortened and the terrace extended. My old bedroom (the add-on bedroom as we called it) is now the dining room. But you'll no longer hear cockerels if you breakfast here. Look out of the window and you'll see an apart-hotel complex, albeit tastefully painted.

I walk to the beachfront. It used to be a gravel track with just a few villas. Now it's a proper pedestrian pathway and heavily built up on either side. I pass by the house belonging to our hard-drinking friends from London. I arrive at the beach and I'm delighted to find it's as magnificent as ever, truly "the beach of light", formed by the unique clash of colour, the ochre and limestone, and Black Rock in the distance. The overhanging cliffs show signs of erosion, when you compare photos from 45 years ago, so barriers are now in place near the edge. But, otherwise, the ocean vista is unchanged.

The municipality made a canny decision regarding Avenida dos Pescadores, the beach promenade. Back in our day, it was a normal road, so my mother would drive along and stop the car and gaze at Black Rock for solace. But now it's all pedestrianized and resplendent with restaurants and souvenir shops. Even on a late autumn day the beach is busy and a few daring swimmers take the plunge.

The boutique once run by the "impossibly snobbish" Zé and Theo, the couple who took a dislike to the native Portuguese, is now closed, but it still retains the same name. The Concha restaurant at its side is still in business. This was the first restaurant my mother took me to in my pram, so she later related, on her first trip to Luz in 1969. It's bursting with beautiful bougainvillea. More little cafés dot the promenade, its clients entertained by a rendition of Spanish guitar. I'm pleased to see so many children playing on the sand, undeterred by the disappearance of Madeleine McCann 15 years earlier and the endless ensuing bad publicity.

I continue up Avenida dos Pescadores until Luz church. Opposite is the Fortaleza restaurant, still offering great views over the rocks. I open the door and the interior looks smaller than I'd remembered. It was here that my would-be "girlfriend" and I momentarily embraced, albeit accidentally.

I turn round and continue up Rua da Praia. Bill's old fisherman's hut, the one from which he'd almost ejected Gerard, has been demolished. But a small side street, Travessa do Bill, still bears our incorrigible friend's name. I can still picture Bill driving off on his last day in his blue Volkswagen van. Further up the street on the right, an establishment now sitting empty, is the site of the former Oxford bar.

I climb up to Rua Direita and turn into Rua da Boa Pesca. It's as secluded and idyllic as ever. I still expect the colonel, "the concierge of Luz", as Gerard used to call him, to greet me from the bridge with "Bow Tie". As I walk along I hear the "clink" of cups and glasses behind the bougainvillea-bedecked terrace walls and the sound of laughing English-speaking voices. But not the cut-glass accents of old. Times change. I wonder if, like my mother and Gerard, they're moving the gin and orange forward of a sunny afternoon.

My mother made a wonderful discovery when she bought in Luz over half a century ago. The place gave me some great all-year-round holidays. Doubtless, I was the envy of many. I can understand, looking out at the beach, and reliving the view from our terrace, the pull of those majestic ocean-plunging cliffs. And, yes, writing this memoir has also helped me to see why she loved it.

Luz was so special that on my second trip back there the following weekend I decide to bring her ashes here and scatter them into the sea. I've been staying in Albufeira, so I get the train to Lagos and then a taxi. I come back to the beach. Yes, this is *the* place.

I have with me a cardboard box which is bound with tape. I don't know what I expected to find inside. Well, alright, I do. I assumed I'd find an urn with a well-sealed lid. I should have opened it up before I left for Luz but, to be honest, I hadn't the heart to do so. I open the cardboard box. That was the easy part. Inside is a miniature fortified safe, a rectangular white canister with four screws drilled deep.

I need a screwdriver and I assume that any respectable establishment will have one. I sit down at a bar on the promenade. A waiter comes along.

"Can I have a diet-coke" and here I lower my voice "and also a screwdriver, please, if you would be so kind?" I ask. "I know it's a bit strange …"

"Of course," he smiled at me.

I sit down at a table. I figure I can surreptitiously open it without drawing undue attention.

A few minutes later, the waiter returns holding a tray, and places two glasses down on my table, a diet coke and an orange juice.

"What's this?"

"You asked for a diet coke and a screwdriver."

Oh God, a giant misunderstanding. The reverse of the old *Fawlty Towers* line. But I decided to drink the vodka and orange – because that is what he brought me. It's all emotional, after all. Just what my mother would have ordered!

I go to a nearby souvenir shop. I show the girl behind the counter what the problem is and ask for a screwdriver. She opens a drawer and produces several. It takes a long time before I find the right one. I don't find it easy to open the box and, in my mind's eye, I see Gerard shaking his head and hissing accusingly. Eventually I manage to take out the screws. Hard part over!

I go on to the beach and head left (west) towards Black Rock. Right before me are the red limestone cliffs. I'm carrying my sandals but wearing my normal clothes, T-shirt and shorts. My wallet and phone are in my trouser pockets and I'm carrying a big bag which now also holds the now open "safe". It's been 37 years since I last walked on this beach. I've forgotten how cumbersome it can be. I get to 100 metres before Black Rock.

The tide is coming in fast and I'm being knocked by the waves. I figure I've got as far as I can. So I empty the ashes by the rocks. But I'm now balancing on a rock to do so. A massive wave crashes against me, throwing me into the sea, scattering my bag and drenching my shorts and T-shirt. I rescue my bag and the box, now empty, that had contained my mother's ashes. But one of my sandals is 10 metres away from me, floating in the sea. I retrieve that too but only after getting drenched again.

I'm now one big soaking, sandy mess, so much so that, when I retreat to the safe part of the beach, a couple of surfers, clad in diving kit, ask how I am. I'm ok but I'm worried if my phone and bank cards will still work. (Jewish thinking, Gerard would have said, but I now tell him to fuck off!)

I change into my swimming trunks. I rinse my T-shirt, shorts, and underwear under the shower and hang them on a wall at the back of the beach. Other beachgoers look on with amusement. I plunge into the sea for old times' sake, reliving the many occasions I swam in these waters as a child, hundreds of hours of endless fun. One time I even took my mother out on a gondola. I see her smiling at me.

I leave the beach and gaze again at that wonderful view, and the intensity of the azure sky. It's such a lovely late autumn day that I walk back to Lagos, along the main road. I pass by acres of orange groves. Time to start squeezing? No! As I continue walking along the road, past Val Verde campsite, I look over my right shoulder and gradually I see the trig point retreating.

Our time in Luz marked the "age of foolishness" as Dickens put it in A *Tale of Two Cities*. Some otherwise sane people took temporary leave of their